RANDOM HOUSE ∽ THE BOOKWORKS

VAGABONDING

IN EUROPE AND NORTH AFRICA

ED BURYN

First Printing, July 1971,   25,000 copies

Cover design, book design by Anne Kent Rush.
Typesetting by Vera Allen Composition Service, Hayward
    (special thanks to Vera and to Dorothy)
Printed and Bound by The Colonial Press Inc., Clinton, Mass.

This book is co-published by Random House Inc.
                             201 East 50th Street
                             New York, N.Y. 10022

                     and   The Bookworks
                            1409 Fifth Street
                            Berkeley, California 94710

Published in the United States, and simultaneously in Canada by
Random House of Canada Limited, Toronto.

Ed and I became acquainted in early 1969 when he came to Book
People seeking distribution of his book HITCHHIKING IN EUROPE,
which he printed himself. He brought me the manuscript for
VAGABONDING in November 1970 but it took me until February of
this year to decide to publish it, and for Ed to agree. Once we set to
work, we made the book together as fast as it would.   *Don Gerrard*
                                                         The Bookworks

The passage from J. R. R. Tolkien's THE HOBBIT used by permission
of the Houghton-Mifflin Company, Boston, and George Allen & Unwin,
Ltd., London.

ISBN: 0-394-70455-X
Library of Congress Catalog Card Number: 74-163471

Random House—The Bookworks books are edited and designed in
Berkeley and produced in New York.

Manufactured in the United States of America

This book is respectfully dedicated to

Stephanie Mines,

who helped in every way you can imagine,
and some you can't. What a girl!

TABLE OF CONTENTS

ACKNOWLEDGEMENTS

The photographs in this book were taken all over the map by friends, relatives, and other good people. Many thanks to:

Julian Curran: Preface; Chapters 1, 11, 14, 16, 17
Stephanie Mines: Chapters 8, 10, 15
Jan Buryn: Chapters 12 & 13
Florence Trone: Cover/Chapter 2
Ted Buryn: Page 179
Jo-Ann Buryn: Chapter 7
Anna Buryn: Chapter 6
Paul Penfield: Chapter 9
American Tourist: Chapter 5
Unknown Spanish boy: Chapter 4
Well-trained self-timer: Chapter 3

Also, special thanks to friends Bert Erickson and Michael McMillan for donating their time and talents along the way.

Prague, Czechoslovakia: GREETINGS, FRIEND!!

PREFACE

This book tells you how to visit Europe as a way of blowing your mind and enriching your life. It says that tourism is bullshit unless you get involved. To do that, you avoid your travel agent like he was the cops, and go find out about the world by yourself, for your own self. Go as a wayfarer open to all experience; go as a courier over the map of Europe, bearing messages to your secret self. All through history, vagabonds have traversed this center continent of Earth, this magic checkerboard of culture, history, language and humanity . . . living the best lives ever known.

This book says you can do that too, because the Age of Discovery is never over if *you* are the discoverer. But how to do it? So many tourists, especially Americans, seemingly do all they can to miss out. In droves each year which increase all the time, they blow it. Living in a television world of secondhand experience, dreaming plastic dreams inspired by rapacious hucksters—no wonder they never see Europe while they're there. They can't. They paid too much money and not enough of themselves.

Yet the magic of Europe is still alive, still working. The question is: Can you make it work for you? Europe is all they say it is if you know how to see it. This book is about doing it by and for yourself, as a free person, as a vagabond. Don't go just to see "things," but to encounter fellow humans and get your life messed with in the process. Go knowing that your travel style may cause you hassles, but in the end will get you closer to the miracle of Europe, of Europeans and of yourself. Can you dig it?

West Berlin, Germany: A vagabond in the park, taking a casual lunch after a night sleeping outdoors. A certain rigor is evident, but so is the feeling of being self-contained, of living an adventure. Right now this bench is home, surrounded by the rest of Europe, of the world. It all beckons, and the vagabond can respond to the call.

1 ANNOUNCEMENTS

INTRODUCTION
ORIGIN
THE VAGABOND DEFINED
VAGABONDING BY THUMB
VAGABONDING BY TRAIN & BUS
VAGABONDING BY CAR OR MOTORCYCLE
VAGABONDING BY CAMPER-BUS

"Whoever you are, to you endless announcements."
— *Walt Whitman*

INTRODUCTION

Conventional "travel authorities" say that the solo tourist—the independent—has just about had it in Europe. The modern tendency to improve every aspect of life in the name of Progress, Leisure, Comfort and Security has made organized tours the only way to go. Individuals traveling in Europe on a solo basis find all rooms taken, all restaurants full, all transportation spoken for and everything in fact completely taken over by the block bookings of the commercial tourist bureaus. Meanwhile, the people on the tours, while getting the beds and meals promised them, are enjoying it less and less. They are routed through clockwork schedules of sightseeing, driven like sheep through museums and castles, hustled from country to country, eat the worst food in the best places and come home skinned and frustrated.

There is another way. Despite this rising tide of obscene tourism Europe can still be a magnificent travel adventure if you're willing to be a vagabond, without preconceived notions about the trip you have to have. By that, I basically mean a way of thinking about travel rather than any specific means of doing it. You can vagabond in a pure fashion by hitchhiking, walking or bicycling; or by using conventional means, such as trains and buses; or by traveling in your own car or camper-bus. All these methods are covered in detail in this book, but the accent is

1

always on how to get the utmost in adventure, discovery and economy.

Did you know that the word "travel" comes from an old Latin root meaning an instrument of torture? And it's no wonder . . . travel used to be an ordeal. The traveler forsook the comforts and safety of home for the perilous road. He learned to fend off everything from bandits to dragons. He faced a world without confirmed reservations. But dig this: The survivors loved it, reporting how high they got, how good they felt to be discovering fabled lands and living adventures that enriched them for all their days thereafter.

In recent times all this has changed. The dragons are gone and the bandits are confirming the reservations. The fabled lands have faded, and the "adventure" comes in a plastic package. The price tag is the memorable part of the trip. Ech!! The thrust of this book is that you can get back the adventure by forsaking some of the comforts, you can discover not only Europe but something about yourself in the process and you can afford to do it without mortgaging your mother.

ORIGIN

This book is based on three trips abroad (1965-66, 1968 and 1970), when I went as nearly everywhere I could get in about fifteen months of knockabout traveling. Hopefully you will find out that's not such a big deal. The world is much grander than one person can possibly know, but I did visit all of Western Europe, Eastern Europe and North Africa. Overall I covered more than 30,000 miles. About 10,000 were in my own car, touring and car-camping. Then I stored the car by a Spanish farmhouse and didn't see it again for six months, while I hitchhiked 10,000 miles across Europe, from Scandinavia to North Africa, from Spain to Turkey. I came back another time to do even more of it. Mixed in between were trains and buses in practically every country of Europe, and miscellaneous airplanes and ferries as well. I did time on rented bicycles and motorcycles, rode hay wagons and horse-drawn sleighs too. And wore out one pair of boots just walking around.

Out of it came this book to tell you about it, based on the premise that you can do it too.

THE VAGABOND DEFINED

Who is a vagabond, and what do I mean by vagabonding? The dictionary says it refers to "following an irregular or vagrant course." Starting with this basic idea, let's examine the implications. A vagrant course is unpredicable, and naturally implies *adventure* en route. Let's include that. "Adventure," says the dictionary, "is a bold undertaking in which hazards are to be met and the issue hangs upon unforeseen events." Thinking about that, it's evident that adventuring, or coping with the unforeseen, must be a special learning experience as well. Out of it has to grow a *knowledge*, a special gypsy knowledge that only wanderers learn. My contribution to the definition is the realization that the knowledge gained and the adventures experienced mostly concern *people*. The concept of human contact and touch is vital, for it is only when you touch people that you are yourself touched. What I mean by a vagabond, therefore, is a wandering seeker who finds adventure and knowledge by personally contacting the world of people.

Vagabonding is the antithesis of being guided. A lot of things you do aren't planned, and you risk, even invite, the unpredictable. You leave things open . . . to experience and learning—or what's the purpose of going at all? Vagabonding is not for those who want merely to take a "vacation" . . . they can get that by lying in a beach chair in their backyard. It's for those who crave living and instinctively realize that Europe is made to order for it. Conveniently there are any number of ways you can travel and still be a vagabond. Here are the main ways that come to mind.

VAGABONDING BY THUMB

This is one of the purer vagabonding techniques, and in some ways the best. First of all, hitchhiking in Europe isn't called that. Would you believe "autostop"? Pronounced *out-o-stop*, from the French. This word is understood just about everywhere in Europe, and literally means to stop autos for the purpose of getting (free) rides. In Germany, hitchhiking is also called "per anhalten."

Hitchhiking in America and autostopping in Europe are not the same thing. Important cultural differences separate Europe and America, and many of them directly affect the free-lance traveler. Vagabonding in Europe is not the moral crime it is here at home, and the motoring public less often equates hitchhikers with criminals, degenerates and worthless loafers. Personal safety is taken for granted, and ordinary people aren't jumpy with fear or beady-eyed with hostility. Europeans, accustomed to motorcyclists, bicyclists, wagons, animals and pedestrians on their roads, don't try to bully anything with less than 200 horsepower into the ditches. Moreover, Europeans understand the spirit and the values of vagabonding. It's been a European tradition for thousands of years.

The lure of adventure, the unforeseen, is one of the big attractions in hitchhiking. It's also the one way that forces you to meet the people of Europe. People are the biggest adventure of all, and hitchhiking makes you need people, react with people and hopefully appreciate people. Coping with the difficulties forces you to depend on yourself, and grow in self-appreciation, too. In addition, hitching costs the least money of any travel method, especially if you camp out. The two biggest costs in Europe for travelers are lodging and transportation. Hitchhiking saves on transportation; camping saves on lodging. Not everyone can do it, but it's possible to travel everywhere in Europe, as I did, for about $3 to $5 per day, including all transportation.

One of the basic rules of travel is that the less you spend, the more you learn about the places you visit and the people who live there. You'll get far more from your bargain travels than most tourists "doing" Europe on $30 to $50 per day, plus their transportation costs. When these tourists pay up to ten times as much as you, they are buying security and certainty. Certainty of schedule, certainty of sensation, certainty of service, certainty of comfort. The price tag for this is dear and not just in money, because this certainty robs them of experience and involvement. But hitchhiking isn't for everyone, so let's see how else you can do it.

VAGABONDING BY TRAIN AND BUS

The problem with hitchhiking is that it can be too insecure and too arduous, so even the most enthusiastic hitchhikers drag their weary bodies off the road at times and head for the trains and buses. This is where most of the other travelers already are, for these are the most common methods of travel in Europe. Public transportation represents a compromise between the pure but rough road of hitching and the much easier but less exciting way of having a private car. European trains and buses are enormous fun to ride if you've known only their American counterparts. They're modern, efficient, exciting and used by people in all walks of life. Rail and bus networks crisscross the map of Europe, making it possible to go virtually anywhere on convenient schedules at reasonable cost. They're an excellent way to meet people, especially if you avoid first class. Their costs can be offset by purchasing unlimited rail passes before you go or, in some cases, by student discounts.

For me and, I think, for most people, European trains are imbued with a heady romance that makes them a delightful means of travel. Rolling across tree-lined plains studded with wagons and farmhouses, chugging up snowbound Alpine passes, gliding along the banks of fog-filled river valleys, being energized by the electric throngs of humanity at the central stations—all are a part of the adventure of European train travel. The possibilities for person-to-person encounter in the train compartments, the opportunity to study and meet other

4

travelers, both foreign and American, the changing panorama of landscape and life surveyed through the window, the very sounds of clacking rails and the whistles going around the bend—all contribute to a great feeling of movement, of excitement, of living.

The buses cost less than the trains but are not nearly so good in terms of routes, schedules and enjoyment. But at their best they are funky and outrageous, especially when there's no other way to get somewhere. Which is fine, because if you take the train when you can and the bus when you have to, you have a good formula for traveling.

VAGABONDING BY CAR OR MOTORCYCLE

These are the commonest forms of private transportation. (Going on foot or bicycle is a special category, about which I have a chapter later.) The chief thing you gain with private transportation is an enormous increase in the convenience of travel. Going along with it, however, is an enormous loss—or at least a potential loss—of contact with people around you. These are, of course, the natives of Europe, the Europeans who contribute so much to the successful tour. Most people don't realize it, but they lower their chances for a really great time when they take their car with them or buy one over there. By arranging to travel too comfortably, in your own car or with a guided tour, there are far fewer challenges and, as a result, much less fun. Therefore, be aware of this and keep it in mind. Enjoy the conveniences of the car but consider how to develop challenges to meet people, to travel spiritedly.

Having your own transportation is going to put dollar signs all over your plans, no matter how you figure it. It costs a lot to have a car at your disposal in Europe. Buying a new car to bring back is a good deal, but means money up front, first to buy the car and then to pay for your European trip on top of that. If you have it, fine. If you don't, you can buy a used car, take your own car abroad or lease one. The latter is economical only if you share the costs among several people. However you work it out, the price of gasoline will put a considerable dent in your bankroll. Gasoline costs two or three times more than here, making long distance touring expensive. On the other hand, with a tent in your car and a sleeping bag, you can camp out easily and thus knock hell out of your lodging costs. So there are a lot of factors to consider, and I'll go into detail in a later chapter.

Motorcycling in Europe is a creative and exciting solution to the problems of the automobile. You enjoy the convenience and freedom of your own motive means, you retain the ability to camp and to explore and you spend less on the purchase and operating costs. Most of all, you get a whole new brand of adventuring to keep it from getting dull. Of which more anon.

And finally there is the campest vehicle of them all. More and more Americans are discovering this method of travel in Europe as being the cheapest and most comfortable way of touring Europe. But too many of these Americans are faking it. They've simply brought America with them to Europe, and tour in a manner which is substantially indistinguishable from how they tour the national parks of America: they go to the ranger museum (substitute Louvre, Prado or Uffizi); they look at and snap pictures of the Big Waterfall (substitute Eiffel Tower, Leaning Tower or other tower power); and they go to the evening campfire talks (substitute guided tours, recommended restaurants and other approved activities). In short, all their travel experiences are interchangeable because they're not really traveling at all; they're doing the same monotonous things in different places.

Don't get me wrong—I do believe in car-camping as a valid way of seeing Europe. I've done a great deal of it. Having your own car and being able to camp can be a great experience because almost every place is accessible to you. You can go where the trains can't and you can go where it's hard for hitchhikers to venture. You can go to offbeat places and have offbeat experiences, and you can do it cheaply. These are the real virtues of vagabonding by car-camper, and will be the ones that I'll stress in the chapter on it later.

✺ ✺ ✺

Try to read all the chapters in this book whether or not you've decided on your own way to see Europe. There are tips and ideas to be gotten from all chapters that will apply to your scene. Bear in mind that the special advantage of vagabonding is the experience of not really knowing what happens next, which you can obtain at bargain rates in all cases. This kind of happy uncertainty keeps you on the *qui vive,* the best stance for seeing and learning. You don't know who you'll meet, what experiences you'll have by staying out of the rut, what things you'll learn that aren't in the guidebooks (this one included). The hardest part is getting started, and that's where this book will help. Once you're on your way, keeping going comes naturally. The challenges you face offer no alternative but to cope with them. And in doing that, your life is being fully lived.

On the Magic Mountain: This is the only picture in the set not taken in Europe. It was just before my second trip to Europe, and I think it belongs here because it somehow relates to "prerequisites." It's a moment of grace, in which my daughter Jan and I project warmth, strength, confidence . . . whatever it is, is good. And necessary. The world floats mysteriously below us, a stage for life, a place to be.

2 PREREQUISITES

IMPORTANT QUESTIONS
STATE OF MIND
SHORTAGE OF MONEY
ABUNDANCE OF TIME
REASONABLE HEALTH
FREEDOM TO TRAVEL
CONFIDENCE
PAPER WORK

IMPORTANT QUESTIONS

Would *you* like to vagabond in Europe, to be free? More than likely, your answer is yes. It's a dream that's somehow involved in the basic definition of "human being." Yet along with that yea-saying, you probably feel timid or unsure that it could be you: too straight, too late, too afraid, too many responsibilities, whatever. Could it be that you're wrong?

On the other hand, maybe you're too gung ho and idealistic, too soft in the head. Better back off and see what's involved. Just what does it take to be a modern vagabond? You better think about it now, before you land and then start wondering why the hell you're there. Obviously it does take something to kick around on the loose. Relatively few tourists do it, although many more could. There are prerequisites, and here's what I know them to be.

STATE OF MIND

Your outlook on life and what you think about this world we live in is the crux of it. That determines how you should go to Europe and even whether you should go. Not everybody should go the same way; not everybody should go at all. Think about who you are and what kind of trip you'd like. Vagabonding is for people who want to be free and adventurous, yet realize it won't come too easily or without

9

knocks. You're not always certain how to go about it, either. You need not be unusual, young, courageous, wealthy, or even insane. But your state of mind must allow for new ideas and new experiences, for tolerance and humor, must be willing to accept some discomfort, insecurity and risk. Basically, you say yes to life, all of it, a whole spectrum, as opposed to the narrow sliver we get to be so content with.

Considering it intellectually is one thing; actually following through is another. We all have stuck in us deep somewhere a keenness for excitement, a savoring for the kooky, a leap-for-life outlook. From this comes the catalytic impetus without which all other requirements mean nothing. Everyday types are as likely to have this *sine qua non* as the obvious icon kickers. The person who strikes off for himself is no hero, nor necessarily even unconventional, but to a greater degree than most people, he or she thinks and acts independently. The vagabond frees in himself that latent urge to live closer to the edge of experience.

Naturally, this can be a hard and heavy number at times, so your head better be ready for that too. You'll be unable to take it unless you understand that it has to be rough at times. Travel in general, and vagabonding in particular, produces an awesome density of experience . . . a cramming-together of incidents, impressions and life detail that is both stimulating and exhausting. So much new and different happens to you so frequently, just when you're most sensitive to it. A day seems like a week, a week a month. The total experience is stoning, and it psychically disintegrates you with its complexity and imagery. You may be excited, bored, confused, desperate and amazed all in the same happy day. Or hour. It's not for comfort hounds, sophomoric misanthropes or poolside fainthearts, whose thin convictions won't stand up to the problems that come along. One of the things to learn is that there's no right way for everybody to handle these problems; there's only your way. And you get better at it as you practice. Everybody, after all, makes their own scene. If you view the world as a predominantly hostile place, it will be . . . any friendly paranoiac can confirm that. If you think it's all rose petals and kitten romps, then you'll be living proof of it. Most people, though, regularly alternate somewhere between these extremes.

The right state of mind allows you to take one thing at a time and dig it. A vagabond learns this. You start really looking at places and reacting to people and finding out things for yourself. This opening-up and reintegrating process is one of the primary values of traveling independently, whether it's to Europe or just into the future. You get the good vibes of experiencing meaningfully, of coping with fear and uncertainty, of becoming aware of the the beauty of all this world and your relationship to it.

Or, how broke do you have to be? Happily, no specific level of poverty is required, but a certain amount is helpful. Meaning that vagabonding is far more attractive if you are short of money and want to stretch it out. This is one of the important benefits: traveling adventurously saves you money in addition to growing hair on your chest.

I can't tell you how much it will cost because there are too many variables involved. Are you a student? If so, then you can save plenty by staying at student hostels, eating at student restaurants and getting student discounts on transportation. If you're not a student, regular hotels and restaurants are going to cost you more. Are you going to be mostly hitchhiking, or taking trains and buses? Or will you be in a leased car or your own car, buying high-priced gasoline? Will you use the car for camping? Obviously your total costs are going to depend largely on how you transport yourself and where you sleep and how you eat and your talent for material self-deprivation. Nevertheless, whoever you are and however you go, the plain truth is that if you go as a vagabond, you're going to do it about as cheaply as it can be done. Again, it's a state of mind I'm talking about: a small amount of money buys the necessities for keeping alive and well. That's all you need it for. Beyond that, *money is useless* and has nothing whatever to do with being able to enjoy, learn, feel or live.

I'll give some cost estimates here and there, but remember that they express probabilities only. *You* may go over and go broke in a few weeks. It can happen. The rate at which different people spend money varies from not-a-cent to shoot-the-works. It's absolutely true that you can live and enjoy yourself on a few dollars a day. But to do it, remember the uses and misuses of money. It helps to hitchhike or camp, to eat in native restaurants when you eat out, to stay in low-cost rooms and hostels and sleep in the fields too. You gratefully accept whatever free hospitality comes your way—food, lodging and friendship. On the other hand, you can regularly guzzle the local poison, smoke the local weed, buy some minuscule but meaningful souvenirs, pay the admission fees to your choice of galleries, castles and museums, buy guidebooks and maps—in short, you can spend a reasonable amount to see Europe, but you waste little on living and travel expenses while you're there.

In what form should you take your money? Carry several weeks' worth of cash at all times and the remainder in travelers' checks. American Express checks are the standard, but Cooks' are cheaper and no harder to cash. Buy them in small denominations (same price). However, my own experience is that traveler's checks are sometimes difficult to cash, sometimes impossible, and looking seedy or beatniky is not going to help a bit. Checks always involve some trouble in cashing—you invariably need to show identification, for example. You usually have to wait in line, especially when you're in a hurry. Sometimes you pay a cashing fee. Pisses you off. And there may be times when you suddenly need cash—for emergencies, for sudden deals (it happens), for black-market exchange—and traveler's checks may not help. Have about fifty dollars in cash money that you can put your hands on, and stash your traveler's checks next to your navel until your next bath. Taking it all in cash is feasible and not really risky, but may be too nerve-wracking for most. Money belts are mandatory if you do carry a lot of cash. In any case, carry a supply of one-dollar bills for those times when you need only a little money to exchange. Always try to exchange your money and cash your checks at a bank-type bank. You get the best exchange rate and pay the least service fees.

Another money concern: see Chapter 17 about how much you need to cross borders.

ABUNDANCE OF TIME

Obviously someone with two or three weeks of vacation can't be a carefree vagabond. You need time—enough to forget that it takes time. Just how long this is depends on you. In two weeks you can hitch, drive or railroad yourself from Spain to Sweden, or vice versa. But with only a few weeks, you'd be better off spending them in one place—say, London, Rome, Istanbul or home in bed. Actually, you might be better off with a tour, and there are some good tours. Any kind of trip to Europe is better than no trip, but don't take one of those two-week, ten-city wonder tours. That's like having a little at a banquet but going hungry because you sniffed every course instead of digging into it somewhere.

A couple of months is a reasonable minimum which makes a free-form fling especially attractive to students and teachers on summer reprieve. The only people more fortunate than students in this respect are non-students, who won't be restricted to summertime alone.

The underlying assumption about vagabonding in Europe is that you save money but squander time. To our so-called modern way of thinking, time is money. As a result, we all have very little time . . . it's so expensive that no one can afford much of it. Yet isn't it curious that the richer you are, the less time you can spare from tending your riches? What's the catch? Catch-22? Not really, because these time-and-money rules apply only when you play that particular game. By switching to a new game, one which in this case involves vagabonding, time becomes the only possession and everyone is equally rich in it by biological inheritance. (Did you know you were born rich?) Money, of course, is still needed to survive, but *time* is what you need to live. So, save what little money you possess to meet basic survival requirements, but spend your time lavishly in order to create the life values that make the fire worth the candle. Dig?

REASONABLE HEALTH

No mystery here. Kicking around Europe, staying in cheap hotels, thumbing now and then, starving yourself here and there so you can go flush occasionally can be a trial to the body, despite the spiritual rewards (or maybe that's just light-headedness). If your travel style keeps you outdoors (hitching, biking, camping), your tiny body will be exposed to Nature's extremes: wind, rain, cold, snow, heat and sun (not to mention tornadoes, waterspouts, whirlpools, tsunami and hot lava flows). At times you'll lack luxuries, such as comfort, cleanliness and companionship, and at other times (or at the same times) you'll even miss out on necessities, such as sleep, food and shelter. Obviously, a sturdy constitution and reasonable freedom from infirmity is desirable. Remember that such adversities are but one aspect of the whole. You will also experience days when to be alive is to be blessed; days in which earthly perfection rests briefly in your lap and glitters incredibly.

What about age? This does matter, but mental age is more important than physical age. Young people are naturals for vagabonding in Europe. They can hitchhike easily, with great confidence in getting rides. They're physically hardly and mentally resilient, so they can take all kinds of crap and love it. But what if you're over the hill—like thirty or forty, or older? My own advice, based on what I've seen, is: Do what you feel like doing. It's enthusiasm, not youth, that makes it. There's a new world coming, old friend . . . Join it!

FREEDOM TO TRAVEL

Most people think they have too many responsibilities to travel, expecially in the way that appeals to their fantasies. The hungry spouse, children, job, mortgage, school, army or Mother needs them. This is bullshit, of course. Most people are simply too afraid to step out of the rut to do something they would like to do. Honest, folks: The world doesn't end when you decide to do what you want to do—it merely begins. It's mostly a question of recognizing the irrational fear elements, and then reorganizing priorities and making arrangements. You can take your spouse or paramour along. Couples vagabonding together can have a beautiful experience, sharing the advantages and reducing the disadvantages. Costs are even lower, loneliness is banished and celibacy becomes superfluous. If you have kids, leave them with your mother-in-law for a while. Better yet, take them along and car-camp. Take a leave of absence from the job, pay the mortgage ahead, drop out of school, and off you go. If you're thinking of dodging the draft or deserting the army, do it in Europe, where you can improve yourself culturally at the same time.

CONFIDENCE

The final intangible thing you need to vagabond in Europe is what this book is about, viz., the knowledge and assurance that free-lance traveling is possible, valid and rewarding. Many Americans who would love to travel freely in Europe wind up taking a tour or not going at all—primarily from lack of confidence engendered by lack of information. For many people, the idea of hitchhiking seems pretty far out; for others, simply the prospect of going over on your own, without forty other people and a travel agent's itinerary, may be too scarey or freaky. Well, it needn't be so. Give yourself a kick in the butt to get started. After that, you're on your own of course. But, wow—that's such a good place to be! You'll find that out for yourself when you try it. From experience comes confidence.

PAPER WORK

If you've gotten through the foregoing intangible requirements, now you're ready to get on to the tangible documents you need to actually get you there.

> *Passport:* This serves to identify you and tell where you've been. You need it in every country in Europe and North Africa. Everyone should own a passport, if only for the feeling of knowing they can split the country on a moment's notice thereafter. To get one, go to a passport office in person (check the phone book or a local post office for location) and bring proof of citizenship, two suitable photographs, some kind of driver's license or ID card that physically identifies you, and $12. If you live in the country or somewhere otherwise distant from a passport office, you can go to a courthouse clerk, who will process the application for you. All passport offices have quickie photo shops nearby that will make the photos for you—fast, but not cheap. If you know someone with a photo darkroom, he'll do it for less, but make sure he

follows the requirements concerning poses and size of prints. (For this and all other passport questions, ask any passport office for their pamphlet "Information for Passport Applicants," or write to: Passport Office, Department of State, Washington, D.C. 20524.) When you have the photos made, get a bunch of extras (six to sixteen) for things like visas, international driver's license, student ID card and giveaways to new friends you'll make. Your passport may take a couple of weeks, so apply well in advance of your departure. If you need visas, apply earlier yet.

Visas: These are entry permits that get you into the countries requiring them. They're normally stamped in your passport, so you'll need that before applying for visas, each of which may take several weeks. Allow yourself enough advance time. They're normally good for one entry and are valid for a designated period of time. Two basic kinds: Transit visas allow you to pass through a country, are usually good for about 48 hours and are cheap. Tourist visas are for a longer stay—usually one to three months, maximum—and cost a bit more.

Fortunately, visas are *not* required by any Western European countries; your passport is the whole shot. But you do need visas for most, if not all, countries in Eastern Europe, North Africa and the Near East. The Appendix of this book notes the countries that require visas at this writing and tells where to get them. For more about which ones need visas, how much it costs and how to get them, ask or write a passport office for their pamphlet "Fees Charged by Foreign Countries for the Visa of American Passports." If you're fairly sure when you're going to be in a certain country, it's best to apply for them in the U.S.A. before you start the trip. Otherwise, you can get them over there, either at their consulate in a neighboring country or at the border. Visa applications generally require one or two passport-type photos and a nominal fee. Some are free.

Immunization Certificate: To get back into the United States after your trip is over, you will need a smallpox vaccination certificate. You can get the vaccination from any doctor or medical center, and some public health departments, who will record it on a standardized international shot card that you should carry with you thereafter. No other shots are required, but it makes sense to be inoculated against typhoid, paratyphoid, tetanus and polio. This especially applies if you're planning to travel in the Near East or North Africa. It's also a good idea for people who intend to rough it in Europe more than the average tourist. If you'll be doing any low-level grubbing, sleeping in fields, walking in the rain or things like that, you may as well get the full complement of shots to keep those foreign germs from eating out your guts.

Student ID Card: It's no requirement, but if you're a student and can get an International Student Identity Card, you'll save money all the way. It gets you into low-cost youth hostels and restaurants; it makes you eligible for student planes, trains, buses, tours, all at worthwhile cost reductions. It entitles you to discounts at theaters, concert halls, shops and museums. Unquestionably, it's worth the dough it costs. The card is good for a calendar year, starting January 1. To get it, send proof of full-time status and one passport picture, with a $1.25 money order, to: CIEE Student Travel Services, 777 United Nations Plaza, New York, N.Y. 10017. Send 25 cents more and ask for the pamphlet: "Student Travelers Information—Europe," which is an excellent quick look at the whole project and tells you where to get more information. Also, ask for additional details on student charter flights in Europe and student tours, hostels and restaurants. CIEE (Council on International Educational Exchange) offers information, travel, work and study services of use to students. All students are urged to get in touch with them.

Non-Student ID Card: What if you're not a student? Is there any way you can get student savings? Yes, there is—by pretending you're a student. Naturally this will be more successful if you can show some kind of student ID card. Borrow a friend's, unearth your old outdated one or forge one somehow. Even lacking any ID, you can sometimes fake your way into student privileges. Pretending to be a student is no moral crime if you need the financial help, and it does contribute towards your education. As a matter of fact, student travelers to Europe tend to have more money than non-student vagabonds. Obviously, the non-students are the ones who need the discounts.

Youth Hostel Card: If you intend to stay in youth

hostels, you'll need the youth hostel card to get into most of them. To get it, write to: American Youth Hostels, Inc., 20 West 17th Street, New York, N.Y. 10011. The cost depends on your age: $5 under eighteen; $8 if you're eighteen to twenty; and $10 if you're over twenty-one. The passes are good for one year and must be purchased in the U.S. before you leave. However, you can buy a hostel card overseas, if necessary, by going to a member association of the International Youth Hostel Federation—there's one in just about every European country. You should also get the handbook listing hostels by country: the European volume costs $2.45. For more information about youth hostels, see Chapter 14.

International Driver's License: If you intend to do any driving, you may want this. In Europe it's not required, except in Spain and the Eastern European countries. But it does serve as a useful ID and is familiar to all police. More about this in Chapter 12.

Camping Carnet: This is for campers only and is not required, either. However, it again serves as identification, and is especially useful because camp directors will take it instead of your passport when you check in overnight. More about this in Chapter 12.

That's about it for paper work (except tickets), but don't forget that Selective Service registrants and reservists technically need permission to leave the U.S.A. If you suspect Big Brother is watching you and may impede your departure, you know what *not* to do.

17

Rome, Italy: Stephanie and I lunching in the Roman Forum, where the Legions marched and the Vestal Virgins kept the sacred flame. One of the world's great places to savor salami and ponder the course of history. It is edifying to look upon such ruins, for they testify to the impermanence of material greatness, and reveal the exquisite greatness of the present moment.

3   WHERE TO GO

IT'S UP TO YOU
OMNISCIENCE SELF-TAUGHT
LIST OF NATIONAL TOURIST OFFICES
RECOMMENDED GUIDEBOOKS
MAKING AN ITINERARY
COUNTRY-BY-COUNTRY RUNDOWN

IT'S UP TO YOU

That's what's great about being a vagabond. Once you decide that you can be a free agent, then that means you're really free to go anywhere you like. You're not dependent on travel agents or anybody else to make arrangements for you. You're the one who's going on the trip, so why not do it from the beginning? Plan it yourself; work it out yourself.

Where you go to some extent depends on how you go. Most places are accessible by public transportation, but some out-of-the-way spots require a private car. Other places will be the reverse: the road ends, but the train goes to it. Sometimes you can make it by bike or cycle; sometimes you have to walk in. Hitchhikers are restricted to well-trafficked roads.

No matter how you travel, however, there's nowhere you cannot go if you want to get there badly enough. But here's the kicker: unfortunately, many good places, out-of-the-way or little-known, are accessible only if you know they exist. This is one of the main reasons for getting information before you go, and the earlier, the better. Make the effort to get as much information as you can. Europe is a big place, and it's possible to miss it all through ignorance: look at the average American tourist. The more you know in advance, the better. Starting a year ahead is not too early. Not just in terms of choosing where to go and what to do, but in being able to better integrate whatever information you'll pick up every day off the grapevine once you're there. The more you know, the more you're able to know.

19

OMNISCIENCE SELF-TAUGHT

The only problem with getting information about traveling in Europe is that there's too much available. Any reasonable efforts made to gather information will pay off with a veritable deluge. Unfortunately, most of it will be tour tripe and tourist hype; at least a lot of it will try to direct you toward traveling the usual ruts, staying in the usual first-class accommodations and doing the usual trip where you insulate yourself from everything European and call it a trip to Europe. Your travel agent will supply you with a lot of this kind of information. So will the various transportation companies. The color photography will be great, along with nothing else. Much better is to contact or write the national tourist offices in this country; you'll find their addresses listed below. You can ask them for any kind of information you want, including special requests, and they will be glad to comply to whatever extent they can. Many of them have such information as railroad schedules, hotel listings and rates, maps of different cities, lists and descriptions of tourist attractions in their countries, and all kinds of good things like that. Write them!

Travel bureaus and tourist offices will provide their information free. Agencies like AAA (if you belong) provide maps, guidebooks and reservation arrangements free. If you're a student, by all means get next to student travel information offices on campus, and definitely with the CIEE (page 16). Another way: rap with people who've traveled in Europe, but carefully consider the source before taking it to heart. You can get all kinds of bum information from people who think they've been there. Get addresses of specific places and people they talk about.

LIST OF NATIONAL TOURIST OFFICES*

Algerian Interests Section, c/o Embassy of Guinea, 2118 Kalorama Road, N.W., Washington, D.C. 20008.
Austrian State Tourist Department, 444 Madison Avenue, New York, N.Y. 10022.
Belgian Tourist Bureau, 589 Fifth Avenue, New York, N.Y. 10017.
Bulgarian Tourist Office, 50 East 42nd Street, New York, N.Y. 10017.
(Czechoslovakia) Cedok, 10 East 40th Street, New York, N.Y. 10017.
Danish Travel Office, 505 Fifth Avenue, New York, N.Y. 10017.
(East Germany) Reiseburo der DDR, Friedrichstrasse 110, Berlin, DDR.
Finnish National Travel Office, 505 Fifth Avenue, New York, N.Y. 10017.
French Government Tourist Office, 610 Fifth Avenue, New York, N.Y. 10020.

(West Germany) German National Tourist Information, 500 Fifth Avenue, New York, N.Y. 10036.

(Great Britain) British Travel Association, 680 Fifth Avenue, New York, N.Y. 10019.

Greek National Tourist Office, 601 Fifth Avenue, New York, N.Y. 10017.

Hungarian Travel Bureau, 1603 Second Avenue, New York, N.Y. 10028.

Irish Tourist Board, 590 Fifth Avenue, New York, N.Y. 10036.

Israel Government Tourist Office, 574 Fifth Avenue, New York, N.Y. 10036.

Italian State Tourist Office, 626 Fifth Avenue, New York, N.Y. 10020.

Luxembourg National Tourist Office, 200 East 42nd Street, New York, N.Y. 10017.

Moroccan National Tourist Office, 341 Madison Avenue, New York, N.Y. 10017.

Netherlands National Tourist Office, 605 Fifth Avenue, New York, N.Y. 10017.

Norwegian Embassy Information Service, 290 Madison Avenue, New York, N.Y. 10016.

Polish Commercial Counselor's Office, 500 Fifth Avenue, New York, N.Y. 10036.

Portuguese Information & Tourist Office, 570 Fifth Avenue, New York, N.Y. 10017.

(Romania) Carpati, 500 Fifth Avenue, New York, N.Y. 10036.

Spanish National Tourist Office, 589 Fifth Avenue, New York, N.Y. 10017.

Swedish Information Service, 8 East 69th Street, New York, N.Y. 10021.

Swiss National Tourist Office, 10 West 49th Street, New York, N.Y. 10017.

Tunisian House, Room 2918, 200 Park Avenue, New York, N.Y. 10017.

Turkish Tourism Bureau, 500 Fifth Avenue, New York, N.Y. 10036.

(USSR) Intourist, 355 Lexington Avenue, New York, N.Y. 10017.

Yugoslav State Tourist Office, 509 Madison Avenue, New York, N.Y. 10022.

---

*This is as complete and accurate a list as I could put together, but it's a drag because the addresses seem to change frequently. It doesn't matter, really—your mail will be forwarded if they have moved. Many countries maintain additional branch offices in selected cities, so check your nearest big-city phone directory to see if there is an office closer to you.

You don't have to buy guidebooks, including this one. Check them out of your public library; look them over; take notes. If there are one or two you think you can't get along without, then go buy a copy. Or rip one off. However, a guidebook is worth whatever it costs if it gives you some real help, and most of them don't cost much.

I always travel with some kind of guidebook, partly because it helps me and partly because it makes me feel better. It's like being lost but noticing you have the end of a string in your hand: you follow the string until you think of something better to do. That's where guidebooks are at. They make decisions for you until you've gathered enough direct information to make your own decisions.

Here's a short rundown on some books I like.

See Europe Next Time You Go by John Keats (Little, Brown and Company, 1968; $5.95). Not really a guidebook at all, but simply the most entertaining and sensible book about going to Europe I've read. Your own trip to Europe will be enormously benefitted if you understand something about why you're taking it and what you expect to find there. This book will help to give you that understanding, and in so delightful a manner that it goes at the top of the list. For reading at home, not for taking along.

Europe This Way by James Steffensen Jr. and Lawrence Handel (Atheneum; $7.95). New edition each year. Never mind that it's intended for students—ETW is the best all-around guidebook I've seen. The cost is high and the book is bulky, but both these disadvantages result from one considerable advantage: it is packed with information. More of it on more countries than any other guidebook, and particularly important, the information is all useful and sensible. It covers trip preparation, working or studying abroad, transportation, food, lodging, entertainment, and the advice given by the authors is consistently excellent. Its country-by-country listings are the best available between one set of covers. If you get it, consider tearing it apart to carry only the pages you need. It's too bulky to carry whole.

Let's Go: Europe by Harvard Student Agencies (new edition annually; $2.25). *Let's Go II*, also by Harvard Student Agencies (1968; $1.95). Both student guides, these are smaller and therefore less expensive than ETW. *Let's Go* is for Western Europe; *Let's Go II* is for East Europe and North Africa (and all the rest of the world thrown in). Both have all the on-the-spot listings you'll need: accomodations, restaurants, night clubs and activities. The accent is on low cost and youthful outlook. Some of the best things about these guides are the descriptive sketches of countries and cities that precede the listings. They also give all the basic data about trip preparations and planning. *Let's Go II* also has sections on skiing, music festivals, art collecting, motorcycling, wine tasting and street singing.

Europe on $5 a Day by Arthur Fromer and *Super Economy Guide to Europe* by Temple Fielding are the standard European guidebooks for most people. As a result, they're slated toward an older, middle-class category of tourists and are not recommended for vagabonds. They abound with listings, however, so look them over.

The trouble with listings in any guidebook is that the specific places often take some time or trouble to find (since you're in a strange town), then turn out to be unsuitable or full, and often are no better or cheaper than you could have found yourself in less time. Another problem is that guidebook-recommended places become targets for all tourists and are soon overcrowded and screwed up for everyone. Don't lean too heavily on the listings.

MAKING AN ITINERARY

As you're gathering your information and forming some idea of what appeals to you, you should make up an itinerary of places you want to go and in what order. Don't expect to keep it to the letter—be flexible. The main virtue of the itinerary is that it gets you involved with the trip beforehand. That is, with your own trip. Not the ones you've read about that somebody else has made, but the one that is just for you. Plan the trip by stringing together the big cities you fancy,

23

along with any other special attractions that grab you. Get some rough idea of how you're going to get from one to the next, and decide which you think you'll stay in and approximately for how long. Get some idea of what you want to see and do there. Try not to lump too much together too fast. Don't make a schedule that has no room for Acts of God or even just changing your mind (Acts of Yourself). Let it be okay if you're forced to stay when you wanted to go (like missing a train connection) or if you want to stay when you're supposed to go (like encountering an adventure as the train is leaving). Getting too hung up in your own schedules is silly. Schedules are to help you think about what you want to do; they have very little to do with what you're actually going to do. The best laid plans of mice and men are often a stone drag if you don't chuck them when they hang you up.

To figure out where you're going, you need a good map. Most likely, more than one. Maps of Europe made by Europeans tend to be the best ones. Kummerly and Frey (from Switzerland) and Michelin (from France) are tops; buy them at good stores everywhere (U.S.A. and Europe). See what other maps your local bookstore or library has. If they're not good enough, try writing to Esso European Travel Aids, Box 142, Convent Station, New Jersey 07961, or National Geographic Society, 17 and M Streets, N.W., Washington, D.C. 20024. Ask them for lists and prices. Good maps are guides to adventure; you should study them carefully and keep them next to you all the time. For hitchhikers and motorists especially, they are positively oracular.

The following comments about maps were written especially for hitchhikers, but really apply to all vagabonds, however they're making their moves. Know what's along the route that takes you to your destination. Merely knowing your destination is not enough. Be ready to decide quickly between alternate routes suddenly presented by a stopped—and waiting—motorist. (Or anybody else with an alternative proposal.) Maybe some Welshman will offer you a ride to Pwlheli, but doesn't know himself if it's on the way to Amlwch, your destination. You've got to know. Remember that this business is made complicated or even impossible when you can't communicate with the motorist because of a language barrier. Having a map to hand him is a fantastic help. Accepting the wrong ride may get you well off the beaten track. Some guy offering you a ride to a funny-sounding place may be the only traffic that ever goes in and out of there—so watch out.

If you're travling with any sort of intentional destination with an approximate time schedule—the usual situation—this kind of mistake can cause you much aggravation and lost time. A good map will also keep you from dead-end roads, from getting stranded in wild and woolly mountains when there was a soft, lowland route; it will get you around congested towns you ought to avoid, may also give you necessary information about boats and ferries, train depots, and so forth. By all means, take a suitable map and study it constantly as you go. Trip on all the pretty colors it has.

COUNTRY-BY-COUNTRY RUNDOWN

The Appendix of this book humbly offers a personalized rundown about all the countries of Europe and North Africa—at least, as far as I've experienced them. It's mostly about hitchhiking and driving, along with personal impressions. Look it over to get more ideas about different places you might want to visit and further travel tips.

Roadside in Spain: Paul and I playing at chess and waiting. "When to go" in this case is a matter of when one can, that is, when it is offered to go. Yet our wait was not mere dull acquiescence. We walked and watched, we talked and learned, we ate and slept in the adjacent fields, we found the slow sultry rhythms of Andalusia.

4 WHEN TO GO

THE BEST TIME
SUMMERTIME
WINTERTIME
SPRING AND FALL
WEATHER TO TOUR

THE BEST TIME

The best time to visit Europe, in my opinion, is as soon as you can make it. The time of year determines the weather, the costs and the services available in Europe, but most important is the fact that you do go. If you can only go in winter, don't feel badly—Europe is uncrowded, prices are lower and it's a lovely time to be there. If you can only go in summer, don't feel badly—Europe is warm and beautiful, everything is open and it's a lovely time to be there.

It's great to be able to choose when to go, but for those who cannot . . . because of school or work or finances or whatever . . . the best time is anytime. With that in mind, let's look at the seasons briefly.

SUMMERTIME

Ah, summertime in Europe! Trees and wild flowers blossoming in the valleys along the Rhine, glittering days in the snowy peaks of Switzerland, swimming in enchanted coves on the Costa Brava, hiking along the windy cliffs of Cornwall. Summertime in Europe is special because weather and place combine into a panorama of grandeur that can never be forgotten.

For the foot-loose ones, summer in Europe is the dream incarnate. The warm days and nights say "go" to hikers, bikers, hitchhikers, campers and other travelers who choose to move close to the earth. The roads are open, the air is clear. Sleeping outdoors in fields and farmhouses is easy, there is food in the fields, and snatches of music thrill the summer air. Your baggage is as light as your heart.

27

Naturally, Europe in summer is a feast of activities for the tourist. Every castle, museum, park and theater is open and ready. Every fete, festival, parade, event is scheduled and on time. Every boat, ferry, train, plane and carriage is operating. Nightclubs, shows, concerts and extravanganzas of every sort abound. In short, Europe really jumps in summertime.

Sounds good, huh? Well, dig this too. Summertime Europe is frankly mobbed nearly to oblivion. People pack the place till you puke. After a while around the main tourist targets, you realize that this is all quite unreal and you are in the midst of a gigantic hoax. A Sunday at the Louvre, for example, is like getting caught in the game crowd leaving the Rose Bowl ... shuffling along slowly in a sea of sports lovers heading for the parking lots ... only, this goes on from opening till closing and you don't even get to see the game, let alone Winged Victory!

The cities are jammed with traffic, soot and shit. The roads leaving the cities are sometimes lined with legions of hitchhikers, and the aura of adventure lessens considerably. All facilities, like hotels and restaurants, are full; travel bureaus and agencies (like American Express) are wall-to-wall carpeted with every kind of idiot imaginable (both before and behind the counters); and everywhere you turn somebody may be hustling you, or perhaps simply hating you. Needless to add, prices are up for everything—from hotel rooms to douche bags. Ah, summertime in Europe!

But don't despair. There is a way, and the vagabond can do it as no one else can. Magic clue: you're free to find the scenes that please you. No itinerary, no tour, has its grip on you. When you hit a bad scene, you split. When you find a good one, you stay with it. You're free, baby. Don't forget it.

The big cities of Europe are good for short stays—for quick once-overs before the crowd-inspired insanity settles upon you. The rest of the time you should be digging the smaller, quieter places of Europe that exist and change from moment to moment as well. Some place that's awful now will be perfect next month, or tomorrow.

I spent a good part of one beautiful summer in a small town at the dead end of a dirt road in Spain, on a Mediterranean beach. It was their tourist season, of course, and there were a few hundred tourists there—along several miles of beach. There was just one American among them, whom I met one day at the local cantina. He was just bumming around too, and later we hitchhiked to Denmark together. All the rest of the tourists were Spanish themselves, with a few French and German as well. Twenty miles down the coast I ran into the only other English-speaker, a retired RAF test pilot who owned a bar. Not bad for summertime Spain.

Earlier that year in England (traveling in my own car then) I picked up a hitchhiker in the rain. (By the way, there is a flood of rain in Europe during the summer. Europe is not California.) He had a pack and climbing rope, and turned out to be an American medical student on a European climbing vacation, doing the heights from the Alps to Ben Nevis. I was going climbing myself (through another story told later) in the Lakes District, so he came along. I can tell you, there were no tourists there as our party roped up and made for the heights. Later we all sang in the car, told tall tales in the pub while putting away pitchers of shandy (lemon-beer), then slept in a field to do it again the next day. Believe me, vagabonds in summertime need not be bothered by tourist crowds.

Visiting Frankfurt, Germany, on my first trip, I couldn't find anyplace to camp. Too many car-campers for the local lot. So I drove out toward the tules and found ... guess what ... the garbage dump! In Frankfurt, it's a huge pit hundreds of yards across, hidden by a small forest of trees. We found a fine campsite in the trees and enjoyed complete privacy for the three days we stayed there. We camped upwind to escape any odors, drove in to sightsee during the day, returned early enough for postprandial perambulations through the collected oddments ... which, incidentally, were fascinating, with everything from big shiny cars to big shiny rats. Recalling my stay in Frankfurt, I would say the cathedral and the dump were the two most impressive sights, though one of them was somewhat flawed by the number of tourists present.

WINTERTIME

Ah, wintertime in Europe! Barren trees silhouetted in vast snowy fields, snowflakes falling past street lamps faintly illuminating ancient winding cobblestone streets, candles burning on the fir trees of Christmastime Europe, a stunningly lovely wonderland illustrating all the visions I had as a child, reading the tales of Dickens, of Hugo, of Hans Christian Andersen.

I personally prefer Europe in winter for reasons of privacy, solitude and the delight of seeing a genuine Europe, less congested and more beautiful. You feel as if you are really there, having it to yourself, along with the Europeans. Gone are the madding crowds, especially the money-pot weirdos. The Americans you meet now you can appreciate much more because they're either vagabonds like yourself, or they have some other good reason for being there (studying, working, etc.). The two-week vacationers—who next year will be at the Jamaica Hilton, the year after at the Royal Hawaiian, and eventually in Hell—are gone.

But, and this is important, winter is something else when it comes to comfort. Being an easy rider requires proper dress: arctic variety in the north, and you'd better have your woolies in the south, too. European winters are infamous for their severity, and for hitchhikers and other travelers who will be outdoors a lot, this means there is no escape from it. More than once I seriously wondered about the risk of freezing to death on the spot if I didn't get a ride. I saw in the Stockholm papers that a stranded Finn froze to death on the same night (minus 30°C) that I slept in a snowbank a few miles away, next to the freeway. I was cold, too, but not that cold—because I troubled myself to sleep in a goose-down sleeping bag, four shirts, two pairs of pants, a sweater, a jacket, a scarf, a cap and a vision of hot southern sands. That last is no idle quip; as I laid there shivering I actually tried to get warmer by imagining myself to be lying in hot Florida sand. It helped. No frostbite, and I woke up surrounded by coconuts.

Merely warm clothing is not enough: windbreaking gear is strongly advised because hurricanes and typhoons will seem common-place in many autostopping situations. Freaky weather is commonplace everywhere, but you don't realize it until you're out there in it all the time.

I could spin all kinds of chilling tales about my various wintertime sufferings from Wales to Warsaw. And you know what? I froze my ass a lot, but I had a ball too. I experienced some far-out times in the snow and ice, and even when I didn't, it was all part of a journey that I had to take whole or not at all.

As to the lesser amount of tourist activities, the shuttered castles, the locked amusement parks ... well, they're not the whole story of Europe, by any means. And seeing them glutted with tourists is sometimes not seeing them, anyway.

In the winter of '66 I lived three months in Copenhagen, during which I didn't visit one museum or castle. Tivoli was, of course, closed. Most Americans would say I missed seeing Copenhagen's sights, but they couldn't be wronger. I lived in five different places (including an abandoned building and an unheated garret), and I fell in with a crowd of folk-musicians who played the clubs. Through them I met many young Danes and expatriates, and got to know a Copenhagen the tourists don't see, had a tempestuous love affair with a married Danish woman that got me into all kinds of trouble, and, in short, had myself quite a time. But I never have seen Tivoli. Tsk, tsk.

In fact, most tourist attractions do stay open all year, and many festivals and activities take place year round or only in winter, when they're uncrowded and probably cost less. Rooms in hotels are easily obtained, there are no lines, fewer people, more leisure and a distinctly genuine quality to life that makes winter discomfort a small price to pay.

Ah, Europe in springtime! Ah, Europe in falltime! You know what I'm going to say. Namely, that those seasons are probably the best. You get the advantage of mild weather, reasonable prices and fewer people. Of course, April in Paris is still damned cold, and it's even worse in England; and the snows in the north start falling as early as October. The best of all is just before school's out (say April—May) and just after it starts (September—October). Too bad for you students.

The pattern of weather and geography in Europe, together with the pace of the vagabond, can be put together in a tour that keeps you following the weather. Simply stated: go south in the winter. Somewhere on the Mediterranean is nice, but it won't be as warm as the propaganda implies. For example, you can't swim all year long in Spain, nor in Italy, nor Greece, either. In Morocco, possibly, if you go far to the south. On the other hand, you may be a ski fan, so you'll do the tour in reverse. Or maybe you'll want to ignore the weather altogether and follow some logical touring sequence: climbing mountains, following music festivals, chasing sports car races or bicycle marathons, doing wine-tasting tours, folk festivals or computer sales conferences. Who knows?

Maybe you'll just go over, as I did, not really into anything except letting it happen as it will. It worked fine for me and it can for you, too. Don't worry about when to go. Just go.

Athens, Greece: Running through the Acropolis to announce, "I'm getting there!" I look a little seedy and crazy, but these are natural and beneficial consequences of vagabonding. The guards here stop you from running about, but I had to indulge one short sprint amongst these wise and joyous stones.

5   GETTING THERE

GENERAL INFORMATION
CHARTER FLIGHTS
REGULAR AIRLINES
IRREGULAR AIRLINES
SHIPS AND BOATS
GOVERNMENT SERVICE
CROSSING AMERICA

GENERAL INFORMATION

You can easily work out the details of getting there by yourself. Do not simply turn your body and your bank account over to a travel "expert." These people are best at the business of selling package tours and extravagant excursions to Americans who are too plastic or too uninformed to know any better. Agents can't help you with low-cost travel arrangements because (1) they don't know enough about them and (2) there's no money in it for them. Any low-cost tours they do offer depend upon treating people as uniform commodities. The popularity of these tours is a reflection of the unfortunate, even tragic, fact that many Americans like to be treated that way because it's so safe.

I worked on the catering staff of a domestic grand hotel a few years ago, providing technical services for conventions. (Now, there was a dumb job.) Among the many insane conventions I served, one was for travel agents. For two days I sat in on their sessions, running a projector and listening to next year's plans and promotions. You wouldn't believe how fervently those cats work at pushing tours on their customers— entirely because that's what brings in the most money. I'm quite aware that being a travel agent is hard work and mostly a thankless job. I know there's little profit in really helping people as individuals; in fact, it's probably impossible. Everything must be calculated in terms of profit margins based on volume turnover of whatever is being dealt. Electric appliances, candy bars, teddy bears and tourists to Europe—it's all the same. As a result, agents really have no time or use for the independent traveler. He's not only unprofitable; he's a threat to the travel "industry."

I've found that by dealing directly with a chosen carrier agency (plane, boat, train), you'll get better service. Or, work out all the details yourself, and then use a travel agent just to make the bookings you've decided on. (There's no cost for bookings.) If you really want to get into being your own travel agent, go to the library for or buy *It's Cheaper to Travel* by Norman Ford (Harian Publications, 1965; $1.50). It's particularly good for explaining all about the travel agent business and how, without a great deal of work, you can save a lot of money by being your own agent.

When you do decide how you want to go, make your reservations as early as possible. Months ahead if by plane, even further ahead if it's by ship. Reservations are simple to cancel if you change your plans, but sometimes impossible to get if you wait too long.

The basics of getting there are covered in what follows. (All prices quoted in this book are, of course, subject to change. What do you think: Will they go up or down?)

CHARTER FLIGHTS

The cheapest way by far is via one of the many charter flights arranged by public and private groups. These groups sponsor literally thousands of European charter flights, called "affinity flights," and the groups themselves are as varied as can be imagined. If you are a student, check with the CIEE (page 16) for student charter flights. Then there are universities (another good student bet), fraternal and religious orders, trade unions, civic clubs, social organizations, store co-operatives, art-lover associations, nonprofit service groups, and you name it . . . so long as everyone in the club has something in common other than a desire to travel cheaply. (Lotta strange clubs get together because of the funny rules governing charters.) In all of these, you must be a bona fide member at least six months before your flight departs, and the costs are prorated among the participants. There is usually a membership fee.

Charters are definitely worth investigating because the cost averages less than half of regular airline fares. Round-trip prices typically run from $250 to $350. There are enough groups sponsoring them for you to be able to find one if you plan at least six months ahead. Organizations sponsoring charters cannot openly advertise their flight plans, but they aren't hard to find. Just start asking around, and you'll find some you can qualify for, no matter who you are. But if you can't, here's an address that will connect you with Overseas National Airways, the largest charter line: Bob Dunne, P.R. Rieber Co., 160 East

39 Street, New York, N.Y. 10016.

Some flights (over ninety in 1970) have been canceled and some clubs disbanded by the Civil Aeronautics Board (CAB) because of procedural irregularities. Be sure your club is not some fly-by-night outfit that will get shot down by the CAB. Don't be afraid to ask questions and request written confirmation of commitments and costs. If you know of people in the group with less than six months tenure, or if you've heard that the club is phoney (that is, originated for travel purposes), there is some risk of flight cancellation at the last minute by a CAB spot check. Another possible problem is a charter flight not fully booked, in which case you may be assessed an additional increment to pay for the empty seats.

There are also clubs formed just for travel, which offer flights at prices equivalent to affinity charters. This is the "inclusive tour" type of charter, but must include hotel costs as well, and therefore is not suited to independent travelers.

However, charter flights have several big disadvantages, especially for the vagabond. The first is that most of them operate only in summer — in some ways the worst time to go. Another disadvantage is the short time between going and coming: most round-trip charter flights allow you about three weeks, some longer, and a few for the entire summer (student charters especially). Outfits that fly winter charters offer only short stays (anyone for the Holy Land at Christmas?). And, of course, you will be tied to unyielding departure and return dates. A few travel clubs offer one-way flights at charter savings, so ask about it. Another little-known piece of information: the CAB allows up to 5% of a charter flight to be one-way trippers. This is a very important provision for vagabonds to investigate. If you can't work that out, you can miss your charter plane home, perhaps sell the return ticket before or after departing (illegal, however) and still come out ahead.

REGULAR AIRLINES

Consider going with a regularly scheduled airline only if you care to take advantage of the free stopovers offered en route to your final destination. For example, in buying a ticket to Athens, you could stop for free in London, Paris, Zurich and Rome — or whatever itinerary you want to work out with another destination and other stopovers. You pay the normal fare to the last city (on a per-mile basis) and are allowed 20% more free mileage to zigzag between other intermediate cities. The disadvantages are that it's going to cost you more in basic fare (to get to Europe) than any other way and, in effect, it limits you with respect to vagabonding. You'll be scheduling yourself pretty tightly, making and keeping reservations, building a whole rigid structure around your free stopovers. Ain't worth it.

As for costs, the regular economy round-trip fare from New York to London is well over $500 in summer (high season) and much more to continental cities further away. By going during some other season, you'll trim around $100 off this price. Then there are the excursion fares (45 days maximum in Europe), which save you a lot — at least $150 over the regular economy round-trip fares. The only problem is that 45 days may not be long enough. However, it will certainly suit students and other people who want a long enough time for an in-depth look but can't make an open-ended trip. You can get one free stopover on an excursion flight and buy one more for $10 extra.

Incidentally, fares are set by the International Air Transport Association (IATA), and are the same for all airlines, except the two I'll describe in a moment. What this means is that you can't shop for prices amongst the airlines ... they're all the same. The IATA has invented a really screwed-up collection of fares and flight arrangements — there are so many combinations and permutations that it's really a matter for the computers. And the IATA changes them every year. Call an airline office to get the exact information that applies to your situation or plans.

IRREGULAR AIRLINES

The IATA rates do not apply to two regularly scheduled maverick airlines that don't belong to it. In the North Atlantic the old stand-by is Icelandic Airlines (Loftleider), flying from New York to Luxembourg via Iceland, with other destinations in Great Britain and Scandinavia. In the South Atlantic, International Air Bahama (IAB) flies from Nassau in the Bahamas to Luxembourg (no other destinations). Fares on both these airlines are the lowest available for any scheduled airlines, and this applies across the board — for regular, excursion or group fares, and they (alone) have a student fare too.* Regular round-trip summer fare is well under $500; student fare is under $400. Excursion fares are lower yet, as are the off-season fares. International Air Bahama does not fly as often as Icelandic, but it has all jets. In 1970, for the first time, Icelandic also started flying DC-8 jets, in addition to the propjets they've used for years. (And charging slightly more for them) I've flown on Icelandic once and on IAB thrice, and highly recommend both. Flying the old propjets of Icelandic will shake you up (a high-frequency vibration modulates your voice into an interesting quaver during the flight), but aside from unimportant weirdnesses like these, good old "Outlandish Airlines" ("Loss Leader") is the budget traveler's buddy. You might consider a circle tour: flying from New

*FLASH: As we go to press Sabena and Pan American Airlines announce new student fares of $220 round trip. Call them or CIEE for info/reservations.

36

York to Luxembourg on Icelandic, and returning from Luxembourg to Nassau on IAB. On the way back (only), the IAB flight makes a one-hour refueling stop at Shannon Airport, largest and best of the European duty-free ports. Icelandic runs IAB too, so you can make arrangements to fly on either one at any Icelandic office. Their main office in this country is: Icelandic Airlines Inc., 630 Fifth Avenue, New York, N.Y. 10020 (other offices in Chicago, Miami, Washington, Los Angeles and San Francisco). For students, the CIEE (page 16) will make reservations.

SHIPS AND BOATS

Steamship fares are higher than airline fares, especially when you consider the miscellaneous shipboard expenses, such as tips, your bar bill and ship's pool losses (unless you win). Figure at least $500 round-trip tourist class plus about $50 for the extras. But if you can afford the difference and spare the time, go by boat — it's the only way to fly. It's fun, glamorous, relaxing and companionable. Sporty, too: on my cruise I battled my way to the tourist-class table-tennis championship — thrills all the way. My prize, ceremoniously awarded, was indeed a foldaway travel alarm clock. (Later on I gave it to a timeless Londoner who befriended me.) Ships have yet other advantages besides awarding clocks: one of the biggest is being able to gradually ease your head into the coming adventure at the proper pace; another is being able to do it with other people, some of whom may help you out or tellingly advise you. They could change your whole trip, or better yet, your whole life. Then there's simply the experience of being on the bosom of the deep for an extended period; the ocean is spellbinding. Shipping also gives you the rare satisfaction of supporting a dying industry. Last but not least, you get to eat like a pig ... shipboard victuals are copious, delicious and included in the price of the ticket.

Incidentally, almost all ocean liners to Europe sail only out of New York City. There are some steamship lines (P&O, Costa and Portuguese Lines) that sail out of Port Everglades, Florida (near Miami), to Lisbon and other European ports, some with itineraries via tropical islands en route. Also out of Vera Cruz, Mexico, on Transatlantica Española to Spain. As with airlines, go off-season (fall and winter) to save money. Take the last boat in April to get the best combination of price and weather. If you are a student, check with the CIEE (page 16). They will get you on a student ship for around $400 round trip, but their biggest advantage is that everybody has a ball (reportedly). Your fellow travelers will all be about your age, many of them oppositely sexed.

Freighters are seldom cheaper than regular steamship lines, but they are more simple, informal and comfortable on a dollar-for-dollar basis. Not to mention slower, smaller and without nightly dance bands. There are several books containing lists of freighter opportunities and travel. Check with *Ford's Freighter Travel Guidebook,* available from Box 505, Woodland Hills, California 91364 ($6 for a year's subscription). Also, Harian Publications, Greenlawn, N.Y. 11740, has a set of three books by Norman Ford for $3.95, or separately priced, as listed: *Today's Outstanding Buys in Freighter Travel* (1969; $2.50) . . . *Travel Routes Around the World,* by Ford and Tyarks (1970; $1.50) . . . *Freighter Days* ($1.50).

Freighters are available from more ports than liners, including Gulf and West Coast ports, which may be more convenient departure points for you. Most freighters nowadays are very classy, but there are still a few grubby and cheap cargo lines left. They're irregularly scheduled, leaving only when they have a cargo, and their destinations are sometimes only approximate.

If you already hold seaman's papers, you could work your way across, and in fact I've known several vagabonds in Europe who've done just that. If you're not now a seaman, forget it; the hassle is nearly impossible. However, *Europe This Way,* the guidebook previously mentioned, suggests some ways it can be done. Then there are private yachts occasionally needing crews, but your chances of getting across this way are about the same as flying over in your homemade biplane. Or try the yellow submarine.

GOVERNMENT SERVICE

Maybe you're already in Europe or nearby, and if so, you're probably a serviceman stationed there. Maybe you're nearing discharge. Why not get paid off in Europe instead of having Uncle ship you home? Or if you're overseas somewhere, use your discharge pay to get to Europe instead. Peace Corps people and all others already abroad may as well stay a bit longer, detouring home through Europe.

CROSSING AMERICA

This can be quite a trip all by itself, especially if you come from California and the West. Europe tends to be toward the East, so a lot of folks have to cross the continent first. If you go by plane and are under twenty-two, you can fly youth-fare at a considerable saving. Otherwise, you can fly stand-by at a saving. Some domestic airlines now have lower fares if you fly by night (Delta, et al.): The cheapest regular carrier, of course, is the bus . . . in America, as in Europe, the people's transport.

The train is out unless you live in the Northwest. If so, check into the cross-Canada trains from Vancouver to Montreal. The fares are lower than American trains ($75, *including* all meals), and the scenery is pleasantly unpolluted and unpopulated. On my last trip to Europe I hitchhiked from San Francisco to Vancouver (if you do this, don't let the Washington State cops see you), then took the cross-Canada express for three days of easy living. (Observation: Canadians sure are straight.) Then hitched from Montreal to New York, where I caught my Icelandic flight.

About hitchhiking in America: there's already one bad book written about this, so I may write a better one, but not right now. However, I will say this: hitching in the U.S.A. is less enjoyable and more dangerous than abroad. The problems are mostly with the occasional freaks, drunks, rednecks and bad-assed cops. Too many assholes, by far. But these are the tiny minority, for you'll meet mostly nice people who'll give you a good trip. Believe it or not, there are lots of warm, wonderful Americans too.

Another traveling suggestion: get a drive-away car (drive a getaway car). Most large American cities have firms that ferry automobiles to places like New York and Miami, and they need drivers. Also, ordinary citizens occasionally want a driver for their car, or take riders to share expenses. For this kind of thing, check the Transportation or Travel Opportunities section in the classified ads of your metropolitan newspaper, or place an ad in it. Sometimes a local radio station broadcasts "personal service announcements." Ads in underground newspapers are another good outlet. Post notices on school and community bulletin boards, in health-food stores, etc.

Taking your own car will work fine if you can store it someplace while you're gone, or perhaps sell it at the point of departure—or give it to somebody. Alternatively, if you can round up a bunch of people at the same time, it will pay to rent a panel truck and drive it cross-country loaded with people sharing expenses, camping out as you go.

Village in Southern Poland: Julian and I met in Copenhagen, where we
got the idea for a grand tour of East Europe. We clowned our way from
Denmark to Turkey, this being one of numerous classic moments. The
Polish Army uniforms belong to a drunken uncle we were visiting, who
bad-mouthed us for being Americans. The pose was our way of
ridiculing him for being such a pain in the ass.

6 WHO TO GO WITH

DOES IT MATTER?
GOING ALONE
TAKE A FRIEND
LOVING COUPLES
FAMILY TRAVEL

DOES IT MATTER?

You bet it does. I've tried all forms of companionship: in quantity, from none to numerous; in relationship, from strangers to relatives; in years, from 6 to sixty-six; and in gender, from male to female. I've gone alone, I've gone with friends, with wives, with girl friends, with children, with parents. Not all at the same time, however. Each outing was extremely different from any other before it, which had to do in large part with my traveling companion(s), if any. One of the basic themes of this book is that the people you meet while traveling are what your trip is all about. A corollary to that theme is that the people who accompany you also play pivotal roles in making your trip.

GOING ALONE

This is the simplest way, the freest way, and is therefore the vagabond's natural mode. It was Leonardo da Vinci that said "If you are alone, you are your own man." (However, he said it in Italian.) Right from the beginning, you don't have to coordinate your trip plans with anyone, you don't have to depend on anyone for anything. Loners are free men and women. There is no compromising, no fighting about where to stop, when to go, what to see, how fast to travel, etc. Oneness is a very flexible state. You can take advantage of many more situations, whether it be picking up a girl or a boy, hitching a ride or just making do. From the standpoint of pure vagabonding, one of the biggest advantages of traveling alone is that you can be as spartan as you can stand. You're not responsible for anyone else's welfare or state of mind, so, if need be, you can undergo all kinds of privations without worrying about anyone else. If you want to sleep out in the snow or starve for a week, you just do it, and with a clear conscience. Traveling alone has always enabled me to live in a manner that I wouldn't dream of imposing on anyone else. And there are times when this helps a lot.

With regard to hitchhiking, certainly it's easier when you're alone. You not only get more rides but you get more attention from the drivers. They're more likely to offer a meal or a bed to one mouth or one body than two. (Hitchhiking for a single girl is a special topic. See Chapter 8 for the details.)

The disadvantage, of course, is that loners get lonely. But this isn't so bad as you might think, for two reasons. The first is that being lonely, while not particularly a pleasant state, does make you much more sensitive to what's happening. That poignant ache you feel serves to engrave experiences into your memory. You think deeply about things, about yourself and about yourself in relation to things. It's worthwhile. That is, if you don't do it all the time. If you've been lonely for as long as you can remember, the point of diminishing returns has probably been reached. Time to find a friend.

Now, the second advantage of traveling alone can be utilized. Namely, you can find a friend and start traveling together. In general, it's much easier to find a traveling companion than it is to get rid of one. Even if you're the type that doesn't meet people easily, you'll find that traveling in Europe is a special case. You'll meet and talk to other travelers in bunches. In hotels, restaurants and travel bureaus, on trains and buses, in the streets and parks, everywhere you turn. It's unavoidable. Wait and see.

TAKE A FRIEND

Taking a friend with you is already more complicated. But hail friendship and damn the complications. Going to Europe is a big adventure, and can be a frightening one. Most people feel much better about having a friend along to bolster their confidence and share the problems. And to share the joys. Remember that in Europe you'll probably experience some alienation, due to the impact of different cultures, foreign languages and new life patterns. Having someone along makes a big difference. Looking at the positive side of it, no one can have more fun than two people traveling together. You share the delight and the newness, you cope with problems and snags together, and every experience is multiplied by two.

But a long trip, especially one studded with privations and challenges, is a severe test of friendship. When things aren't going too well, when you're stuck somewhere, when you're miserable or uncomfortable or embarrassed, you're going to find yourself blaming either your travel companion or yourself for your troubles. Either way, it's rough. After a while, long-time travel companions just naturally start hating each other.

So, be prepared to split up if incompatibility sets in. It may not come to that, but keep it in mind as a possibility before you start. No blame need be involved. The way to handle this is to split up every so often, making arrangements to meet again later on. You can do this for hours at a time, days at a time or weeks at a time. Highly recommended to keep the proper perspective. (Only in extreme circumstances should you agree to split up forever.)

There are many other advantages to traveling together. Certainly cost-sharing is one of them, especially as regards hotel rooms. Paying for a double room almost always costs you proportionately less than for a single. You also save in buying food at grocery stores for communal consumption, for books and magazines, etc.

Another advantage of togetherness is diversity: two heads are better than one. Take languages. Traveling with Stephanie on my last trip, I found her command of French, though limited, made all the difference in communicating with Arabs across North Africa. And her rudimentary Russian could conceivably have been useful, too (when meeting exchange students or espionage agents). On an earlier trip I traveled with Julian, who spoke French and Danish while studying Greek and Guitar. I speak a little each of Spanish, German and Polish (all of which I learned in Europe), so between myself and a linguistic companion, we can go most anywhere in Europe and have suitable sounds to make. (Grunt.)

Another time, I traveled with Paul, a flash-fingered folk singer/guitarist/harmonica player. His talents quickly made friends for us and in a pinch could provide us with an income (street-singing, for example). In the same way, my camera helped along the way to make contacts, and I did earn a few kroner with it as well. Pool your talents.

Diverse personalities help in a similar way, provided you can get along with each other first. People you meet will often respond to one of you more than the other, which may result in, say, an invitation to dinner or a place to sleep for the night or a guided tour of some local attraction. For hitchhikers, if often means a ride a few miles further into the center of town rather than the outskirts, or a longer ride than first agreed on.

Hitchhiking for two people together can be good. Whatever your sex, from the standpoint of rides alone, you'll be better off if the second party is a girl. For example, assume you're a girl: by traveling with another girl, drivers will see you two as even more of a good thing than one. Of course, having a guy along brings other compensations, one being an increased sense of security. Now, assume you're a guy: unquestionably you should be hitchhiking with a girl. She'll be your passport to lots of rides, so take good care of her. Going with another guy is generally better if you plan to rough it, but you will have more trouble getting rides. More about this in Chapter 8.

One of the things to remember if you're traveling with a companion of the same sex: you will find yourself competing with each other for members of the opposite sex. It's no big thing, but it's one of the ways that disagreements start. Talk it over or work it out in order to keep resentments down.

Finally, what about more than two people traveling together? This is an excellent arrangement if you have the right means of transportation. Definitely out for hitchhiking. Okay if you're using public transportation. Best of all if you're using private transportation: walking, bicycling, motoring or camper-bus motating. If you can handle the crowd, the general rule is the more, the merrier—especially for good friends.

LOVING COUPLES

(If you're unmarried, see Chapter 14 about checking into hotels.) This is like taking a friend, only much more so. When you travel with a lover, whether shipped from America or newly found on location, both the advantages and disadvantages of traveling with a friend are accentuated. Pleasures become raptures; disagreements are crushing. It's unquestionably the best way of really getting involved in the experience, because the ups and downs all make it memorable. The emotional drain is considerable, but you won't be bored. If you're not particularly involved with your travel companion, this tepid relationship tinges the things you do together with ennui. But if you love someone, particularly with the freshness of a new love, or if you just care for someone as a friend, the things you experience together will have a quality of richness that will make your trip memories last a lifetime. And the fights! These will be magnificent. In the course of them, try to avoid becoming violent: Europeans have already heard enough about American violence without your giving them any demonstrations.

FAMILY TRAVEL

Is it possible to vagabond in Europe with a family? Definitely, but there are obstacles. Traveling with your spouse is okay because that's generally like traveling with your lover. However, a special note.

As we all know, married couples are frequently not lovers at all. They live together for mutual convenience but enjoy no worthwhile relationship with each other. Taking a standard tour of Europe will be okay for them, but attempting to vagabond will put strains of reality on the relationship that may disrupt it. In fact, this is the way my own marriage broke up. My wife and I car-camped all over Europe, and the stresses of aimless traveling upset what had been a delicate balance. Finally, it was in Spain we let it all hang out, and went separate ways. I don't regret that trip even a little bit; it just happened that one of the casualties was our marriage. Oh, well.

On another trip I went to Europe with my parents. Frankly, I had a lot of trepidations about how we'd get along (after all, you can always get another wife . . . but another mother?). I have to hand it to them. We covered a lot of ground, taking trains, buses and planes, and the only problem was that they tired more easily than I did. However, they sensibly went to sleep when they were tired, leaving me free to roam around as I pleased. They are unpretentious and practical people, for which I am thankful. They took relatively little interest in cathedrals, museums and other tourist attractions that they would never visit in America either. Instead, they were interested in the everyday details of European life and made efforts to meet people wherever we went (in fact, I met many older people I probably couldn't have met by myself). In short, they were as full of enthusiasm and excitement as anyone could reasonably expect. My dad is a baker, and all through Europe he walked into the back of bakeries to look over the equipment and premises and meet some of the bakers. Far out. We had a grand time, and I would unhesitatingly travel with them again. So it is possible. In the end, it all comes down to personalities, as usual. Some people travel badly, whether they're five years old or fifty years old, whether they're parents or pubescents. Especially if you're of high school or college age and your parents invite you on a trip to Europe with them, I'd say:

1) Go in any case, but
2) consider who they are and what they're like, so that you can
3) work out reasonable compromises that take into account what you *each* want from the trip. Among other things, make certain to
4) arrange time for yourself to do some things *you* want to do. It's important to have some time away from your parents, and vice versa (though they may not realize it).

Traveling with children is the most difficult of all. But even this can be done successfully, even brilliantly, providing that special consideration be given to the needs of the children en route. This means they must be able to nap, they have to be able to be fed easily, changed if they're at diaper age—in other words, all the myriad necessities must be fulfilled so that they will be kept receptive themselves. They need attention and

45

love, with a minimum of being dragged about and nagged at. Crying children, whining children, unhappy children, will easily destroy your trip.

What this means is that in actual practice the only feasible means of transportation is the camper-bus. It's the only way you can nap your children, keep them enclosed, feed them whenever they need it, give them a sense of "home" for security and still keep moving on any kind of free schedule. I traveled with my six-year-old daughter in Europe for six months, so I know whereof I speak. The camper-bus also will put you in contact with peer companions for your kids, especially at campgrounds. Kids need other kids, too, and, as a result, two children travel better than one. In fact, if you have an only child, I'd seriously consider inviting his or her best friend along if it can be worked out.

There's one fantastic advantage in having children along. Europeans adore children. By pulling one out into the open now and then, you've got the best ice-breaker in the world. Your child is a magic midget who will make acquaintances, dispel hostility and put you in direct contact with Europeans. By the way, a trip to Europe can be a great boon to your child's education. For a growing child to see another culture, realize that other people are different, that other languages are actually spoken, is to enrich his or her education as no school can ever do. But it works only if you are willing to make whatever modifications in your own plans necessary to keep the children happy. If they're not happy, if they're merely resented baggage, the worm will turn and eventually it will be you and your spouse who are dragged . . . through hell.

Chamonix, France: One of the models for the mountaineer's fashion show? No, it's just one of the commuters on the cable car that runs up to 12,000 feet on the side of Mt. Blanc. Far up, non?

7   RAGS AND BAGS

RAGS, OR HOW TO DRESS
APPEARANCES ARE REVEALING
BAGS, OR WHAT TO TAKE
PACKING LIST FOR MEN
PACKING LIST FOR WOMEN

RAGS, OR HOW TO DRESS

Packing clothes for a vagabonding trip to Europe means taking as close to nothing as possible, while being ready for as close to everything as possible. Your rags should be suitable to the climate (more likely, several climates), hard to wear out, resistant to soiling, washable in cold water, neat in appearance, adaptable to city or country and light in weight. Whatever you wear, the paramount rule is to travel light. As a brief summary of what follows: take a few pairs of socks, a couple of changes of underwear, the clothes on your back, plus one and a half changes of clothes.

I recommend that your basic outfit be for the city. For men, a pair of wash-and-wear tough-weave slacks, a long-sleeved dress shirt (formal with a tie, but sporty open-necked) and a sports jacket that looks pretty good but which you don't mind rolling up into a ball to go into your pack. For women, a wash-and-wear skirt (maybe wraparound), a long-sleeved blouse, with perhaps some bodice frills to dress it up, and a cardigan sweater or light, casual coat. This is your basic outfit for any occasion. Your other outfit should preferably interchange piece by piece with this one, but will be more dressy for dining out, theater-going and other occasions where you want to be better dressed than just casual. This especially applies to women, because a man with a dress shirt and sports jacket is presentable on a majority of occasions, but the woman's other outfit should probably be a dress or perhaps a light suit, and a pair of shoes to go with it. The remaining one-half outfit should be Levi's and a tough shirt for both men and women. Everybody should bring a sweater, and in wintertime one more to wear over the first one. Definitely take a raincoat. It

49

should be one that can be worn as a light overcoat in cold weather, or as a windbreaker on the road. Bring a water-resistant cap or hat and a colorful wool scarf. Europeans wear short shorts a lot (not Bermudas), and so can you. This will also be your bathing suit. Women can make a top when needed out of boy-scout type bandanas, which is another thing everybody should take. Now you're just about all set. Very important: make sure your footwear is comfortable. For vagabonders who are going to be on the road a lot (hikers, hitchhikers and others), the main concession to the road is a pair of hiking boots, instead of or in addition to ordinary street shoes (which won't survive country mud, snow or rain). And throw in a pair of sandals. A last planning note for winter travelers: pick your clothes so that as it gets colder you can put on more and more of them; ideally, you could wear them all at once without looking too much like a clothes rack.

Car campers are about the only people who should bring a little bit more, because they have the room and they may as well. But not much more. Remember that if you need clothes, you can always buy them. Clothing is everywhere cheaper than in the U.S.A. Buy what you need when you need it, give away or sell what you're through with. Detailed check lists for guys and girls appear a few pages ahead.

APPEARANCES ARE REVEALING

"When in Rome, do as the Romans do" is okay advice, but don't expect anyone to think that you're Roman just because you're trying to do whatever it is that Romans do. You're a tourist, baby, and everything about you will announce it to the world. The important thing is not to get uptight about it. It's cool to be just what you are: a tourist. It's uncool to pretend to be anything else. Don't try to hide it to spare yourself embarrassment. Play the role and enjoy it. The point is that if you don't put anybody on, you're free to make dumb mistakes at times, to mispronounce all the words and garble the meanings, to look confused when in fact you are, and so forth. Traveling in a foreign country automatically means a lot of hassles, because through ignorance of people and places you will constantly be making an ass of yourself. But only if you're pretending to be a native or know-it-all. That's the point. To be a tourist is to be expected to make mistakes; there's no way you can avoid it. But you can be graceful about it by knowing beforehand that you are a tourist, and they know it and you know it, so it's nothing to hate anybody over. Find time to laugh at yourself and join in on the occasions when others will laugh at you.

The people I see having the most fun in Europe are young people who are obviously tourists and are freed by it. A good example: the occasional bands of roving gypsy/hippies who dress and act like they came from outer space. Wearing fantastic Afros three feet around, bedecked in iridescent jeweled coats made by stoned tribesmen from distant unknown continents, tinkling and jingling and laughing, nobody mistakes them for natives of anywhere. The result is that nobody can classify them; no code of behavior exists that they unconsciously have to adhere to. Hence, they are the freest travelers I've ever seen. That's an extreme case, but it exemplifies what happens if you just be yourself—a vagabonding American traveling through Europe to see, to learn, to experience.

By the way, regarding freaky appearances: it's okay. Europeans by and large are more tolerant than Americans about this. But it's stupid to look like a bum, or to look cruddy or unsavory. Europeans everywhere tend to dress better than Americans at home, so being neat and reasonably clean will work to your advantage and spare you unpleasant incidents with officials and citizenry. The trick is to look neat but "interesting." For example, be bearded or long-haired if you like, but dressing neatly at the same time will make you presentable instead of preposterous. Or dress differently—mod, outdoorsman, cow-hand style or whatever—just don't overdo it. Long hair on guys is a special topic that I'll talk about later—see Chapter 17, and also the Appendix, under "Morocco."

BAGS, OR WHAT TO TAKE

First, and most important, how are you going to take this stuff? For me, the most practical, the most flexible and the most interesting hand baggage is a rucksack or back pack. For hitchhikers, it's practically a requirement. A pack has the air of adventure, of faraway places, and will help you to get rides. Travelers with suitcases, duffel bags or no bags don't excite as much interest, and get fewer rides.

There are a couple of problems with a back pack, however, that may incline you otherwise. For one thing, you'll be stared at a lot wherever you carry it—on trains, buses, walking down the street, especially in hotels, and so forth. You may not like this, but you *can* get used to it. Even so, the youthful adverturer with back pack is an unwelcome visitor in some places. It's not too common, but it is starting to happen wherever lots of money is normally made shucking the ordinary tourists. This hostility is mostly from establishment types: police, border guards, hotel and restaurant keepers, etc. No big deal, but if these things will make you lower your regard for yourself, take suitcases instead. But keep the following in mind. However you choose to carry your load, be prepared to do it easily by yourself for at least a mile or two. Next, be able to do it frequently. As a traveler, generally

51

you'll walk with your baggage much more often than you want to. Your luggage should also be crush-proof, hard to lose, easy to spot and to all appearances not worth stealing. This all points to a back pack instead of a suitcase.

Here's an important tip: don't take a frame pack—that is, the rigid metal-frame type used for mountain hiking. This type of pack is intended for really heavy loads, and if you need it, you're taking too much. Also, the frame is bulky and you'll have trouble getting it into small European cars, getting on and off trains and maneuvering on crowded city buses. A frameless pack is easier to store when empty and can be used as a ground cloth underneath you when you're sleeping out. Try doing that with a frame pack!

Whatever kind of luggage you wind up taking, take it in two pieces: a big one for your clothes and other bulkier, less-used items; and a smaller shoulder bag or purse for your valuables, such as money, passport, camera. To be really handy, the latter bag should be large enough to carry maps and guidebooks, maybe a lunch (at least some fruit) and perhaps your camera and some film. The best bag I've found for this use is a small army-surplus bag about a cubic foot in size, with variable strap arrangements, so you can carry it on your shoulder, around your waist or in your hand.

Just about everything else you'll need is listed on the following pages in the packing lists. Most of the items are self-explanatory, but I'll comment on some of them here.

Sleeping Bag: This is a must for hitching/vagabonding. Requirements are given in Chapter 14.

First-Aid Kit: A simple collection of things you may need, but which may be inconvenient to find at the time. Suggested contents are given in Chapter 17.

Camera and Film: See Chapter 17 again for recommendations.

Poncho: This serves mostly as a ground cloth when sleeping out, but is handy as an emergency shelter or as a covering for your luggage. The familiar army type is good but heavy; get a lighter nylon one (about $15) if you can afford it.

Bota: You need something in which to carry liquid refreshment, preferably collapsible, and the Spanish wine bag (*bota*) made of leather is perfect. Any outdoor outfitter here sells them, but they're much cheaper in Europe. Without one, you'll get unpleasantly parched on the road in areas lacking convenient waterholes. Also, bear in mind that in most of Europe you pay a deposit on any container or bottle, which adds up after a while.

Pocketknife: Innumerable daily uses if you have one that contains blade, can opener, corkscrew, scissors, tweezers and all those neat things. Almost the only one to have is the famous Swiss Army knife, sold everywhere, but cheaper in Europe and especially at duty-free stores.

Clock: A small folding travel alarm clock is worthwhile if you're sleeping out or car-camping and want a wake-up service to get an early start on the road or the day.

Flashlight: Again, for sleeping out this is a necessity. Take the miniature kind. Unless you reverse the batteries when you don't need them, you're certain to discharge them accidentally in your pack.

Marker Pen: For making hitchhiking signs—next chapter.

Soap: This is a rare item in cheaper European hotel rooms, and you'd better bring it with you if you expect to see it. Bring some way to conveniently carry it (soap dish). Soap will not only be for your face and feet but for washing clothes, so pick a medium-strength bar.

Toilet Paper: Again, an infrequently encountered luxury. Unless you enjoy using the back of your hand, you should start off with a small roll. Afterward, replenish it from bathrooms that do have it. European toilet paper, by the way, can be very weird. Some of it is like sandpaper, some like wax paper. Of related interest: wait until you see the bathroom fixtures of Europe. There's the bidet (bee-day), which is found in most hotel rooms without toilet or shower, and is a useful substitute for both. Hmmm. Then there is the German-style toilet, where you deposit your feces for inspection on a platform before flushing away. Finally—voilá—the French-style (Turkish) toilet, the end achievement of Gallic art. You squat on a porcelain slab with a dark hole in the center, and hope your aim is good. When you flush, the water inundates the entire slab, including your feet. You'll love it.

PACKING LIST FOR MEN

Basic Items

Back pack, frameless
Shoulder bag, army-surplus
Sleeping bag, down-filled
Wallet
Watch or clock
Passport and health card
Tickets

Simple first-aid kit (see page 170)
Camera (and lenses)
Film in cans
Ground cloth (poncho)
Bota
Swiss Army pocketknife
(Student card)

Clothes

Lightweight dress raincoat
Wool jacket (safari-type—lots of
    pockets) or sports jacket
Pullover sweater (2 in winter)*
Long-sleeved dress shirt and tie
Long-sleeved cotton shirt
Corduroy pants
Levi denims
Belt
3 pair cotton socks
2 pair wool socks*
3 pair underwear

Long-sleeved wool shirt*
3 undershirts
Gloves, leather or wool*
Lightweight dress shoes,
    comfortable
Hiking boots
Sandals
Wool scarf*
Wool cap*
Brimmed hat, crushable
Bandana/handkerchief
Shorts (swimsuit)

Other

Small flashlight or Penlite
Felt marker pen
Soap bar and dish
Toilet paper
Comb, pocket
Towel, small
Toothbrush (?)
Shaver and blades (?)
Small American flag (?)
Pocket dictionaries/phrase books
Map(s)

Sewing kit (needle, thread, safety
    pins)
Extra passport photos for visas and
    gifts
Guidebook(s)—or selected pages
    therefrom
Address book
Journal or diary
Pen and pencil
Sunglasses and case
Smoking supplies (?)

Suggestion: Waterproof all garmets and cloth articles with Scotch-Guard
or other spray.

---

*Winter trip. Asterisked clothes discarded or mailed home when winter is over.

Basic Items

Back pack or rucksack, no frame
Large canvas purse with shoulder
   strap
Sleeping bag, down-filled
Wallet
Passport and health card

Tickets
First-aid items (see page 170)
Birth-control pills or
   diaphragm (see page 170)
Pocketknife
Camera and film
(Student card)

Clothes

Lightweight trench coat
Wool suit or dress*
Drip-dry dress
Pullover sweater (2 in winter)*
2 blouses, long-sleeved
Skirt
Slacks or jeans
Jacket (windbreaker)
Underwear
Tights, several pairs—useful as
   long underwear, too
3 pair wool socks*

Medium-heeled shoes,
   comfortable
Rainboots—calf-length and/or
   hiking boots
Gloves, wool or leather*
Sandals
Scarf, wool*
Cap, wool*
Brimmed hat, crushable
Bandana/babushka
Shorts (bathing suit)

Other

Small flashlight
Soap bar and dish
Toilet paper
Toilette/cosmetic articles in
   small kit
Towel, small
Tampax
Sewing kit, simple
Map(s)

Guidebook(s)—or just the pages
   you'll need
Address book
Journal or diary
Pen and pencil
Extra passport pictures—for visas
   and keepsakes to new friends
Sunglasses and case
Pocket dictionaries/phrase books

Suggestion: Waterproof your clothes and things with a suitable spray.

*Winter trip. Asterisked clothes given away or mailed home in the spring.

Somewhere in Morocco: Not much to say about this: The photo says it. Hitching actually does bring you to spots like this, where the unknown and the exotic become everyday, where you stand at some far-out spot and feel it's right where you belong.

8 WHAT ABOUT HITCHHIKING?

WHAT IT IS
DANGERS OF HITCHHIKING
THE HITCHHIKING GIRL
WHERE RIDES COME FROM
MORE HITCHHIKING TALES
WHICH COUNTRIES ARE BEST?
TOO OLD TO HITCHHIKE?
A MOMENT OF TRUTH

WHAT IT IS

Hitchhiking is a much misunderstood means of travel. Mention hitchhikers to most people, and images of crime, violence, tramps and general unpleasantness clog their heads. On the other hand, most people who have actually engaged in hitchhiking have mixed feelings about it, but wind up thinking about it as an enjoyable experience. In fact, it's hard to say what hitchhiking really is because it's different for everyone. Unquestionably, it's a heavy experience, which accounts for both its advantages and disadvantages. The advantages are fantastic: you can travel as far as you want to go for no money at all; you don't have to worry about your vehicle breaking down, being stolen, or any of that usual capitalistic possessiveness trip; you're forced to meet all kinds of people in every walk of life; and mostly as a result of them, your travels are adventurous and joyous. Like, wow! If those incentives don't stir you even a little, then it's getting very late for you, pal. Go back and watch the boob tube some more.

However, the disadvantages are considerable. But they're also interesting. The very same thing that makes hitchhiking an adventure— namely, the uncertainty, the challenge of the unknown— is also hard to take after a while. How long it's going to be before the insecurity buckles you depends both upon yourself and the kind of experiences you have en route. But it's not entirely unpredictable. There are some certainties about it: you can be sure you will be uncomfortable, discouraged and disturbed. You'll get rained on, you'll get sunburned,

57

you'll be stared at and you'll be very soul-weary. I'll elaborate on these things more in the next chapter, but for now let me just say that whatever happens to you, you'll live.

DANGERS OF HITCHHIKING

Speaking of living, a lot of people think that they are in danger of ceasing to do so if they take up hitchhiking. How dangerous, exactly, is hitchhiking? Let us be clear about this and admit that hitchhiking does involve some dangers. When reviewing it, however, bear in mind the old truism that the most dangerous place in the world is your own home.

Probably the biggest danger to the hitchhiker is that of being struck by a car. By continually standing next to a traffic stream and sometimes unwisely getting involved in it or exposed to it, you run the risk of being struck. This is something to bear in mind always; this danger can be greatly minimized by your judicious selection of hitchhiking locations. I discuss this in detail in the next chapter.

The next biggest danger, but the one paramount in most people's minds, is that one arising from your helplessness in the face of people who deliberately want to do you in: robbers, murderers, rapists and weird people like that. The hitchhiker, frankly, is more vulnerable than most to these encounters, but considering it on the basis of statistical likelihood, there really isn't a hell of a lot to worry about. Especially in Europe, where violence is not a way of life. Even if you should meet one of these people, you are by no means robbed, raped and murdered just because you've met them. The specific personal interaction that takes place is all-important, and the odds are excellent that you can handle a potentially unpleasant situation if things come together that way. But to go around worrying about it is really dumb. If you honestly believe that you should not go hitchhiking because it's too dangerous, then let me advise you that your fear is irrational, and perhaps you should consider facing that fear by trying some hitchhiking yourself. In fact, hitchhiking is no more dangerous than a hundred other things we do all the time, most of which are far less rewarding.

Some other less-than-wonderful people you'll meet might be an occasional homosexual, the weekend drunk, the East European smuggler, and if you're a girl alone, the cat who insists on feeling you up. Of course, the longer the trip, the more you autostop, the greater the chances of encountering these types. This is part of the adventure, but you want to avoid crossing over the line between adventure and disaster. Probably the best single response to people who hassle you or disturb you is to ignore them as best you can for as long as you can safely do so. In any case, stay calm and get out at the earliest opportunity. To show disgust, indignation or fear is often to provide them with an emotional response that feeds their hang-up. They want a response.

If they don't get it, they'll lose interest and let you out. By the way, don't carry any lethal weapon with you. The European police will make you exceedingly unhappy if they ever pick you up with it, and they should. The chance of actually needing it to protect yourself is much smaller than the chance you'll hurt someone or yourself with it.

In general, you have to consider these "dangerous" aspects of hitching in a philosophical way. However, Europe is not a dangerous place. Compared to America, crime and violence are insignificant. With very few exceptions (some Mediterranean port cities, primarily), Europe is "safe" for individuals anywhere and at all hours. You can roam deserted back streets at night in complete safety and can trust strangers; you can experience a delightful freedom from fear that is virtually unknown to Americans.

THE HITCHHIKING GIRL

Ah, the painful truth . . . men can do anything they want to, but women can only do what they can get away with. Certainly this applies to hitching. It comes down to who you are and where you are. Sweetheart, *you* might be able to hitch alone through Italy, Spain, Morocco, Turkey and other places where the masculine-machismo insanity prevails, but don't count on it being easy. In these places, women are still literally behind the plow, the veil and the cradle. The emancipated lone woman hitchhiker is first and foremost a sex object. Her existence will be viewed by some as deliberate provocation: she can't escape being hassled.

Nevertheless, lots of women do hitchhike alone. They're the ones who are good at life games and are willing to write off an occasional failure to experience. As a matter of fact, there isn't much physical danger, but you might frequently be uncomfortable. A lot of men will make some advances to check you out as a sexual possibility . . . that's why they gave you the ride in the first place. Coolness and pugnacity will almost always fend them off. Just about every one of these guys are playing out their fantasies, and prove quite harmless in the end. In extreme cases, however, the end may not come until you've had to push, slap, scream, etc.

Incidentally, don't look for help from local women. For example, a girl hitching in parts of Spain may get spit upon by the village women, which isn't all fun and games. To these over-Catholic ladies, you can only be a *puta*, a whore come to corrupt their men.

Girls, you can vastly improve the odds by hitching only during the day (especially if alone) or hitching with another person. Another

59

girl is fine, but not foolproof. Hitching with a guy is the best way, but when you do this you should generally pass yourself off as man and wife, whether or not you actually are. Many foreign men will give a couple a ride but ask you if you're married. If you are not, they will consider the girl to be fair game.

For the single girl, more tips: before you get in, try a few words with the driver. This way you can check out the vibes, see if he's drunk and generally look the scene over. Keep alert, and if it doesn't hit you right, don't get in. After all, there'll be another one along in a few minutes. If your would-be benefactor doesn't want to accept this and hangs around, walk the other way. On general principles, be wary of cars with two or more men in it. I'll have more to say about this in the next chapter, but the truth is that the people-dangers are either negligible or can be dealt with. Don't worry about it.

WHERE RIDES COME FROM

The people who don't give a damn also don't give rides. Every person who stops for you has quickly made a positive decision about you, and that's already a kind of involvement with you. And, by the nature of the beast, this involvement is basically a selfish one. Drivers pick you up because they want something from you. Short list of wants:

1) They're bored—you're to entertain them or vice versa.
2) They're curious—you're to provide information about something, usually yourself.
3) They want to feel charitable—you're the chosen recipient.
4) They need something tangible—you're to share expenses or help drive, etc.

Recognize that normal, healthy people basically behave in selfish ways. It gives you a base of understanding that you can turn to your own advantage—being yourself normal, healthy and selfish. For example, my earlier advice on dressing interestingly is partly predicated on this—you'll be more of a draw to the bored and curious. Remember, however, that once you have the ride, you're obligated to the driver. He may want you to talk, to listen or, perhaps, to just sit there companionably. So don't get in, mumble your destination and go off to sleep. Not only is it impolite, it's stupid. Showing some (preferably honest) interest in him is a nice expression of thanks . . . makes him feel better about picking you up. (And will incline him to pick up other hitchhikers.) Offer a cigarette or piece of chocolate to break the ice and show friendly intentions. Remember, a lot of drivers will be nervous about you and are looking for assurances too.

A driver whose friendship you've won is a good thing to have going for you. He may take you further than he'd first planned to—very common. In fact, many drivers originally announce a closer destination than they're actually going, just in case you turn out to be bad company. On becoming friends, you often get a longer ride. Or he may drive you through a large town to save you a long walk or some other problem (very helpful when you don't know the town or the language). Or drive you directly to a desired address. Or offer you a meal or a bed. Or give you a sightseeing tour out of pride and friendliness.

In Denmark, leaving Copenhagen on a rainy windswept day, I took a 70-kilometer ride offered. We conversed animatedly, he reached his turnoff and just kept going for 80 kilometers past his destination. He explained he had nothing else to do and liked my company enough to keep me from wet discomfort as long as he could.

In Zurich, a Swiss gave a friend and me a 100-kilometer ride across the German border, right to the start of the northbound autobahn. Originally he was only going part way. Not only that, but he stopped along the route to show us some Roman ruins, gave us a short tour of Basel, helped us change money at the border, bought us a meal and beer on the German side and insisted we take some money from him (a few dollars each). As we left him (somewhat dazed), he pressed on us whatever he had left in his pockets: a partial pack of cigarettes, pipe tobacco, some gum, and then apologized for being unable to do more. Why all this? Yes, he was a good guy, but it was also because we tried to answer all his (many) questions about America and we didn't laugh at his fumbling English.

In West Germany, a young engineer gave us a short ride in a rattletrap Mercedes, and we talked about his work (using basic English and basic German). At ride's end, he invited us home for lunch, where we met his pregnant wife. The "lunch" took all afternoon and was followed by an invitation to stay the night. We had a great evening of conversation and good feelings, and next day went on a motor tour of old castle towns thereabouts. This included a tour of Büdingen, a fairy-tale walled town, where we had tea with our hostess' parents, who turned out to be count and countess of the town's ancient royal family. Earlier we'd visited a bleak hilltop castle in which our host's wife was born, ascendant over snowy woods, and another where she grew up. We spent one night more and then were driven back to the autobahn with a near-tearful goodbye. How can this kind of memorable friendliness be repaid? By being yourself a friend, by being interested in the people you meet, by wanting to see what they want to show you. The best way to truly repay a good host is to be a good guest. And later, to be a host yourself for others.

In Holland, a teenage boy gave me a short lift to the German border on Christmas Eve night. He left me at a coffee shop, where I stopped to get out of the snow for a while. Ten minutes later he suddenly reappeared, in a rush to invite me to his parents' home to wash, eat and attend a Christmas Eve party. (He'd had to ask his mother first, hence the delayed offer.) I gratefully accepted, and emerging from a fantastic hot bath, found myself honored as the traditional holiday guest. The party was memorable—a dozen young people reciting (in Dutch) from the Bible, caroling, then eating in a hall illuminated solely by the light of many hundreds of festive candles about the room and on a twenty-foot fir tree. A pot-bellied stove roared in a corner, the snow outside silently banked on the panes, and I was amidst friends. In the morning, I breakfasted with the family, then hit the road again, laden with fourteen (yes, 14) ham sandwiches, which lasted me three days more, till Copenhagen, my destination on that trip.

Another time, a girl and I had just hitched over the Brenner Pass (in February) and found ourselves in Verona in the north of Italy. At the entrance to the Venice autostrade, standing in slush . . . an hour went by, then two hours. I began to curse my fate and worry about frostbite. But suddenly . . . succor! A beat-up delivery van stopped and a smiling little man hauled us in. The truck was laden with wine casks, and it was clear from the way we meandered from lane to lane that the driver sampled his cargo. And so we met Alberto Boscarolo, a political idealist and man of heart. Shouting above the engine noise in several languages, we gradually learned that Alberto had only five years of schooling, was from a family of eighteen kids, had been interned for a year at Matthausen death camp because of partisan activities, and worked there with the burial squads. After the war Communists couldn't find work in Italy, so he immigrated to South America for ten years. Back in Italy he married, had a family and nurtured in his mind a vision of a society without oppression and war. At one point he pulled into a rest stop on the freeway, ordered a round of drinks and we drank to the workers of the world. Back on the highway he began to sing, and then wrote down the words for us (in Italian) so we could sing along. The song extolled the world of tomorrow, a world without borders, in which black and white will clasp hands in unity and happy young people will never again be deprived of the sun. At ride's end in Padua, despite our objections (because he was obviously poor), he bought us a small lunch of wine and sandwiches, during which he cursed the police, denounced the Church and castigated Nixon. And melted us with his concern for our well-being, charmed us with his humanity and soul. In parting, he asked that we send him a photo from San Francisco showing black and white Americans together in friendship.

Hitching out of Casablanca one afternoon, a big Citroen dodged through the traffic and stopped for us. The driver, a handsome middle-aged Moroccan in a business suit, spoke no English, but we gradually tuned in to each other in French. Bad French, of course. He talked about the countryside we passed through, stopped to let me take a picture and, after a while, asked if we wanted a bit to eat. But when he pulled the car over, it was to an elegant roadside restaurant with outdoor tables and servile waiters. We ate very well indeed, including two bottles of Morocco's best wine. He paid the tab with a flourish, and now well greased and gassed, we sped away into the night to Rabat. He apologized for not being able to invite us into his home (something about his wife not understanding), but said he knew a nice hotel in Rabat, which he took us to. Indeed, it was the nicest hotel I've stayed at in three trips abroad, and he paid for the room in advance. He bade us goodnight and said he would return the following evening. We spent the next day digging Rabat. At the appointed hour he actually showed up again, treated us to another full evening of food, drink and friendship. A wealthy, intelligent and educated man, he contributed much to our knowledge of his country and its people. Much later at the hotel he paid for another night and insisted we take some spending cash as well. How can you travel better than this?

Another time in Morocco we talked two gruff soldiers into giving us a ride in their army truck. Taking rides is against orders, so they hid us in the back, closed all the flaps, and we spent one whole afternoon bouncing around in the dark. After some hours they turned off the highway onto a dirt road into the forest. We thought they might be getting ready to roll us, but when they opened the back we were confronted instead by a huge picnic lunch—fresh roast meat, fish, cheese, fruit, bread, butter, milk, wine.

In Turkey I met two American students who drove me to Athens, where we all boarded ship for Crete, just for kicks. I eventually went all through Yugoslavia and to Venice with these guys, sharing expenses for rooms but not for their auto gas and costs. I never saw them again, but during the time we traveled together we were good friends and had some far-out times.

And so it goes. I can recount similar experiences in virtually every country I visited—a civil servant in England, a schoolteacher in Sweden, farmers in Poland, a railroad worker in Hungary, a student in Czechoslovakia, peasants in Spain. The human race is full of great people, and that includes you—if you give them, and yourself, a chance.

WHICH COUNTRIES ARE BEST?

You can, of course, hitchhike anywhere that there are cars and traffic. But some places are better than others, and below is a list in which I've attempted to rate various countries according to ease of hitchhiking. Naturally, it's only a rough guideline, but it may help you in planning transportation or building expectations. Look at the Appendix for hitchhiking details on each country. Remember that you can get stuck in the best, and luck out in the worst. Much depends on your karma, as always.

BEST:	Israel	FAIR:	Switzerland
	Great Britain		Denmark
	West Germany		Greece
	Algeria		Turkey
	Tunisia		Luxembourg
	Morocco		
GOOD:	Italy	POOR:	France
	Sweden		Spain
	Holland		
	Belgium		
	Austria		
	Yugoslavia		
	Norway		

TOO OLD TO HITCHHIKE?

How old is too old to hitchhike? I think it's safe to say that young people have a better chance of getting rides than old people. But what separates old people from young people is hard to tell. Especially for a driver going by. I think the drivers tend to stop for you on the basis of a quick first impression they receive. Young people are favored at least in part because they tend to dress young. Thus, an older person who chooses to hitchhike should see what the kids are wearing and dress the same way. My guess is that if you are an older person hitchhiking, you already know this. I don't think there's any great prejudice against picking up older people, and I don't think that being "over the hill" is a reason beforehand to discard hitchhiking as a means of travel. I know this: *all* of my European hitchhiking was done after I was thirty years old. And I don't see any reason why I couldn't keep hitchhiking successfully until I am at least forty or fifty. I think that someone even older than that will get rides fairly consistently. You will be able to get the rides as long as you want to get them. I suppose that older people don't hitchhike because they're afraid or embarrassed to, not because they're unable to get rides. Buck up, Grandpa . . . let's hit the road.

A MOMENT OF TRUTH

This may be the appropriate place to speak about the personal implications of actually going to the roadside and putting your thumb out. (Or hand. Or sign. Or whatever—customs vary.) No doubt about it, it's a moment of truth. The road has a life of its own, and to join it is not always an easy thing. You don't make a gradual transition from where you were before to where you are now. It is an abrupt experience, a what-the-hell leaving behind of mother self, when you select a spot and decide to do it. It means giving yourself up to whatever comes. When you first put your thumb out, you go through changes as you realize the nakedness of your appeal.

You offer the frailty of your humanity to juggernaut forces swirling by, seeing you, searching you and then ignoring you. You feel shamed somehow; your valuable ego-self-me wonder is by-passed again and again while you stand frustrated. Hey, see me, take me, redeem me with sedan or truck, grant me recognition and acceptance. This soul-testing is very much part of hitchhiking, and you must make your peace with it in whatever way you can. Some can't, and give up what they feel isn't worth it. The first time is the hardest, but the discomfort passes as the time passes and you become accustomed to it . . . for that time and that place. But it does recur in other places and other times, because each new time is to some extent a new declaration of commitment to the road. It is a humbling position, a time of being stared at, a time of declaring to every passing motorist and to every bystander that you willingly give up certain controls over your fate, that you have confidence all the same. Of course, the starers are not really staring, nor are they aware of your insecurities . . . but you are, because you are "on the road" in a way they cannot comprehend. This you must experience for yourself, and it is a root experience of life.

Somewhere in Germany: This is not an ad for frozen food; it is an illustration of technique. The clothes are right (several pairs each of socks, pants, shirts-sweaters, headgear), the luggage is compact, the sign readable, and the location good. It didn't take long to get a ride straight to Hamburg.

9 TECHNIQUES OF HITCHHIKING

TELLING IT LIKE IT IS
THE PLACE TO DO IT
THE FREE WAY VS. THE FREEWAY
CITY TIPS
THE SIGN OF THE HITCHER
BAGGAGE
TIME OF DAY
CROSSING BORDERS
TAKE EVERY RIDE?
PERSONAL CONTACTS
TRUCKS
FOOD AND DRINK
ON BEING DISCOURAGED
ON MAKING TIME FLY

TELLING IT LIKE IT IS

Hitchhiking does not require much preparation. You don't need a college degree, you don't need journeyman's papers and you don't have to be able to paint the Mona Lisa. Hitchhiking takes more verve than brains, more nerve than skill. Nevertheless, it is practice that can be done badly or well, that can be made difficult or pleasant, depending on how you go about it. The intent of this chapter is not to teach you how you to hitchhike, but to help you do it better and enjoy it more. There isn't much learning involved, but what learning there is you have to do for yourself.

THE PLACE TO DO IT

Why don't we do it in the road? Picking the right place to hitchhike is both important and difficult. Usually you'll have to compromise in some way or other. There are two main problems in choosing the spot: the first relates to the cars and the second is about

67

you. How easily can you get to this spot? Is it safe (or legal) for you to be there? Is it sheltered and comfortable in case you end up there a long time? And what do you do from there if you can't get a ride?

Looking at each of these matters a bit further: cars beget rides, usually in direct proportion. So, study your map(s) to figure out where the most traffic would be. Figure it out on the basis of which roads you would take if you were driving. Next, lots of traffic won't help if it isn't going your way. For example, there may be lots of traffic within a city, but only a small percentage leaving town. You can't stand at a downtown intersection and hope to get a ride to the next town. You must make the outskirts where a majority of cars on the highway are going in the same direction you are. To get there, don't be afraid to ask for directions . . . it's the easiest question there is. State the name of the place you're going, point in any direction and shrug your shoulders questioningly. Ideally, you should always try to get to a spot at which all traffic is going to the same place you are.

Stand where drivers can see you. They need a long lead time to look you over, change lanes if necessary and bring the car to a stop safely. In practice, this means you shouldn't stand behind a curve, amongst other people, in the shadows, and so forth. If you're hitching at night, get under a streetlamp or some other illumination, not just for a ride but for your own safety. When hitching, never lean out or step into the road to attract the attention of a driver—it's dangerous for both you and him. Furthermore, this maneuver only annoys drivers. They'll see you if they wish to see you and believe me, they'll refuse to see you if they don't want to, even if you jump up on the hood and make faces. A good place to be noticed is near or under a traffic or road sign, which all drivers tend to glance at anyway. By implication, of course, you are also going in the same direction or to the same destination stated on the sign.

Finally, the spot you choose has to have a runout for cars nearby, or it's no good. Sometimes there simply isn't one—for example, on the entrance ramp of a freeway—and you have to hitch anyway, but you'll get far more rides if you give the motorist a place to stop for you. If you've stood at a bad or marginal spot for some time, consider leaving it to find a better one. However, as this may involve considerable exertion or uncertainty on your part, making the decision may be hard.

Next are the things you have some control over. Getting to a suitable hitching spot often is the hardest part of hitching. If you're any distance from where you have to start, allow yourself lots of time. This may mean walking through a small town, catching a bus, or buses, through a big city and just plain wandering around lost and confused almost anywhere. You may have to compromise with a poorer spot because the better one is too hard to reach. Choosing a safe spot makes good sense. Hitchhikers do risk being struck by cars, and this is a real threat, not just good-intentioned paranoia. On superhighways anytime, or at night anywhere, there's always some danger in standing by a roadside. Also consider whether your spot is legal—that is, whether the police will dig it if they see you. Pedestrians are always prohibited on freeways, and sometimes at the on-ramps, too.

Next to consider: how much personal discomfort will you be exposed to at this spot? Depending on what weather is happening, does this place give you any protection from the wind, sun, rain and poison-tipped arrows? Is it a pleasant locale to spend a couple of hours, if need be? (Days?) At least some of the places you hitchhike from should be enjoyable for their own sake, and you should look for them. Lastly, can you beat an orderly retreat? What if you can't get a ride? How easy is it to get somewhere else? Where will you sleep? Which way and how far to food, warmth and girls? (Boys?) Be wary about getting yourself out on a limb—that is, to some spot that will be difficult to back out of.

THE FREE WAY VS. THE FREEWAY

The freest way to hitch is to avoid the turnpikes, but this is difficult because they are the fastest main routes. And many European countries now have them or are building them. Germany and Italy especially. England, France, Switzerland, Austria have some, and more are coming fast. It's the old problem: having plenty of time to enjoy yourself and taking the country byways, or having less time and taking the way that is more direct and less fun. To hitchhikers, the freeway is a mixed blessing: rapid but revolting. To start with, it's illegal to walk on them and quasi-legal to stand near them. So there's police to be nervous about. Next, at any given on-ramp, the ingoing traffic will be slight compared to the total of traffic on the freeway itself. Finding the best on-ramp and getting to it by foot or bus is complicated because you will usually be in a strange city without adequate map and without sufficient linguistic skills to properly fill the information gap. To get to your spot, you may have to walk miles or go through nerve-racking omnibus episodes (where is it going and where do you get off?). If you can get anyone to drive you out there to get started right, go out of your way to make it happen. If you've stayed over in the city, this might be someone you contacted or stayed with there. If you're just passing through, try to get the driver who brought you in to take you all the way through as well. Alternatively, ask your driver to tell you the best way to the city limits (or outgoing freeway) from the spot where he's depositing you. In freeway hitching, once you've gotten to your spot, you may still have a bummer on your hands. You will sometimes find yourself standing on the edge of or in the middle of some vast concrete desolation, your ears assailed by the roar of traffic and your lungs filled with smoke and soot from the infinite exhaust.

All the other hitchers are doing the freeways too, so if you have the option, why don't you do something else? Take the time and go another way, on the older roads through the smaller towns. You'll move slowly but see far more.

CITY TIPS

Anytime you can get city maps, do so. Not only for sightseeing information, but you will find them either useful or necessary for getting across town so you can start hitching. Especially if you're on foot, the weather is bad or threatening and time is short, some kind of route-finding efficiency is mandatory, and you need a city map. Get them at tourist offices, railroad information offices, in some guide-books (for example, the Green Michelin series) and bookstores. They will also show you the way to the railroad stations, which make the best bases of operation in almost any city. Always ask for a ride to the (main) railroad station when someone is bringing you into a strange city. Invariably, it will be in the center of things, near information, lodging and transportation. Once there, you can sit down and think about what you want to do, and get maps and sightseeing information, have a meal—either at the station restaurant (often inexpensive) or from a fruit/candy/sundries counter, catch forty winks if you need it, store your luggage or pack, or just watch the funny-looking foreigners go by. About storing your pack: if it's beat-up looking enough, you can leave it in any corner or on top of a locker for hours or days without checking it or worrying about it.

THE SIGN OF THE HITCHER

In many if not most European hitching situations, don't hold your thumb out at all—show a sign instead. A little skill at sign-making will go a long way, literally. Carry a large felt-tip pen or grease pencil (preferably one that won't smear if it rains) as a part of your traveling kit. Signs should be big enough to be seen—at least twelve to eighteen inches long, with large, thick letters. Points to note:

1)   Use cardboard of some kind; fold it for stiffness in the wind.

2)   Keep your eye peeled for sign materials; when you see a good piece of sign material, store it in your pack for future use.

3) Use large lower-case letters if you can print them well enough (they're more readable than capitals—like freeway signs).

4) Use the European spelling of your destination, not the English (München, not Munich; Roma, not Rome). Check your map for the right spelling.

Signs are often a necessity. For example, when you stand at a freeway entrance that feeds in all directions, you've got to inform the motorist which direction you want. He'll be reluctant to stop and ask you. Signs are almost always useful in any case. They make you easier to spot, and tell something about you. Most of the time, it will help to have a flag on your bag or sign, or "U.S.A." in capital letters. This will enable you to meet both friendly and unfriendly natives who want to praise and revile America, respectively, or most often those just curious about America and wanting to talk about it. Another ride-getter (sometimes) is a musical instrument, such as guitar, banjo, harmonica (the latter is best). Show it by the roadside, or maybe play it as you hitch. Mere possession will help, but you may be asked to play it in the car.

BAGGAGE

As mentioned before, having baggage is an asset. It makes you a serious traveler rather than some untrustworthy dilettante. However, more than one bag or pack is too much. From the driver's viewpoint, picking up a hitchhiker is one thing. Helping him relocate his household possessions is another. When hitching, don't hide the pack, but do stand in front of it. If you do have too much, try to compress, stack or otherwise make it look smaller. In North Africa, I met an American couple actually planning to hitchhike with frame packs, suitcases and skis! Leave your toboggan at home, too.

TIME OF DAY

For some reason, catching a ride is easiest in the morning. In countries where the going is worst, the very early morning hours are the best. I suppose it's because there is more traffic on the road then, as everyone goes to work. Hitching after dark is certainly possible, but your ride chances are reduced. If you wish to, or have to hitch after dark, do so under a street light. You not only enhance your ride chances but your chances of survival till morning.

Particularly in the south of Europe (and North Africa), night traffic falls to zero, or close to it, and hitching is mostly a waste of time. Better catch some sleep instead. This also applies to the hot afternoon siesta hours.

CROSSING BORDERS

Rides at a border are harder to get because the majority of road traffic in a country is internal. Lots of cars go to or near the border, but few cross it. If you get stuck at a frontier, as the Europeans call it, try to intercede personally in your own behalf with the motorists. Inquire about a ride as they go through the border formalities. You'll get out much faster. And take even a short ride; it may be all you'll get. Furthermore, every mile penetrated into a country increases the amount of internal traffic as opposed to across-border traffic, thereby increasing your ride chances. Sometimes it's worth walking away from a border, especially if there is a horde of hitchhikers, as there often is in summer. Many motorists will balk at giving a ride when confronted with a dozen or more hitchers thrusting their thumbs, but may well pick you up if you hike a few hundred yards past the beseeching mob. When you're in such a crowd, don't expect the first party to get the first ride. The fifth in line may have a better chance than the first. It depends on the spot you have (is there enough room for a car to pull over?), how you look (crummy?) and on the motorist himself. Let's face it, the average European motorist confronted with a rogue's gallery of hitchhikers will select someone who looks reasonably clean, doesn't have too much baggage, indicates with a readable sign where he wants to go and perhaps has a good-looking girl with him. Wouldn't you?

TAKE EVERY RIDE?

The general rule is to accept every ride offered, but there are exceptions. Don't leave a good hitching spot unless you're reasonably sure of getting to another good one. If you're out in the tules somewhere, a short ride going a few miles further doesn't count for too much. You have to weigh strategic advantage against mere distance. Also, you're hitching not simply to cover distance; shorter rides can prove as interesting as long ones. Nearing a large city or leaving a border, every ride is as good as gold. Freeways are again the main offenders here: accepting a short ride to some small town a few miles ahead may leave you stuck at an on-ramp that gets no traffic. In the countryside without freeways, accepting short rides is okay because one spot is as good as another and short rides may be all you get, anyway.

Always be alert to get rides by making personal contacts with drivers, wherever they may happen to be stopped. For example, gas stations, restaurants, truck stops, rest stations, picnic areas, campsites, etc. Every so often you'll run into motorists with flat tires, vapor lock or other short-term troubles (including a need to empty bladders on unsuspecting trees) that you can turn into rides for yourself.

Study the license plates of cars. Often you can relate them to where they're going and, as a result, will be able to more efficiently ask for rides. For example, in Germany license plates bear letters designating region of origin: M for München, H for Hamburg, etc. Also, American military personnel and their families drive cars with red or green U.S.A. license plates; the cars themselves are almost always the standard oversized Yankee chrome barges. You'll seldom get a ride from one, even when carrying a U.S.A. sign and waving and hollering. Demoralizing, but common. American troops and tourists aren't much on giving rides at home, and they're worse in Europe. Most of your rides will come from Europeans, although there are thousands of American motorists on European highways. When I refer to tourists/motorists in this book, I generally mean European nationals, not Americans.

In truth, the Americans aren't all that bad. I've gotten rides from Americans, but there is a trick to it. Americans simply aren't in the habit of picking up strangers, especially foreigners (ugh), so you have to make personal contact with them. If you can do that, you're in. Speak to them at gasoline stations, at border gates, on ferry boats, in restaurants, etc. Identify yourself ("Hi, Yank, me Yank too, yes?") and name your desire ("Hey, buddy, how 'bout a lift to Corsica?") and you'll make out okay. But don't expect miracles of national brotherhood. U.S. troop movements in Germany are good for back-of-truck rides if you can catch them while they're stopped for gas or pisscall, but you don't see them every day.

TRUCKS

Generally speaking, make hitching overtures to almost all vehicles passing by, including trucks. You rarely get rides from trucks, especially large trucks, but this has to do primarily with company regulations and insurance policies. Truckers are forbidden to pick up riders, but they occasionally break the rules. Smaller trucks in particular, driver-owned or small-company operated, are much more likely to give you rides. When you get them, truck rides are something else because they vary from panel trucks to grain wagons to army transports, enclosed rides,

73

open rides, and with all manner of cargoes. They can range from your most comfortable rides to your most miserable. Truckers tend to be more down-to-earth and horny everywhere, so girls or guys with girls will get more truck rides than just guys alone.

FOOD AND DRINK

If you fail to go food-shopping on your hitchhiking days, you will rue it. Always try to keep an emergency stock of food and drink in your pack—a can of sardines, some bread, a few oranges and wine in your *bota* can make all the difference. You will swear that these humble items are amongst the most delectable morsels you've ever eaten. Life on the road keeps your appetite sharp, and you will enjoy these improvised snacks enormously. Always buy a little more than you need so that you'll have some left over in case you aren't able to replenish by the next meal. And to offer to drivers who pick you up or people you meet on the road. By such simple means, you will be able to keep smiling . . . and, like the song says, when you're smiling, the world smiles with you.

ON BEING DISCOURAGED

But what if you're not smiling worth a damn? What if you're discouraged, unhappy, freaked out, hysterical and other interesting if unpleasant states of being? The first thing to know regarding this is that you will be. Hitching is not exactly a totally pleasant joy ride through fun land. Everyone who hitches can recount moments of despair from being rideless, uncomfortable, lonely, embarrassed, endangered. Whatever it is that you personally react adversely to, sooner or later you will experience it in hitching. And yea, that too shall pass away. Not only that, but you'll probably recall it as the very height of the good old days.

> "Now it is a strange thing, but things that are good to have and days that are good to spend are soon told about, and not much to listen to; while things that are uncomfortable, palpitating, and even gruesome, may make a good tale, and take a good deal of telling anyway."

> *—The Hobbit* J.R.R. Tolkien

Remember that although you can travel almost anywhere by hitching, it's wrong to think that it is somehow comparable to the train or bus.

You meet guys who say, "Oh, yeah, I made it from there in four hours," or, "Sure, it only takes two days to get there," or whatever—the implication being that it always takes that long or is always that easy. Of course it ain't so, as you will perceive when you're on the road attempting to do it. Hundreds or thousands of cars may pass by before you will get just one ride. In other words, the ride probability factor is shockingly low. In any given place at any given time, you're hoping for certain drivers to come by. Of all the people in the world who might conceivably give you a ride, perhaps none at all will pass by. Chance being what it is, one or two probably will, but there's no guarantee. This chance factor is completely unpredictable. The type of traffic going by can be guessed successfully. For example, businessmen going to work, workers on their way home, farmers, tourists, whatever . . . but the driver who picks you up often turns out to be someone unpredictably individual. You constantly meet people you wouldn't even guess existed, frequently just when you've about given up hope.

I know how discouraging it can be. I've been there often. But I also know and wish to assure you of how quickly it can all change for the better. If you're freaked out at some point (and don't think it can't happen to you) and feel you're at your limit, then the right thing to do is do something. It almost doesn't matter what you do, as long as you do something. Action precludes despair, so if you get to that state, make movements. Walk to another spot, give it up for the day, get on a bus, crawl into a hole and sleep. The main thing is to get into a different head so you can carry on another time. Plan to use public transportation occasionally, not only to save your life at times but also to keep yourself sane.

ON MAKING TIME FLY

Despair is one problem of hitching; just plain boredom is another. Standing idly by a roadside for hours might seem an unproductive use of time, especially of your hard-won vacation time. In fact, this waiting time is never really wasted. Wherever you turn up as a hitchhiker, you are basically detached from your own environment—just a passer-by. This is an ideal position to observe whatever scene is around you. By standing around for a while, particularly in a town or village, you'll get some insights into a place—its people, its style, its rhythm. Watch what goes on around you. It merits your interest. Never mind the people looking at you—they won't eat you.

Another worthwhile activity, especially at low-fascination spots like freeways or in open country, is to think and talk. Surprisingly, hitchhikers enjoy a lot of privacy of thought, although very little privacy of person. Everybody sees the hitchhikers, but no one ever knows what they think and what they say to each other. It's that same detachment again. So, if you're alone, you can contemplate any subject with serenity.

For example, standing by the road is a marvelous place to contemplate your trip, to digest and integrate all the experiences and impressions, to consider your prospects and weigh choices ahead. A trip to Europe usually embroils you in such a stew of activity that you greatly profit by any time taken to rest from it and sort it all out in your head.

On the other hand, if you're traveling with someone, the opportunity for worthwhile communication is exceptional. People hitching together feel close to each other and rely on each other. They are sensitive to themselves and their environments. They are eager to share thoughts and feelings. The result can be the most provocative and stimulating conversation possible between people. It's one of the little recognized but important side benefits of hitchhiking.

Besides that, clowning and skylarking convert the listless hours into fleeting moments. Joke-telling, poetry recitals, Indian wrestling, contests of skill with stones and snowballs, calisthenics, are all there is. Be silly sometimes . . . what the hell. If all this is to no avail after a few hours at one spot, why, do try another. Walk a hundred yards, a kilometer, or ten kilometers. It may help your chances, and is a worthwhile activity in itself. See at least some of Europe on foot—and the more, the better. You'll see more in a mile of walking than in a hundred of riding, which we all know. So stop knowing it already, and do it—live it.

Pompei, Italy: Hiking in the rain through the streets of yore. In winter and in the rain may be the only way you'll find these streets deserted, but it's worth it. As often as possible, do what the others are not doing: go off-season instead of on, go in bad weather instead of good, walk when others ride, laugh where others cry . . .

10 WALKING AND BICYCLING

LIKE TO TAKE A WALK?
HOW TO WALK
BIKING FOR BEGINNERS
RENTAL BICYCLES

Both of these travel means are now considered old-fashioned, even in Europe. At one time there was a considerable vogue in bicycling and walking. It is over now, and has been since World War II. There is a quality of innocence, romance and patience characteristic of the long-distance biker or hiker that died in Europe with the wars. Of course, on the streets, on the highways and in the fields of Europe everywhere you will see the natives bicycling and walking. But they're going to work or going home, and you'll see few tourists doing it. Therein lies perhaps the best reason for considering it. All the other travel means are well known and overused; even hitchhiking in the last few years has lost its novelty and is becoming a standard travel means. Certainly the same thing is true of car-camping, which has become enormously popular in recent years. But walking and cycling are practically unknown, and made to order for vagabonding.

LIKE TO TAKE A WALK?

Walking is probably the oldest known form of transportation (antedated only by crawling and being carried by your mother), and in certain important ways has never been improved upon. Unquestionably, it's the purest of all vagabonding methods. If you want to see the most, experience the most and be the most carefree, look inside your shoes to discover the ultimate travel tools: your feet. It is the pace of walking i.e., its slowness, that is at once its beauty and bane. The foot traveler first of all sees much more; he notices hundreds of things the auto traveler doesn't, he has the time to integrate them and, perhaps best of all, the opportunity to stop whenever he likes to investigate further. It's ridiculously easy to meet people, and they'll be far more receptive than if you arrived in, say, the usual brightly painted steel box. When people see a hiker shuffling down the road, they have ample chance to look him over and work up a few questions in their minds, and by the time you get to them, they already feel they know you a little bit. Also, a hiker appears to be harmless, so people are naturally more open. In fact, the cross-country hiker in Europe can expect to be offered more free lodgings by friendly and curious Europeans than any other traveler. This will bring you even closer to a European ultimate experience, and at very low cost.

Hiking is also extremely flexible. Start off hiking with a few clothes in a back pack. If you get tired of doing that, you can easily start hitchhiking by the simple means of stilling your legs and activating your thumb. Or just take the train or bus until you're ready to walk again. For my money, I think some combination of hiking, hitchhiking, train riding and bicycle renting is the ultimate way to move throughout Europe. Certainly, you can walk anywhere, but in many cases walking might not be the best way to travel in terms of the rewards obtainable from it. For example, the south of Europe generally consists of large countries, long distances between cities, much barren or open land and hot climates in summer. It would seem reasonable to avoid these countries, at least until you've been to northern Europe, where villages and cities are close to each other, scenery is characterized by great variety and quantity of sights and the weather is ideal for walking. For an American, England is probably ideal. The sylvan countryside is speckled with farmhouses and inns, abbeys and castles, and the existence of a tradition of walking will bring you plaudits from the people you meet. And they speak English there, so you'll be able to communicate also.

HOW TO WALK

It's characteristic of the problems of our society that few people really know how to walk any more. And certainly not for any long distance, carrying with them the basic necessities. An excellent beginning would be to walk down to your local library and read a book called *The Complete Walker* by Colin Fletcher (Knopf, 1969; $7.95). If reading this book doesn't both convince you of the worth of doing it and also tell you exactly how to do it, then you can quit right there (and take the bus home from the library). This classic book not only gives you the *Weltanschauung* of walking, but it tells you how to do it in every detail right down to how to defecate outdoors.

The next step would be to gather particular information about a walking trip in Europe. Get some idea of what countries you'd like to visit or what parts of which countries you'd like to walk around in, and then start getting detailed information. In writing to the national tourist offices, tell them specifically that you plan a walking tour and ask them to send what information they can that would apply. In particular, ask them about where to obtain detailed maps suitable for hikers, especially ones that might show existing trails or paths; the addresses of hiking clubs in the country that might provide further information or offer their services after your arrival, perhaps even for accommodations; and the like. Hiking clubs are popular in northern Europe especially.

A variation on the walking theme, and one that all vagabonds can practice, is that of hiking in a particular area after you've used other transportation means to get there. Thus, you could hike only the West Country or the Cotswold region of England, the valleys around the Jungfrau in Switzerland, a maritime province of France, or innumerable other places. It would be something like driving to a national park in America, then going hiking after you got there. The difference in Europe is that you wouldn't be restricted to a natural environment for exploration; you could choose to hike around villages and farms, or explore islands like Capri, Guernsey and Ibiza, as well as hike to the top of Snowden, around the fjords of Norway and through the lakes districts (of England, Sweden, Poland). In all European cities walking should be your chief means of transportation when sightseeing. You can walk everywhere in Paris, in Rome, in Madrid, in Copenhagen and in most others as well. European cities were originally built for pedestrians, and they still have a human scale. If you do anything but walk, you'll miss a lot.

BIKING FOR BEGINNERS

Cycling through Europe is probably not going to interest you a lot unless you are already a biker, in which case you'll have your own ideas on the subject. Nevertheless, here are mine. The bicycle is one of man's greatest inventions, particularly because there's hardly a bad thing you could say about it. Unlike the automobile, it doesn't kill people, either violently through accidents or insidiously through poisoning. In fact, the exercise makes you healthier. It covers distances quickly but not so quickly as to remove the involvement between you and your immediate environment. Bikes are relatively cheap to buy and easy to maintain. And cycling has just about the same social advantage as walking: the ease of meeting people and sharing something of their lives, and the freedom and ease of travel.

There are only about two disadvantages, but they weigh heavily. The first and lesser one is that you're responsible for an awkwardly shaped possession, something that is always hanging between your legs or hovering helplessly nearby. It needs to be cared for in case it breaks down, it needs to be watched over to prevent stealing, and so forth. However, bikes will be accepted as cheap baggage on all European trains and buses (not planes, however); you can also hitchhike with them counting on trucks for lifts. But in general, responsibility for the machine reduces your flexibility and, furthermore, imposes its own disciplines.

This is the other disadvantage, for the disciplines imposed upon you are fairly stern ones. Mostly, you've got to be in excellent physical condition. Riding a bike mile after mile, day after day, requires that you be in condition for it. This is why you must not be a beginner if you're going bicycling in Europe. Start cycling in America first and see if you'll enjoy it—or if you can stand it. Assuming that you can and will, undertake a conditioning program before you go to Europe. You'll need about thirty days, starting with learning how to sit on the bicycle and ending up with a fifty-mile ride with a full load of luggage. Cycling also affects how you'll dress and how much you'll perspire.

To get started, get interested or purchase a bike, buy the *Complete Handbook of Cycling* ($2.10) from Big Wheel Ltd., 310 Holly Street, Denver, Colorado 80220, or the encyclopedic *The Complete Book of Bicycling* by E. Sloane (Trident Press, 630 Fifth Avenue, New York, N.Y. 10020; $9.95). Then subscribe to the monthly "Bicycling!" from H.M. Leete & Co., 256 Sutter Street, San Francisco, California 94108. Before you decide to tour, also read "Cycling in Britain," available from the British Travel Association (page 21).

The best touring bike to have is the so-called club or touring bicycle, with high-pressure tires, *dérailleur* gears (10- or 15-speed), dropped handlebars, narrow seat and lightweight frame. Prices in America go from about $100 to $400, but you can better this by buying it in Europe, where most of the best bicycles are made. If you do want to buy a bike here, look at the bicycle page in *The Whole Earth Catalog* ($5 at your bookstore) for a list of top American dealers around the U.S.A. (Moneysworth Newsletter rates the Peugeot U08 bike sold in America for $95 as a best buy.) If you already own the bike and want to take it with you (perhaps even ride it to your place of embarkation), it's quite cheap to ship over. If you go by boat, it's free. If you fly over, most airlines will carry it at the excess baggage rate—a good deal if your other baggage weighs in at under the normal baggage allowance of 44 pounds. Or you can ship it over as air cargo for about $25. Either way, the bike will go in the cargo compartment and probably will have to be packaged in some way: in cardboard sheeting with handlebars and pedals removed and everything taped closed. Check with the specific airlines to get exact information and also to find out whether you'll have to reserve cargo space on your plane.

Part of the traveling outfit with a bike should be a kit containing extra parts and repair items. Besides a tire repair kit, this should include friction tape, cable wire, brake blocks, valve stems, chain links, extra spokes and some required tools. Rain fenders and rain cape, too, for you-know-what. And a luggage rack with saddlebags. For security from thieves, a single chain and lock is probably adequate.

Getting information for your trip is important. Go through the same procedures as for walkers. Write to the national tourist offices and tell them your plans, get in touch with the bicycling clubs in the areas you're going through and obtain sources for good detailed maps of the terrain. If you're not already a member of American Youth Hostels, then you should join to find out about hosteling in Europe. The entire setup of youth hostels was originally based on bicycling and is still better suited to bicyclers than probably anyone else. Their annual handbook is full of information pertaining to cycling, including ads for places to buy them and sources of information. See page 17 for address.

Weather conditions and type of terrain are going to prove important factors in bicycling: Switzerland, Scotland, Austria, Yugoslavia, Greece and mountainous parts of other countries might warp your enthusiasm if you aren't in good physical or mental condition. Uphill grades are hard work at best and sometimes impossibly steep or long; downhill grades can be deadly. Mountain weather is also unpredictable and difficult.

All in all, take on the tall ones with care. On the other hand, countries like Holland, Belgium, Denmark are well suited to easy cycling, and even have bicycle paths along the highways. Most of France, Germany and England are also excellent cycling regions.

By doing some topological and meteorological research before you embark, you should be able to have a great trip, without throwing your bike or yourself off a cliff. Use the trains to haul the bike across the long intermediate distances.

RENTAL BICYCLES

Without exception, all able-bodied tourists should rent bikes for making short tours around the cities and into the neighboring countrysides. Bikes can always be rented easily and cheaply. The local tourist office can tell you where. Pack a lunch.

ഗ   ഗ   ഗ

To be quite honest, my experience with bicycling in Europe is scant. In Gibraltar I bought a new English "high-riser" bicycle that I peddled across into Algeciras, but its small wheels made it unsuitable for the dirt roads of the Spanish village I lived in. My only other experience comes from a cyclist I met at the youth hostel in Delphi, Greece. He was a wild-eyed ex-sailor from Manila, who was plane-hopping to Singapore, Calcutta, Bombay and various places in the Near East. He bought himself a super touring bike in Lebanon, and was having one adventure after another on his way to England. He never owned a bike before, so was still in the process of figuring it out. The mountains in that part of Greece are steep and inescapable, so he was having some difficulty. But he dug it, and planned to go all the rest of the way on it. He was a really kooky guy who talked constantly, waved his arms to illustrate his stories, pounded on the table, had a tremendous exhilaration for life and the writings of Henry Miller. I was hitchhiking at the time and frankly envied him his trip over mine. If he'd invited me to go with him (which I secretly hoped), I would have bought my own bike and gone on with him. But he didn't, so I didn't, and that was the end of my bicycling experiences in Europe.

Rzeszów, Poland: Here's the picture, snapped at the train station, that got us landed in jail. I must have looked too much like a CIA agent because both Julian and I were both picked up by the police right after this was taken. Train travel isn't perfect.

11 TRAINS AND BUSES

AIRPLANES ARE NON SEQUITURS
GETTING RAILROADED
PASSES AND DISCOUNTS
TRAIN TIMES
BUSING

AIRPLANES ARE NON SEQUITURS

Speaking of trains and buses, it doesn't follow that I should talk about airplanes, but I will digress to them briefly. Traveling by air as a way to explore Europe once you're there is not recommended. The chief objection is that you will see nothing. The second objection is that it will cost you plenty to do so. If you do take any intra-European flights, you'll get the picture fast: the planes are full of tourists, businessmen and the usual pastel air-conditioned sterility. The stewardesses speak some other languages in addition to English, but otherwise it's indistinguishable from the Cleveland to Chicago run. Aero-planing nowadays is a strange activity: hundreds of bodies are strapped into giant metal containers that then are jet-propelled from one concrete terminal to another. Use aero-planes only if you must save time. But remember that most of the time you shouldn't be saving time.

GETTING RAILROADED

When train travel is used in conjunction with other travel means, I can't recommend it enough. Forget any experiences you've had with American trains—these are different and wonderful. Much of the excitement invested in European trains derives from their widespread use by all types and classes of people. Train stations are literally and figuratively in the center of human activity. As a result, the train systems are vital, lively and exciting in a way now almost forgotten in America. In every country the depots are kaleidoscopic phantasmagorias of sight, sound, smell, touch, taste and people-people-people. By contrast, in America a train station is a ghostly place of rotted glory, fatally infected with decrepitude and ugliness. People in America got to be in too much of a hurry, and that was the end of trains (among other things). Europe is still much slower, so the trains are great.

In case you haven't seen them, most European trains are constructed on the compartment system, usually eight people each (six each in first class), and everyone gets to know everyone else before the trip is over. When boarding, what you do is stroll the corridor till you find a compartment (in your ticket category) that contains both interesting-looking people and a spot left for you. If you have to spend the night on the train, or want to in order to save money, the accommodations will be uncomfortable, but there may be compensations, depending on your compartment companions. Aboard trains is a good place to meet the people of Europe, and they will impress you with their friendliness and humanity. As for meeting the opposite sex, it is hard to improve upon the opportunities provided by train travel. Unquestionably the best way for the knockabout traveler to meet nubile numbers, male or female.

European trains don't always have dining cars, which is irrelevant because you should feed yourself by other means, anyway. Bring food and drink aboard with you (bread, cheese, wine, for example) or buy it from the vendors on the station platforms. Often it's up to you to leave the train, buy the victuals and dash back aboard just as it's pulling out.

PASSES AND DISCOUNTS

Eurailpass is a way to get unlimited train travel at a fixed price and can be a big saving if you intend to travel a lot. It also gives you numerous free bus, boat and ferry services thrown in, with reduced rates on many Europabus routes. Nevertheless, I don't recommend Eurailpass for several reasons: the first is that you can only travel first class with it. (Exception: this year—1971—for the first time, for students only (fourteen to twenty-six), a second-class pass is available—Student Rail-Pass. Two months for $125. You can get it through the CIEE.) But non-students will be forced to pay the first-class rates (like so many other Americans—forced to do everything first class). And more important, you'll meet only other tourists traveling on Eurailpass. All the good people of Europe, the burghers and the "folks," are in second class—be there!

Another objection to Eurailpass, including the student version, is that it is good for only thirteen countries. If you count countries on the map you'll find there are lots more than that. The pass is good in

Austria, Belgium, Denmark, France, Germany, Italy, Luxembourg, the Netherlands, Norway, Portugal, Spain, Sweden and Switzerland. But it is *not* good in: Bulgaria, Czechoslovakia, East Germany, Finland, Great Britain (England, Wales, Scotland and Northern Ireland), Greece, Hungary, Ireland, Israel, North Africa (Algeria, Morocco, Tunisia), Poland, Rumania, Russia, Turkey and Yugoslavia. Even if you don't want to visit any of the latter countries, you might change your mind after you get over there, and you should be free to do so.

The last objection to the Eurailpass has to do with another limitation: it not only restricts you to certain countries but it restricts you, of course, to traveling by train while you're in those countries. What if you meet some people and want to go hitchhiking or car-camping? What if you find some place of some scene you like and want to stay there for the duration of your trip? Having that big money investment in the Eurailpass is going to make you less free in the end. It's a good deal if you use it, but it isn't cheap—especially since you have to pay for it all at once in the U.S.A. (buying it from a travel agent or European rail rep here) before you ever touch down in Europe. Once you use the pass at all, there are no refunds. Ditto if you lose it or have it lifted. You can get (at this writing) 21 days of travel for $110, a month for $140, two months for $200, or three months for $230. Great Britain has a similar pass, called BritRail Pass, with the major advantage that you can buy a second-class version: 15 days of unlimited rail travel (unlimited except that it does not include Ireland) for $40, 21 days for $55 and one month for $70. If you're a student fifteen to twenty-two, you can get the Youth Pass version: 15 days for $35, available from the CIEE. Britain also has another rail plan (Thrift Rail Coupons), in which you buy a certain amount of miles: 1,000 second-class miles for $40 or 1,500 miles for $60. These coupons are transferable and therefore particularly useful for splitting them among friends traveling together. Finally, Ireland has its own Overlander Ticket at a reduced price.

Other countries often have rail discounts you can use if you know about them. For example, French National Railways offers 20% discount for round-trips on weekends, 30% discount for round trips on Sundays. And a 20%-off tourist ticket if you buy at least 1,500 kilometers of round trips within France. Denmark also offers 25% discount on round trips. Ask about such discounts at national tourist offices and agencies in route.

The best way to use the trains is in conjunction with your other travel means. For example, after a period of hard-at-it hitching, riding the trains is something you can really appreciate. Take the train for a while to ease your aching feet, to soothe your shattered nerves, and as a womb-like retreat from the rough and tumble of travel.

The too-sudden juxtaposition of hitching and train travel can be eerie. I remember one stark evening in a whistle-stop village in northern Spain at the end of two days, hitching north from Madrid. I'd spent the whole of that weary day, from sunrise to sunset, alone on the road, feeling down. A frigid wind blew up and the sky perforated, letting loose a torrent of water. I huddled in a dark doorway. Traffic was nil neither pedestrian nor vehicular. After an hour of this, a little boy opened the door behind me and pissed out into the street. Reaching bottom now, I asked him where the train station was. After wading a mile through unlit streets, past shuttered windows, I found the little station and wetly bought a ticket to the French border. The train shushed into the tiny depot, stopped a moment and rolled off again. I had stepped aboard the Madrid-to-Paris express, and the effect on me was profound. Suddenly here was this warm, dry place with electric lights, full of laughing, drinking, well-dressed travelers in the twentieth century. There were beautiful women, and they wore dry clothes. There was gaiety, music, clouds of cigarette smoke, crowds of humankind— talking, eating, reading, writing, sleeping. Outside was a faraway place that none of these people knew, though it was just outside their windows. If I had been on the train for eight hours from Madrid, instead of hitching two days from there, the train would have seemed normal. Instead, it was a magical vehicle—a space capsule from Mars or somewhere (Madrid, maybe). And I was the only one who knew what it was really like outside there in the rain.

Then there may be times when the rain is in the train. Going from Fez to Marrakech in Morocco, I found that I couldn't hitch because the direct route skirting the High Atlas Mountains was closed by snow. I was tired of hitching anyway, so I took the train to Marrakech (hardly the fabled Express, since this one chugged a lot but moved quite slowly). After buying a third-class ticket, I found myself in an ancient and tiny wooden rail car that the wind howled through all night. Later it began to rain and the roof began leaking all over the car. I spent the night huddled under a seat dripping with water, lying in a wintry draft and bouncing constantly on the floor. A conductor came by twice to inform me it was forbidden to do that (I was never quite sure what he was referring to—perhaps it is necessary after all to sit under the drops for the price of the ticket). Ah . . . adventure!

In general, traveling by bus is not so good as the train (!) but okay once in a while. In some countries the local buses will strain your credulity concerning the accommodations, routes, patrons and/or general ambience. Europabus, the European equivalent of Greyhound, offers luxury bus travel at about the same price as second-class railroad fares. However, Europabus usually requires reservations, and as a luxury service, will be full of Americans and tourists again. So don't use it. Take the local buses, which are, of course, cheaper as well. There are some bus passes. For example, Britains Coach Master ticket: 8 days' unlimited travel for $20.

Occasionally you may do better to go by bus than train, especially when more convenient insofar as schedules, or if there is no train. Most of southern Europe and North Africa, especially, have no public transportation other than bus, including all the remoter villages and mountain towns. Sometimes your bus route between major cities is the villagers' local that will take you into the mountains via strange routes over winding roads, perhaps causing you to lose your *bon appétit* out the window. Anyway, since the buses are the true people's transport, they're usually inexpensive. Sometimes so cheap that it's not worth hitching. Inquire.

In the so-called more backward countries such as Poland, Turkey and Morocco, the buses are often over-aged, under-powered, over-crowded and under-ventilated—so they're not over-comfortable, which is under-standable. They do a space-compression trip by first filling the seats and then letting down auxiliary backless seats to fill the aisle. The result is a complete stew of bodies, babies and BO, with no way to get out. If you have to relieve yourself, too bad. I had to hold my bladder one evil day on a Turkish bus, and I would rate that as probably the second or third most agonizing experience in my life (after being hit by a truck and falling down a mountain). The bus rolled on and on without stopping. After some hours I began quivering spasmodically—sweat-covered, speech already paralyzed—when the driver unexpectedly stopped to check for a possible flat tire. Somehow I crawled through or over or around the wedged people without wetting my pants, and then deluged one of those life-saving tires. Lordie, what a memory!

Another time, in Poland, there was such a bus shortage that a mob of angry Poles literally attacked the door of the bus, already overcrowded, to force an entry. The driver gripped the doorhandles in both hands, with his feet wedged against the sides, attempting to hold it closed while a howling maelstrom of ragged-looking brutes clawed at the outside. They finally forced it ajar, screaming, and surged forward. At this, the frantic driver kicked the lead gorilla right in the chest and shoved them all back, giving him a chance to lock the door and drive away. No one else thought this was unusual. Strange but true bus experience.

You should know that figuring out some of the bus systems is challenging, to say the least. In some countries, each destination is serviced by a different bus company, each with a different loading/departure point and/or different ticket offices. Sometimes there will be one place where all the buses depart from, but each has a different ticket office and it's hard to tell where any particular bus is going because of a general chaos in progress. The best way to get any information is to simply plunge in somewhere and start asking questions; don't stop or lose heart until you have multiple assurances that you're in the right spot or on the right bus.

Although the foregoing applies to intercity buses, you'll find that traveling by city bus is adventurous also. Getting on a strange bus in a strange town, using strange money and not knowing the strange language, may strain your brain at times. If you have a map to point to or a name to keep repeating, it will be easy for the money-taker to alert you when your stop is at hand. By the way, you always go into the back door of the buses, where you'll find the conductor seated. Don't try hitching through the large cities. Use the public transportation—bus, subway, train—to get to the outskirts if you're hitching through, or just generally to get around town if you're not. If the city has subways, these are the best means of transportation because they are the easiest to understand. All subway systems have excellent maps at each station, enabling you to figure it out. If you're spending any time in places like Paris, London, Berlin or Madrid, you'll love the subways because you can use them without the necessity for a major international brouhaha every time you want to cross town.

Somewhere in Europe: Protecting the magic bus from flies and other tourists. This snapshot speaks about the easy-going informality that's possible when you have your own vehicle. This kind of picnic site — a patch of forest just off the road — is easily found throughout Europe. Don't fetter yourself to high-speed dashes between capital cities; learn to swat flies in the forest, wearing sandals and BVD's.

94

12 TOURING BY CAR OR MOTORCYCLE

INTRODUCTION
HOW TO VAGABOND BY CAR
EUROPEAN AUTO CLUBS
HOW TO VAGABOND BY MOTORCYCLE
BRINGING YOUR OWN CAR OR BIKE
BUYING YOUR OWN CAR
BUYING A USED CAR
RENTING OR LEASING A CAR
BUYING A MOTORCYCLE
ABOUT CAR-CAMPING
NECESSARY DOCUMENTATION

INTRODUCTION

For most people, getting some motorized wheels underneath them is the best compromise as a way to see and enjoy Europe without being driven to tears by the challenges and frustrations. In truth, private motorized transport can be the key to free-lance, long-distance vagabonding. Furthermore, it opens the way to camping throughout Europe, whether at regular campgrounds or just by the roadsides . . . and thus can cost very little. Such costs as there are can be further reduced by sharing them with a group of people who all travel by car together. Americans in particular are used to traveling by automobile and, in fact, feel unnatural traveling any other way. Fortunately there's a choice of automotive options that can fill just about any need: bringing your own, buying a new or used one over there or leasing one. I'll go into each of these along the way. The only real problem with the car or the bike is that same old one again: it's so easy to keep moving, so easy to use the car as a traveling womb, that it stands between you and the experience of Europe and its people. However, there are relatively easy ways you can keep from doing this. Let's see.

Most of the known world is paved, including Europe. (Hurrah and sob!) However, by far the majority of tourist traffic is never seen off the main highways connecting the capitals of Europe. A lot of Americans take particular pleasure in exploring the back country of America, whether it be the farm lands of their own localities or back-country mountain and desert roads when they go on a national-park vacation. Therefore it's odd that so few of us do that in Europe. I suppose it's the fear of the language or the alien culture, but motoring Americans are scarce in the European tules. It's a pity, for this is one of the ways to have a memorable trip. Europe is literally crisscrossed with a network of secondary roads that go to fascinating backwaters, populated with folks as easy to meet and friendly as you can imagine. This is the beauty of having your own transportation, for it enables you to do what no one else can do when traveling by bus or train. Even hitchhikers are forced to keep pretty much to the main roads, because they depend on a certain minimum of traffic that back roads don't provide.

Next suggestion: when you visit the major cities of Europe, and of course you should, get rid of that car. Having your own wheels in the countryside means freedom, but in the city it's slavery. European cities were obviously not laid out with the automobile in mind. Even if you have a map, it's difficult to get around. Streets are narrow and winding, laid out in no particular order, traffic jams are frequent and unbelievable, parking is at a premium or impossible. European drivers in the cities are notoriously impatient and will take every opportunity to weave through traffic, dart ahead of you, jam on the brakes, take ridiculous chances, and after they bash your fender, will give you a tongue-lashing you won't forget. They're right . . . you shouldn't have been driving anyway. If you want to enjoy yourself in the city, check into a hotel or campground, stash the car and forget it for the rest of the time you're there. Use the public transportation, which is efficient, cheap and fun. And also, walk as much as you can because European cities are a walker's delight. All these cities were originally built for people instead of Progress, and walking is the best possible way to see them. Go to the official tourist information offices in all European cities for the best and most convenient sightseeing information.

Here's an excellent suggestion: pick up hitchhikers! American motorists in Europe don't realize it, but hitchhikers can do them a lot of services. First of all, many of the hitchhikers will be Americans or English, or at least English-speaking and will provide you someone new to talk to. Hitchhikers, of course, get around quite a bit and are up on the interesting places to stay, off-beat things to see and do, and are frequently just plain interesting people. Besides keeping you company and giving you all kinds of tips, they can also help drive your car and perhaps even share your expenses—not just gasoline, but room costs if you're all going the same way. If they're European hitchhikers and don't speak English, you will at least have a chance to meet and communicate with young Europeans you'd never hope to meet otherwise, and you can do so on your own terms. By which I mean you have a captive audience, and you may as well make the most of it.

The encounters can be interesting: while I had a car in Great Britain, I picked up a young man with a pack and some climbing ropes on his back in the rain in Wales. Turned out he was from Liverpool and had been out climbing the local crags for the weekend. A little further on we spotted some more of his friends and picked them up too. I drove them part of the way into Liverpool and got addresses and an invitation to visit when we got there. Which we did a few days later. One was the son of a widowed longshoreman, who was poor but proud to have us as his guest. We stayed for dinner, eating in shifts because the kitchen was too small to seat everyone at once. Afterward the family all stayed up until two in the morning talking about British life and politics. (Particularly interesting because just a week earlier we'd stayed with a friend's parents, who were wealthy industrialists. There we'd also talked politics, hearing about it from the other side. Vagabonds happen onto this kind of population sampling all the time.)

Before we left, the boys invited us to meet them the following weekend in the Lakes District for some rock-climbing together. Far out! We agreed, and the following week met them at Ambleside, whence together we all ventured into Langdale Valley with its surrounding peaks. The next two days were something else, clambering over and hanging onto such things as Gimmer Crag, Oliverson's Variation, Bracket and Slab, and Bowfell Buttress. By the time we said our last goodbyes, there were ten of us loaded into the car. We all sang a great deal in chorus, pushed and tackled and kidded each other lovingly and departed with a deep feeling of fraternity.

Another suggestion for car touring is to bring someone abroad with you who has traveled in Europe before and will show you around. Along the same line is to talk a European into accompanying your party. This could be someone you already know in the States who'll go with you, someone you know there with whom to rendezvous or someone you encounter along the way who wants to adventure with your little band of roving riders. The advantages are obvious.

EUROPEAN AUTO CLUBS

Another tip for vagabonding motorists is to get a lot of information about your target areas. You'll feel much better about leaving the main roads if you have some good maps. They'll give you hints about what you're likely to find, thus providing incentives to forsake the beaten paths. Whether or not you have the maps, you should visit an office of the local automobile club as you move along. Virtually every European country has their own automobile clubs. They will provide information about what to see by car as well as their own maps. To get the most cooperation, you should be a member of some American automobile club, such as AAA—sometimes this gets you free honorary membership in a European club. Or you can join a European auto club for a nominal fee. Besides the information and map services, they stand ready to help in the event of car trouble, accidents or any other problems requiring sympathetic assistance and knowledge. This includes assistance in buying or selling a car and arranging the necessary documentation. You'll frequently see signs on the highways indicating the presence of a club office or representative nearby. Sizeable towns usually have auto club offices and most major border entry points, as well.

Major European and North African Auto Clubs

Austria:	Österreichischer Automobil und Touring Club (OAMTC), Schubertring 7, Vienna 1
Belgium:	Royal Automobilclub de Belgique, 4 rue de Luxembourg, Brussels
	Royal Touring Club de Belgique, 44 rue de la Loi, Brussels
Bulgaria:	Bulgarian Automobile and Touring Club, 6 St. Sophia St., Sofia
Denmark:	Kongelig Dansk Automobil Klub, Nyropsgade 47, Copenhagen 5
	Forenede Danske Motorejere, Frederiksborggade 18, Copenhagen
Finland:	Finnish Automobile Club, Fabianinkatu 14, Helsinki
France:	Automobile Club de France, 8 Place de la Concorde, Paris 8
Germany:	Allgemeine Deutsche Automobil-Club (ADAC), Königinstrasse 11a, Munich 22
	Automobilclub von Deutschland (AvD), Wiesenhüttenstrasse 2, Frankfurt a M
Gr Britain:	Automobile Association (AA), Fanum House, New Coventry Street, London W.1
	Royal Automobile Club (RAC), 83 Pall Mall, London S.W. 1
Greece:	Automobile et Touring Club de Grèce, 6 Odos Amerikis, Athens
Italy:	Automobile Club d'Italia, Via Salaria 243, Rome
Luxembourg:	Automobile Club de Luxembourg, 180 route de Longwy, Luxembourg

Morocco:	Touring Club du Maroc, 3 avenue de l'Armée Royale, Casablanca
Netherlands:	Koninklijke Nederlandsche Automobil Club (KNAC), Sophialaan 4, s' Gravenhage
Norway:	Kongelig Norsk Automobilklub (KNA), Parkveien 68, Oslo 2
	Norges Automobilforbund (NAF), Kongensgate 5, Oslo 4
Portugal:	Automovel Club de Portugal, Rua Rosa Araujo 24, Lisbon
Spain:	Real Automovil Club de España, Calle del General Sanjurjo 10, Madrid
Sweden:	Motormannens Riksforbund, Sturegatan 32, Stockholm 5
Switzerland:	Touring Club de Suisse (TCS), 9 rue Pierre, Geneva Automobile Club Suisse (ACS), Laupenstrasse 2, Berne
Tuninsia:	Touring Club de Tunisie, 15 rue d'Allemagne, Tunis
Yugoslavia:	Auto-Motor-Savez Jugoslavie-Savezni Odbor, Ruzveltova 18, Belgrade 66

HOW TO VAGABOND BY MOTORCYCLE

This is similar to vagabonding by car in that your mechanical slave does the hard work and bears you effortlessly into all kinds of scenes. But the style is entirely different, which leads, therefore, to a unique kind of experience. One big reason is that motorcycles— especially big touring bikes—are far rarer than automobiles wherever you go, and most of all in the back country. People-reactions are therefore stronger: more curiosity, more attention. An Australian I met in Denmark and got to know quite well was fond of telling me stories of a trip by motorcycle into East Europe. He did it with little money on a used motorcycle bought cheaply (and later resold easily) in Denmark. His tales were characterized by a sense of amazement at how much he saw and how many people he met and what a great trip it was.

Motorcycling does require more than just the machine. Besides getting yourself internally straightened out, you must also externally prepare properly for it. This means a fiberglass helmet, padded leather suit, good gloves, high boots, goggles and a rain suit. A silk hankerchief is strongly recommended to wear over your face for protection and a touch of Zorro. Your traveling environment will be populated constantly by bugs, sand, wind, rain, dust, dirt. You'll need more baths than most travelers. As for your gear, with a luggage rack and saddlebags you'll have ample space to take all you need, including tent and camping equipment. You'll need a rudimentary tool kit. However, routine service and repair of the bike won't be difficult. Stop and talk to local motorcyclists to find out where the facilities are. As the ultimate in baggage, also consider taking a companion of the opposite sex.

Driving a motorcycle is not difficult. Even the big bikes can be handled easily, and on the open road, the bigger they are, the safer you are. Bikes are especially convenient to have inside cities, where their small size and maneuverability make them more than a match for their grosser four-wheeled cousins ... not just in traffic but for ease of parking.

Of course, motorcycling is more dangerous than most travel means, but alertness and common sense will reduce the dangers to a tolerable level. Remember that the serious accidents in all dangerous pursuits—from skiing to skin diving—generally happen to the experts, who take more risks and become careless through overconfidence. So don't push the odds and don't become careless, and you'll be okay. Particular tips: always beware of anything that could spill you and your bike (sand patches, wet spots, oil slicks, rocks and pebbles, ice, potholes and small to large animals). Be particularly cautious in the rain or better yet, don't drive at all. Ditto on being tired. Long-distance days can literally mean murder. Plan on short driving days with frequent rest stops. Quit when you're tired. Don't tailgate cars or trucks. This is asking for it. And whereas drunken driving with either an automobile or a motorcycle is stupid and dangerous, the difference is that a car endangers others while the bike endangers you. Save yourself for something better. Drowning, maybe.

Despite the hardships, there's nothing else that even approaches the sheer joy of motorcycling; To quote Robert Hughes (*Time* magazine), "Instead of insulating its owner like a car, a bike extends him into the environment, all senses alert ... It is this total experience that creates bikers." Exactly! And vagabonds and other free people. I've never biked extensively in Europe, but I did rent a motorcycle in Crete one glorious day: drove up into the mountains past the birthplace of Zeus, then crossed down the other side to the sea and turned off onto some dirt road. Going mile after mile through the olive groves on the rutted road, passing waving peasants and cart riders, smelling the sea tang and searching for remnants of old ruins ... what a life!

If you're interested in doing this, get hold of *Let's Go II*. There's a fine section on motorcycling in Europe in it.

BRINGING YOUR OWN CAR OR BIKE

This is not recommended for car owners because the shipping costs too much and the chances are that your fat American car will be too big to haul around the smaller European roads and streets. An exception is if you already own either a camper-rigged car (a small one like a VW bus) or an ordinary one you can use conveniently for camping, *and* are going to stay in Europe a long time. This way the costs of shipping the car come to very little on a monthly basis, and the possible savings from camping out are considerable. In this case, see the next chapter for some tips on bringing your own car and the story of how I brought mine. For bike owners, shipping yours over is feasible since it'll cost only $50 to $75. And if you go by ship, you can bring the bike free, as baggage (though it'll have to be crated—and should be for safe arrival).

BUYING YOUR OWN CAR

The only problem is money. If you have the bread, then there's no problem . . . buy your new car in Europe. You won't be able to pay for your trip on the savings you make, not after you get through paying shipping, taxes and duty, but you will have all the convenience and advantage of your own car in Europe. There are all kinds of people eager to make the arrangements. In fact, you can buy the car, have it financed, get your insurance, international driver's license and whatever else you need through one of many firms. (See list below.)

There are two purchase plans: outright purchase and sell-back purchase. When you buy the car outright you order it at least two months in advance, pick it up in Europe and bring it back with you when you return. The broker through which you buy it arranges for shipping, documents, accessories and insurance. In general, on small cars—the Volkswagen, for example—there is little or no money to be saved by buying Europe once you include all the additional costs. You can save money if you buy an expensive car like a Porsche or Mercedes, but that's talking a lot of money up front.

If you buy it to sell back, you get a new car with all documents, accessories and insurance, and at the end of your trip you return it for a guaranteed price to the place where you picked it up in Europe. If you're going to make a long trip (six months or longer) with a lot of mileage, the repurchase plan is cheaper than leasing a car for the same period. For more information on ordering and costs, contact some of the following car brokers:

AAA International Division, Seventh Avenue and 33rd Street, New York, N.Y. 10001 (AAA members only)
Auto-Europe, Inc.:
    1270 Second Avenue, New York, N.Y. 10021
    307 N. Michigan Avenue, Chicago, Ill. 60601
    1623 Wilshire Boulevard, Santa Monica, Calif. 90403

323 Geary Boulevard, San Francisco, Calif. 94102

3047 - 78 Avenue S.E., Seattle, Wash. 98040

Avis International Division, 1860 Broadway, New York, N.Y. 10023

Auto Foreign Service, 3500 Fremont Avenue N., Seattle, Wash. 98103

British Leyland Motors, Inc., 600 Willow Tree, Leonia, N.J. 07605

Car Tours in Europe, 555 Fifth Avenue, New York, N.Y. 10017

Citroen Cars Corp.:

209 Post Street, San Francisco, Calif. 94102

40 Van Nostrand Avenue, Englewood, N.J. 07631

12616 Beatrice Street, Los Angeles, Calif. 90066

Euro-Car, 5430 Van Nuys Boulevard, Van Nuys, Calif. 91401

Europe By Car, Inc., 45 Rockefeller Plaza, New York, N.Y. 10020

European Auto Travel, 323 Geary Street, San Francisco, Calif. 94102

Fiat Motor Co., Inc., 375 Park Avenue, New York, N.Y. 10022

Foremost Euro-Car, 5430 Van Nuys Boulevard, Van Nuys, Calif. 91401

Kinney Europe, 535 Fifth Avenue, New York, N.Y. 10036

Nemet Auto International, 153-03 Hillside Avenue, Jamaica, N.Y.

Renault, Inc., Overseas Delivery Depot, 100 Sylvan Avenue, Englewood Cliffs, N.J. 07632

Ship Side Delivery, 609 Fifth Avenue, New York, N.Y. 10017

VW of America, Tourist Delivery Depot, Englewood Cliffs, N.J. 07632

The information that I received from one of these companies at random (Auto-Europe) is impressive. It includes a question-and-answer section on buying a car, a free European travel kit that is quite extensive in what it offers, ordering information for literally hundreds of models, plus information about leasing, renting and financing arrangements.

BUYING A USED CAR

This is really the cheapest way to have the use of a car while you're in Europe. You can buy them from about $100 up. The procedure is fairly easy if you contact and join an auto club in the country where you'll buy the car. They'll recommend reputable dealers (who are mostly new-car dealers with some used cars hidden in the back somewhere) or turn you onto a public auction (where you'll pay about half what a dealer will charge). Plan on spending a week or so to find and buy the car. If you're buying it in England, the language may make the process considerably easier. Also, you can check the classified ads to find private sellers. One good place to look is the weekly classified newspaper *Exchange and Mart*. Once you have the car, the auto club (which will probably have some English-speaking personnel in whichever country you select) will arrange the insurance and documentation for you. Also check at American military bases.

RENTING OR LEASING A CAR

This is made to order for people not wanting to have the responsibility of hauling their own car around Europe, or without the financial means to buy a new car there. However, a large deposit may be required. Renting a car (as opposed to leasing) is intended for people taking a short trip with little mileage. Not much of a deal. Rentals run from about $3 a day for a VW to $11 a day for a BMW, plus 5 to 10 cents a kilometer. Cars available for rent generally tend to be bigger and more powerful (needlessly) than you get in the leasing arrangements.

Leasing costs at this time for a small Citroen (33 horsepower, four-seater) typically run $260 a month, $355 for two months, $415 for three months, $465 for four months, $515 for five months, $575 for six months. For the big Citroen sedan (115 horsepower, five-seater) comparable leasing costs run from $600 to $1,300.

The beauty of leasing, however, is that if you load a bunch of people in the car to share the costs, simple math shows you can do quite well, especially compared to commercial transportation. There are no mileage costs on the leasing plans, either, except of course that you buy your own gas. However, don't overlook the fact that European gas costs a lot more than American gas. It varies from country to country, but goes from around 50 to 60 cents per gallon, ranging up to 80 cents (Portugal), 90 cents (Greece) and $1 (Finland). Looking at the best possible case of a small Citroen leased for 6 months and carrying four people, the costs per person per day would be less than $1 each. If you camped out in addition, your costs for everything (car, gasoline, food, lodging and the rest) could be quite reasonable: under $5 a day if you didn't drive every day. But four people in a 2CV (Deux Chevaux) for 6 months is incredible, if not impossible. More realistically, let's assume two people for 60 days; the cost works out to about $3 per day per person. Not bad, but remember that gasoline costs can double that on driving days. For more information on leasing, contact the same firms listed above in the section on buying a car. Some lease, too.

103

BUYING A MOTORCYCLE

You can most likely buy it right off the shelf anywhere in Europe, although London and Munich are the best places to do so. Try Savile's Cycle Stores, Ltd., 97 Battersea Rise, London S.W. 11, which sells both new and used bikes, and rents them too. Another is Claude Rye's on Fulham Road in Chelsea, London. For your liability insurance and international insurance certificate (about $40) try the Motor Union Insurance Co., Ltd., 7 St. James Street, London. To buy one in the states before you leave, write to any of the following:

BMW machines: Butler and Smith, Inc., 160 West 83rd Street, New York, N.Y. 10024

BSA's or Triumphs: Harvey Owen, 181 Walworth Road, London S.E. 17

or write to the various government tourist offices in New York to get information about European manufacturers and their American representatives. Another excellent source of information, including bikes for sale and rent, is: *Motor Cyclist Illustrated,* Aldwych House, 81 Aldwych, London W.C. 2, England. (Send a dollar to cover the cost of mailing a sample issue.)

If you're unsure about it, wait until you get over there. It's easy to buy a bike in Europe, especially a used bike, from either a dealer or a private party. As a vagabond, you'll probably run into lots of people riding cycles who'll tell you where you can buy them. For example, from students at universities. In England, don't forget to look in the *Exchange and Mart.*

ABOUT CAR-CAMPING

I'll get into this in detail in the next chapter, but if you're going to have a car you may as well go car-camping, either part of the time or all of the time. It is certainly not necessary to have a camping-type vehicle to go camping; just bring along a tent and some basic camping gear, and that's it. The stuff isn't that much trouble to set up, it's fun to cook out if you eschew gastronomical masterpieces and you save money by the barrel.

Any kind of tent at all will do, and you can buy one from about $30 up. The more you plan to camp the more elaborate tent you may want in terms of features—such as space, flooring, mosquito netting and construction conveniences. Even if you decide you want a fancy rig, cost per night is going to amortize out to be low if you use the tent a lot and if you're sharing with a couple of people. If you're only going to camp out occasionally, or if you really want to rough it, then you only need some kind of ground cloth. You can sleep next to the car on the ground, with the ground cloth under you. If it starts to rain, string the ground cloth overhead from the side of the car, or simply crawl underneath the car. I've done the latter at times, by the way, and don't recommend it a bit—there's no room to turn over and you only get greasy trying. For a motorcyclist, a one or two-man tent, or just that ground cloth, can be carried quite easily in your saddlebags. I've camped out frequently in Europe without either a tent or a car, making use of whatever expedient shelter was available. This is always possible, but having your own shelter with you is certainly more reliable.

It is possible to lease a complete camping rig in Europe, either with or without a car. One kind is a camping trailer that hitches behind; another is a luggage-rack package (called an auto tent) that unhinges and unfolds into a canvas home. Ask anyone who leases cars about these camper rigs.

NECESSARY DOCUMENTATION

To drive a car in Europe, here's what you need:

Driver's License or International Driver's Permit: Your ordinary state driver's license is fine everywhere except in Spain, Turkey and some of East Europe. Germany and Italy require translations of your license. However, get an international driver's license anyway, since it serves as alternative identification (instead of your passport), is printed in five languages and looks official. Send $3 and two passport photos to AAA, Seventh Avenue and 33rd Street, New York, N.Y. 10001.

Liability Insurance: Called the Green Card, this meets the insurance requirements of most European countries (for those where it won't—such as Spain, Bulgaria and North Africa—insurance can be bought at the border). Consult your auto club or insurance broker. Or you can buy it through a European auto club. When you lease or buy a car, the dealer normally arranges for this insurance. Required for motorcycles, too.

Carnet de Passage: This identifies your car or motorcycle, but is seldom asked for any more (though it was once an important document). Get one from AAA if you bring your car; otherwise, bring your title and registration. If you buy or lease a car in Europe, the carnet will be delivered with the car.

International Camping Carnet: Optional except in France and Denmark. Besides serving as identification, this is a document you can deposit with campground directors instead of your passport. You can get one through your auto club, or through a European auto club or camping club for $4. If you join the National Campers and Hikers Association (NCHA), 7172 Transit Road, Buffalo, N.Y. ($5 membership), your camping carnet will entitle you to discounts at European campgrounds through the association's affiliation with the International Federation of Camping and Caravaning.

Maps: For trip planning, any standard map of Europe will do, but when you get into the nitty-gritty reality, be sure to have some good ones. The Michelin series is good, as is the Kummerly-Frey series. For more details, write the addresses on page 24, or buy the maps sold in European service stations (notably, Esso). An all-in-one road atlas might be more convenient, and a good one is *Collins Road Atlas Europe* (published in England).

Gas Coupons: Some countries offer gas discount coupons to tourists to help beat the high cost of gas-petrol-*essence*-benzine—or whatever they call it what your car converts into smog. Italy and Morocco are the only ones I know of at the moment, however. Buy them through your auto club, through the national tourist offices or at the border. The discount is 30% in both places.

Dirt Road in Spain: Jo-Ann and I pause to barber the brute at a sun-splashed casual campsite in some rural heaven. Spain abounds with such places, but expect to meet occasional shepherds and civil guards. Offer them a glass of wine, or maybe a haircut.

13   ABOUT CAR-CAMPING

SOME UNPLEASANT THEORIZING

There are stacks of guidebooks written about car-camping in Europe. I guess the reason has to do first of all with the popularity of car-camping. Secondly, this market consists mostly of people who feel they need to be guided. Unfortunately, all the guidebooks to car-camping, without exception, stress the comfort and convenience of car-camping in addition to its low cost. It's a magic formula: nothing could appeal to the average American more than buying comfort at a low price. The only problem is that they're buying the wrong commodity. What about you? I'm presuming you're in Europe seeking a sense of *adventure* at a low price, not a sense of comfort.

My first car tour was done in England, and after a month there I wrote in my journal: "Feel right at home now—too much so. It's certainly easy to travel in isolation from the country being traveled, and I see the danger of this . . . insufficient contact with the people and the real content of the country. Too much ease makes for too little broadening. Without the few addresses we started with and the contacts we made with the hitchhikers, the trip so far would have been much less rewarding." That doesn't mean that difficulty is therefore the highest good—you can have trouble and still miss everything. Nevertheless, a first trip to Europe should ruffle your feathers a little bit and, hopefully, even pluck a couple clean out. Trying to cope with other languages and life styles can certainly be fun, but it can't be easy. If you find that it is, you better start suspecting that somebody's putting you on, perhaps even yourself.

Anyway, I'll shortly recommend some of those guidebooks for their campground listings and factual data, but I repudiate the attitude that underlies them. Car-camping in Europe is a way to save money, be mobile and flexible, and open new opportunities for creative touring. It is also a way to travel in real comfort, and that is a snare that most car-campers get caught by. Yea, leap willingly into. It's no big thing, except that they invested a lot of money in their trip when they could have saved it and stayed home for even greater comfort. The real shame is that they might have genuinely seen Europe if they had been aware of the subverting aspects of car-camping and had made some minimum efforts to counteract them.

TYPES OF CAMPERS

There are numerous ways you can go camping: with an ordinary car or motorcycle, with the disadvantage being that you're less prepared for a camping experience than a motoring one; using a larger vehicle not especially equipped for camping, but easily converted to it (this could be any kind of station wagon or van-type vehicle); using a full-rigged camper-bus, such as a VW or one of the super English campers; or by hauling a trailer rig of some kind behind your car.

In my estimation, camper-buses and trailers become increasingly less suitable as they become more and more specialized. For example, hauling a trailer is some kind of abomination—a contrivance so specialized to provide comfort and convenience that it's worthless for anything else. Reject. Similarly, if your camper-bus is too fully equipped, too self-contained, you will be over-isolated from your surroundings. A camper-bus or any other vehicle so well equipped that it has all the comforts of home is a conspicuous contradiction. If you want to travel, it means you want to leave home. That's what travel means. Obviously, if you take home with you, you're not traveling . . . you're involved in some kind of perversion. I don't know . . . maybe that's your trip. All I'm saying is that if you want a better trip than that, one that retains the best aspects of motoring and camping but which still involves you with people and places, then don't go the deluxe-camper route. Get some sort of general-purpose vehicle that's adaptable to camping, and with all the money you'll save by that choice, you can stay in Europe longer.

In order to use campsites with any comfort at all, certain things are needed. The first requisites are a sleeping bag and ground cloth. If you'll always sleep inside the vehicle, you can skip the ground cloth, but you'll still need the bag. The colder it is, the better bag you'll need, of course. (I discuss sleeping bags more in the next chapter.) If you can afford it, a down-filled bag is best by far. Good sleeping bags will be cheaper in Europe than in the U.S.A. In addition, you might want to take an air mattress. This is too heavy and bulky for most travelers, but if you're car-camping you'll have the room. Better yet is a polyurethane foam or ensolite sleeping pad. They're comfortable, provide superior insulation, cost less and, best of all, they don't spring leaks and deflate in the night.

Next, camping implies cooking. By all means, prepare to cook meals and have the right equipment to do it. But don't plan to eat all your meals off a camp stove. Your cost savings will be offset by your time losses, and you'll miss out on the experience of European cuisine. The main reason you want to cook out is for those occasions when there's no restaurant near or you really would like to have a "home-cooked" meal. First off, you'll need a stove. Don't buy a Coleman: they only burn white gas, which is rare in Europe, and they're clunky and inefficient. The Swedish stoves are best: either the Primus or Optimus. Some models will burn ordinary leaded gas; others will burn kerosene. Or you can get a propane or butane stove using disposable cylinders, or a refillable tank. Probably the best stove arrangement of all is the two-burner International Gaz butane cooking stove that is familiar all over Europe. You buy the gas bottles in two-or three-kilo sizes for around $10 and then get refills for around $2. Almost all campgrounds sell refills.

Then you'll need some pots and pans, bowls and plates, utensils and things like that. Keep it as simple as you can. One thing I recommend very highly, no matter how simple or extensive your rig, is a supply of water in the car. You may already have one built into your rig, but if you don't, then take along a five-gallon plastic jerry can. Having water along means that you can make camp anywhere at all, and not just at a designated campsite. This is important. There are miscellaneous odds and ends you should have along, like:

flashlight
folding table and stools
tarpaulin
plastic bags and jugs for food storage
rope for tent-building, clotheslines, etc.
good pocketknife
towels and washcloths

To get your various camping supplies, some good American outfitters are listed below, followed by some European ones:

Camp and Trail Outfitters, 112 Chambers Street, New York, N.Y. 10007 (free catalog)

The Ski Hut, 1615 University Avenue, Berkeley, Calif. 94703 (Excellent supplier of lightweight quality goods; free catalog)

Recreational Equipment, Inc., 1525 11th Avenue, Seattle, Wash. 98122 (A cooperative that offers about 10% dividend refund on purchases. Membership and catalog: $1. Also offers European charter flights for members!)

Other sources are: Sears, Roebuck & Co., Montgomery Ward & Co. and army-navy surplus stores in your area. Overseas suppliers:

France: Au Vieux Campeur, 48 rue des Ecoles, Paris 5

Amis Campeurs, 105 Boulevard Beaumarchais, Paris 4

Trigano, 44 Avenue Jean-Jaurés, Paris 19

England: Eaton's, 100 Haydons Road, Wimbledon, London S.W. 19

Thomas Black & Sons, 22 Grays Inn Road, London W.C. 1

In England, you should also look for used equipment in *Exchange and Mart.*

Other countries: any auto club, auto camp or American Express agency can direct you to local equipment suppliers. Since camping is so popular with Europeans themselves, any big department store will have a camping section ... and most likely an English-speaking salesman.

USING COMMERCIAL CAMPGROUNDS

Every country in Europe has a network of commercial campgrounds. Most are listed in popular directories, such as *Europa Camping and Caravaning* (several thousand listings) and *Guide Europe Caravaning* (covers sites in twenty-nine countries in three languages), among others. A good place in Europe to buy them is: Geographia Ltd., 167 Fleet Street, London E.C. 4. In addition, some of the other popular car-camping guidebooks I'll recommend later have site listings as well.

In general, campgrounds are so numerous and so easy to find that you really don't need listings of them. Sometimes it is worthwhile to know of some super site up ahead and to aim for it (or to avoid it). A standard rule is that most major cities will have large auto-camping sites on the outskirts, or sometimes even right in the heart of town. As you approach any large European city, you will see signs directing you to the sites (CAMPING or the letter "C" with a tent symbol).

Commercial campgrounds in Europe are something else. Generally they tend to the luxurious side, and sometimes come complete with restaurant, stores, free showers and toilets, cocktail lounge, bank, post office, beauty salon, barbershop, laundromat, playgrounds, athletic facilities, golf course, swimming pool, etc.! Of course, some camps are rinky-dink holes in the wall or little ragged plots of scorched earth, which sometimes I preferred to the super plots. Needless to say, car-camping is extraordinarily popular in Europe, especially with Europeans. In catering to mass number of campers, many of the campgrounds are also monuments to mass taste. They give you no sense of privacy, no sense of uniqueness, no feeling of being anything but some kind of automaton who sleeps out at night. But such places are fun once in a while, and useful when you want a hot shower and a cold brainwash—a safe and plastic environment. If you really like this kind of place and want to stay in them all the time, you've elected for comfort instead of adventure. Why is it you came to Europe again?

Fortunately, many European campgrounds are relatively simple and thus more individual and interesting. Generally, you can see what kind of a place it is before you enter, so you'll know what to expect. (Or ask to look around first.) They're all quite cheap, certainly less than hotels or pensions, and they can be fun. When you stay at these camps, by all means try to get around and meet some of the other people, and not just those with English or American license plates. Or those who speak only English. With any luck at all you'll strike up some friendships with Europeans who'll give you their addresses and invite you to visit them when they return home after their vacation. This kind of invitation is worth following up.

Insofar as costs go, on the average you will pay from about 40 cents to $1.50 a night for two persons, car and tent. In most camps the total fee is based on separate charges for your car, your tent, the number of persons and the number of nights. No other commercial accommodations even approach the low costs of car-camping.

USING OTHER CAMPSITES

The other way to car-camp in Europe is to find so-called casual campsites. This means just pulling off the road wherever you can and parking for the night. There are a lot of if's that go with this procedure, however. First of all, you can (generally) do it only if you are prepared to sleep in your vehicle. There's often not enough room to pitch a tent, nor do you want to attract attention to yourself by doing so. Furthermore, many countries are too small or too crowded to afford much opportunity for this kind of free camping. Although some countries and some places specifically prohibit casual camping, in most countries it is allowed, though sometimes frowned upon. Casual campsites are easiest to find in large countries with mountainous, wooded or coastal areas. In looking for them the best means is to get off the main highways onto secondary roads or dirt roads and investigate what lies along them. If this doesn't yield any sheltered, secluded or private site, you can sometimes pull off the road onto a field or other suitable area, preferably one out of sight. As a last resort, simply park on the road shoulder or a turnout.

If you do this frequently (as I did), you must expect some encounters with people who will want to know what you're doing there: property owners, police and suspicious citizens. If you camp anywhere along the coastal regions of Spain, you can almost depend on encountering the Guardia Civil nightly. They never asked me to move at once (some ordered me to leave in the morning), but they always awakened me, no matter what the hour, to ask questions and check my papers. I also talked to the police once or twice in Germany and calmed some irate citizens in England, but nothing traumatic enough to make me consider giving up the activity.

The advantages of casual camping are numerous: the very encounters with the citizenry and officials that you might think frightening or forbidding turn out to be highly interesting. Frequently the people who approached us (often farmers and shepherds) stayed to share a glass of wine and bravely struggled through a linguistic maze that finally led to some kind of rapport. This kind of camping is quite cheap: it doesn't cost anything at all. Often it's solitary and beautiful, besides. This included beaches at which I could swim woods for hiking and exploring after dinner, sometimes a river or lake.

This kind of camping is only possible if you are fairly self-contained. You must have your own water, be able to cook inside the car if necessary (due to inclement weather or an inadequate site) and be able to sleep inside the vehicle. Sometimes it is difficult or impossible to find a casual campsite, and you will waste hours looking for one. Although it didn't happen to me, I'm sure that in some cases you will be chased away or possibly even threatened with arrest. The U.S.S.R. and most East European countries (Bulgaria, for example) have officially designated campsites and you'd better camp there, or else.

In any case, you wouldn't want to use casual campsites exclusively, if only to get a hot shower once in a while. Over a period of time, they're more isolating than any other means of travel. Alternate with regular campgrounds and hotels frequently. You'll certainly save enough to be able to splurge now and then.

One of them involves having the responsibility of the car. You have to keep it running and serviced. This may tie you up once in a while, because you'll find that service appointments often have to be made in advance. The new motoring public of Europe is growing by leaps and bounds, far faster than the capacity of service organizations to keep up with it. This means planning ahead. When you arrive in town to do some sightseeing, immediately arrange to get your car serviced if it needs it. Go directly to the dealer and make your appointment, then look for a campsite or other accommodations.

If your car breaks down, what do you do? If you belong to an automobile club, you can use the services of European automobile clubs at little or no cost. Many European clubs have full-time patrols for cars in trouble on the major highways. You'll also find auto-club representatives along international borders and ports of entry to help you in any way they can. Watch for telephone call boxes along the highways to put you in touch with a local automobile club. If you intend to do any significant amount of driving on the continent, check into joining a European auto club directly. The main offices of the major European automobile clubs are listed in the previous chapter.

Another problem of camping: You will find yourself spending all your time in the routine of camping, with little left for anything else. Car-touring is hard work. Great enthusiasm is needed to overcome the routine of constant travel, especially if you're preparing your own meals or spending time hunting for campsites. It will seem that each day is a succession of meal-making and ground-breaking efforts, and you'll be lucky to squeeze in anything else. The solutions are obvious, but may be hard to bring about, simply because of the nature of routines.

Building up rigid routines is one of the insidious dangers of car-camping. Almost no other method of traveling allows you this dubious luxury. Once your routines have been established, you use them as a bulwark against the foreign hordes outside your car windows, as a security blanket to keep you from coping with new experiences. If your housekeeping (car-keeping) routines don't allow you any freedom to do what you want, then you're being defeated by your means of travel.

First of all, go slower. Don't prepare all your meals. Don't use commercial or casual campsites only—stay in hotels occasionally. Park the car and forget about it sometimes. Meet and talk to other campers at the commercial campsites. Do pick up hitchhikers, as suggested in the previous chapter. And by all means, look up any people whose addresses you have in Europe. These include addresses you brought from America with you (see Chapter 16) as well as any addresses you can pick up from people you meet enroute.

Well, Mom and Pop, car-camping is one way you can vagabond in Europe and still take your kids. But better give it some thought before you jump to it. It's not going to be as easy as you might think. Special efforts will be required to keep the youngsters from being bored, no matter what age they are. All ages of children couldn't care less about sightseeing. Nor are they too anxious to drive every day cooped up in an iron box, watching the mile markers go by. Kids like to play, especially with other kids, and you will be constantly challenged to entertain them if you don't satisfy these basic needs. My advice is to leave them home if you can do so, especially on a short trip. The mother-in-law or grandmother will love to take them for a month or two—or three. You should probably let her.

If you're going on a longer trip, that's another story. But then go in the full knowledge that you won't be entirely satisfactory as your child's playmate, no matter how good a parent you are. In this respect, bringing two kids is better than one, especially if they're about the same age. Plan to use the commercial campsites more, because there's a supply of other children there. And do give your child the run of the camp when you're there. If he or she is too shy to approach the other children, then it's up to you to breach the gap and do it for him. Likewise, a long trip is going to put a strain on everyone, and you're going to have to pay more attention to junior than perhaps you'd like. Warning: if you don't do it, you're risking disaster. Little kids instinctively know more ways to spoil trips and to give grownups a hard time than you could possibly imagine . . . as you may find out for yourself.

On the other hand, the family that car-camps together lives much more closely than might be otherwise possible. You have to rely on each other to cope with the challenges and problems of travel. You build up an interdependent unit. If all goes well, you'll find yourself digging each other far more than you could at home. By all means, you should take turns reading stories in the evening, talking about the day's experiences, practice your newly burgeoning languages on each other and, in general, make it a family adventure. On a long trip, the parents will have to act as tutors for the children, and this can be a positive activity if everyone takes part in it.

And, as I've mentioned before, children can be your open sesame to meeting people.

The procedure for ordering and buying one from America is the same as that outlined in the previous chapter for buying an ordinary car. Contact the companies listed.

In addition, however, there is an entire line of British specialty campers that Americans have never heard of, but are worth considering. Called caravans or motor caravans, these are generally manufactured by specialty firms using stock chassis converted to campers, ranging in price (new) from just over $2,000 to around $10,000 (but most under $3,000). You probably wouldn't want to buy one outright, since they'd be weird back in the U.S.A., but it might be okay on a guaranteed repurchase plan (or leasing—see below). To get some idea of what these are like, go to the library and check out *Continental Autocamping* by Derek Townsend (Fernhill House Ltd., 1968; $3.75). It has specifications, pictures, prices, lists of manufacturers, etc. To get some information right from the horse's mouth, you could write one or more of the following:

Wilson's Motor Caravan Centre, 36 Acre Lane, London S.W. 2. (Mostly Commers and Fords; has a stock book for $1, and several hundred models always in stock. A good place to get personal or mail advice.)

J.P. White, Alexandria Works, Sidmouth, Devon (mostly VW conversions).

Martin Walker Ltd., Tile Kiln Lane, Folkstone, Kent (produces the popular Dormobile VW conversions).

Guaranteed repurchase normally requires a minimum term of 3 months' use. Refunds start at 60% and go down the longer you use the car. Thus, a $2,500 camper would be worth a $1,500 refund after 3 months, or about $11 per day for the time kept. If you keep it for 6 months it works out to be less than $8 per day. Plus gas costs. Most of these campers sleep four people for cost sharing. This compares quite favorably with leasing the same vehicle for the same time. Leasing charges are even higher in summer, too. If you do want to lease a camper, or a car with tent and camping equipment included, you can do it in advance through one of the auto agencies listed in the previous chapter. (Auto Europe, for example, offers Commers for lease and has a booklet that spells it all out quite clearly.) Or write to: Geo. Collins Ltd., Hersmonceux, Sussex, England (has the Dormobile type— converted VW buses).

Buying a used camper is another way, and may be the cheapest of all. As with any used car, better see it first. So wait till you get there and start shopping around. It is certainly possible to get a good car at a good price this way, especially something for just tootling around. Don't expend your life savings or go in hock forever just to have the dubious pleasure of driving a couple of tons of new, solid comfort around. To start with, check at Wilson's (mentioned above) and Simpson's Caravan Centre, N. Circular Road, London S.W. 2. Also stop in at an auto club for advice. Check army base bulletin boards.

BRINGING YOUR OWN CAMPER

My wife and I did this, and it worked out fine. Consider the facts. It was a VW van beautifully decked out for camping, and I paid $1,000 for it (used, of course) in California. Having the car at the start enabled me to plan and pack everything perfectly, without worrying about doing it in Europe. No outfitting problems either, of course. Since we knew the car well before we ever started, we also saved ourselves a lot of hair-tearing later.

Next, we drove the car to the point of embarkation on the East Coast, thus saving money transporting ourselves to the ship. By taking the car as accompanied baggage, the cost was kept reasonable (then $200). Now it costs about $300, with only $50 more for the round trip.

From the very first day off the boat, touring worked out beautifully because we were already packed and accustomed to the vehicle. After a few months we started having engine trouble. Well with Germany sitting right there, it was quick and not too costly to just replace it ($200). End of problems. Finally, after months of vaga-bonding and traipsing, we finally settled in Spain (completely exhausted, I might add). It was after this that I stored the car for six months and went off hitchhiking for the first time—and otherwise carousing around the map of Europe. To make a long story short, when I came back to retrieve the car (now layered with dust) I had just enough money to bail it out of that farmer's garage. But by selling a few possessions to the peasants (like a new $80 bicycle for $10), I raised enough gas money to drive it to Madrid and leave it with a friend. Some months later he sold it for $400, and that was that. I was robbed, of course, but it didn't matter since I had been prepared to junk it anyway. Even so, my total investment in the car was $600 net cost plus $200 (shipping) plus $200 (new engine). Total: $1000 for one year's use of a fine VW camper bus, or less than $3 per day. And if I'd round-tripped the car on the original ticket, much better yet. Incidentally, handling the necessary documentation is simple: AAA can do it—see the previous chapter.

Here are some car-camping guidebooks, with comments. None of them are necessary, but they may be helpful.

Camping Through Europe by Car, by Ann Grifalconi & Ruth Jacobsen (Crown Publishers, 1963; $2.95). This is the one that I liked the best, even though it's one of the oldest. It gives a lot of campsite listings, along with maps that indicate their locations. Has a light-hearted touch that makes it easy to read.

Camping Guide to Europe, by Paul Lippman (Holt, Rinehart & Winston, 1968; $3.95). This one gives more information about how to get started, plus miscellaneous reference data, with a section on selected listings. But it's a straight, middle-class, all-American approach that leaves me unmoved.

Europa Camping and Caravaning (mentioned before, page 112). This is the standard reference book listing the most European campsites (several thousand). I haven't seen a copy so I can't say much about it. Also in the same category are *Guide to European Campsites* (Hewitt) and *Guide Europe Caravaning* (Popular International Guides).

There are quite a lot more than this, but look them over before you buy. Some are simply trip reminiscenses of not too much value.

Berlin, Germany: Long moments of weariness and defeat in a flophouse with a difference: This one is run by an order of nuns, and is full of international drifters and characters. A classic place to feel depressed and save money, too.

14   FINDING A PLACE TO SLEEP

THE SITUATION IN REVIEW

How and where you sleep relates directly to how much money you have to spend. For most travelers, the cost of their sleeping arrangements is the biggest single expense on the daily tab, although food is not far behind. Your per-person per-day cost in Europe will be less than $5 only if you can beat the high cost of sleeping. Fromer's book *Europe on $5 a Day* can be made to live up to its title, but only if you set out to prove it can be done. Excluding car-campers, no one I've met actually using his book could make it on $5 per day. However, I have met lots of people not using his book who do make it on less than $5 per day. The answer is not in the guidebooks but in your style.

Before getting into the subject of hotels, a word about food costs: these can be knocked down a lot by shopping at the grocery stores instead of the restaurants, but don't take this too far. For one thing, food preparation will be difficult and/or time-consuming, but the main objection to this is that you'll miss the restaurants of Europe. And you shouldn't—European food is so good compared to most of the denutrified gook you get at home that you should let yourself experience it. But . . . you do have to beat the hotels. How do you do it?

One way is to tour Europe in a camper-bus, which automatically gets you bedded at very low cost. However, remember that cars themselves cost money and they need worrying about; you tend to stay in them too much, and it can be all too ordinary.

Card-carrying students should take advantage of student hotels, restaurants and assorted services. There are substantial savings available, especially in the expensive countries of North Europe. Similarily, you can stay in youth hostels if you're young enough and you can take it.

Another way to save money is to spend most of your time in the cheaper countries of Southern and Eastern Europe, and/or North Africa. The low cost of hotels (and generally everything else) makes you and your money go further. Every two- or three-dollar day in the south helps preserve the average by reducing each eight- to ten-dollar day in the north.

Another way is to travel with one other person to share the costs, especially the hotels. This can be your spouse, lover, friend or somebody you just met on the road. Share costs whenever you can. Often you can share costs with the people who give you rides.

Finally, the cheapest and most adventurous way is to find free overnight lodgings in whatever way and wherever you can. Sleep outdoors in the fields, miscellaneous shelters, stay with old or new friends, accept invitations from drivers who befriend you, etc. This is the best way to save money and have fun, but it will get hairy at times, of course. It's not all that difficult if you're prepared for it, and you need not do it all the time. Don't be afraid to ask the people you meet where you can stay; they may put you up or know someone who can, or may know of a good barn to crash in, or something else along that line.

Miscellaneous other tips: sleep on the night trains and buses and, in effect, pay for a fare instead of a hotel. Hitch at night and sleep in a traveling car.

WHAT KIND OF TRIP DO YOU WANT?

Where you sleep determines the entire character of your trip. Suppose that two people or two groups travel the same route at the same time . . . one sleeping in youth hostels, say, and the other sleeping in the fields. They will have rather different conceptions of their experience because the choice of slumber shelters forces the action and thought patterns of the two parties into different areas.

The hostel-user enjoys more security—he knows his sleep will be graced with an overhead-type roof and that he'll be warm and snug and full-bellied. He'll likely meet other travelers and socially indulge. Hostels are also great to make new scenes, gain, lose or trade companions and meet sex interests. Some of this particular crowd are the cream of the phony crop from four continents, but others will be real people. Through this human contact may come friendship, love, profit, fun, information, experience.

The hardy outdoorsman misses at least some of this and knows greater uncertainty and insecurity. Counteracting this is a sense of greater closeness to nature, a greater freedom and self-reliance. He experiences the pageants of sunset and sunrise more as a participant than an observer. For the hitcher especially, sleeping out always gets you off to an early start. Also, the field fellow often sees and touches the natives as they are, not merely the tourist service types and the other tourists. And it's free.

I vividly recall awakening outdoors to a Spanish sunrise, misty and mysterious. And people beginning their day—farmworkers on foot and burros through the shrouded olive trees of the dewed fields; factory workers on foot and bicycle through the side streets of Murcia and Valencia. And commuters waiting for buses in the flat countryside in the south of France. And waking on a snowbank in a Berlin park amidst a passing throng of valise'd schoolboys and shopping-bagge'd hausfraus. Or the eerie thrill of slipping to sleep in an ancient Roman crypt across the street from the Colosseum. A barn in Holland, a hayloft in Denmark, a highway tunnel in Norway, a freeway overpass in Sweden, underneath a truck in Germany . . .

My own recommendation is to do it both ways, which is the real freedom. Have enough money to buy a room when you need or want one, but also bring enough gumption to sleep out when there's no reason why you shouldn't or it's indicated that you should. Every vagabond should bring a sleeping bag anyway—he'll use it many times, even in youth hostels, where it is often required.

CHOOSING A SLEEPING BAG

Make every effort to buy a down-filled bag. It's the best possible investment you can make. To be able to sleep warmly and well is a necessity beyond all others. You can keep going without food for a while—water, also. You can be hassled, tired, sick, or whatever. But to really keep going in all circumstances, you've got to make it with old Mister Sandman. A top-quality sleeping bag, especially if you're winter traveling, is what will do it for you. It will also last for years and years, constantly being a tool for living freely, not just on this trip to Europe but in the big one through life. I can't conceive of not owning a down-filled bag any more: it should be among the two or three most necessary things you own. Putting it another way, if I were forced to get rid of everything I had except what I could carry, would I include a good sleeping bag? You better believe I would.

123

Sometimes army-surplus stores have used army- or marine-issue down bags, but they are usually in cruddy shape. The best ones (but expensive) come from mountaineering supply stores. (The ones listed on page 112 have good lines of equipment—and catalogs, if you write.) They also sell lots of other things you might need or be interested in. You can also wait until you get to Europe, where—in London, Paris or Scandinavia—you can get equivalent bags at better prices. However, a bag is something you can use immediately, so I'd say buy it here and take it over. Also, it'll be your bulkiest packing article, so it would be wise to have it before you fill the rest of your pack. Plan to pay between $50 and $100 for the right bag.

CAMPING OUT

By this I mean staying at the commercial campgrounds. (See the previous chapter.) I mention it again here as a suggestion for people without a car. You can go to a campground by motorcycle, bicycle or on foot, too. Generally, however, you will need some kind of tent or shelter to qualify at the gates as a camper. If you're a biker (with or without motor), you might consider bringing a small lightweight tent on your luggage rack just so you can use these campsites. It will save you a lot of money and be fun in the bargain. A hitchhiker or walker won't be able to get to these campsites very easily, so it won't be worth carrying a regulation tent. But the back-packer can carry a large sheet of vinyl plastic from which to rig a makeshift but serviceable tent. The best kind is a plastic tube of about 8 feet in diameter and 10 feet long. This is a standard item at many outdoor outfitters, costing between $2 and $3, weighing about a pound. (There is also a two-man size, which is 12 feet in diameter.) To use it, you pass a cord through the tube to form the tent ridge. You and your sleeping bag form the floor. Bring enough nylon cord to tie between even fairly distant trees (about 50 to 100 feet).

If you use these campsites this way, your cost is much less than hotel rooms, but you can still get hot baths and the other amenities. Most large camps have either a good store or restaurant, or both, so dining is no problem either. By circulating about the camp and meeting the campers, you'll also have no trouble getting rides if you're a hitchhiker.

YOUTH HOSTELS

Many people like them; each to his own opinions. I've found them disappointing as a general thing. Too many restrictions (early closing, for example, and petty policing policies), limited duration of stay (3 days), age limits sometimes (under twenty-five when they do have a limit), often crowded with guided tour youth groups (especially during the summer season), too many travel dilettanti in the ranks, often hard to find or to get to, unreliable information as to when they're open (despite what it says in the official handbook) and not always the cheapest accommodations around, either. Remember that youth hostels in theory are for hikers and bikers only. People who drive up to them on car or motorcycle—or who hitchhike—are not allowed across the thresholds. In practice, most hostels don't check your boots or bicycles for use factor, but quite a lot will turn you back if you look suspiciously motorized (maybe by appearing with a faceful of smog). Remember also that the youth hostel set is mainly for Baden-Powell boyscout types, who are not a little horrified by the scabrous hippie set.

Hostels I did like among the ones I used: Warsaw, Poland, and Iraklion, Crete. But I liked these for the staff—the facilities were okay, but not nearly so swell as some hostels that were dogs otherwise. In Warsaw the operation was a scraggly, run-down, fifth-floor barracks across the street from Communist Party headquarters, run by a bunch of rough and tough Slavic characters who turned out to be warm, lovable and permissive. The offbeat hostels are usually the best. The large ones tend to be impersonal youth factories.

I've been referring to IYH-affiliated hostels so far when I've spoken of youth hostels. If you plan to use these, it's best to join here in the U.S.A. Write to the address on page 17. You can also join anywhere in Europe, but they may give you a hard time about it. I tried to join first in Norway, but the nurds turned me out into a snowdrift on New Year's Eve because they said on-the-spot membership wasn't permitted (not true)—and they had available rooms that night, too. I finally was able to join in Poland, but it did take two visits and the linguistic help of a new-found and patient Polish friend. However, in the off-season you can stay in most hostels without a card; they only want the jack.

FINDING ROOMS

Rooms can be had cheaply anywhere in Europe, any time of the year. However, in certain cities at certain seasons, finding them may take some scrounging around. Holiday seasons in the tourist capitals (for example, Easter week in Paris) are particularly bad. Needless to say, so is summer. As a general rule, always take the cheapest room available. The resulting privations, if any, will not ruin your life or spoil your trip. (However, paying a bit more than the very least will usually disproportionately increase the quality of accommodations.) Never get a room with bath (use the joint john down the hall), or, usually, with breakfast. Ask about the price of breakfast; you can often get it cheaper at a nearby café (especially since it always consists of just rolls and coffee). But sometimes not; it depends on the hotel. One hears so much crap about the need for reservations. I suppose it's true for American-type tourists who wouldn't dream of going anywhere without a confirmed reservation, but short-order workingman's rooms, students' quarters, plain but clean hotels and private homes are always available to you as a non-gold-plated human being. And carrying a sleeping bag always assures you of a place to sleep. (Namely, in it.)

The main railroad station of a large city is usually the place to begin. In the station area you will usually find the cheapest hotels in town. Check or just leave your pack at the station and scour the area for a few blocks around. Asking at different hotels will give you some idea of room price, availability and quality. Instead or also, go to the hotel booking service in the railroad station and inquire about rooms available. If there isn't one, inquire at a tourist information office. They will get you into a place for a small fee, but their listings often will not include the cheapest hotels. Ask them (there's always an English-speaker on duty) what is the lowest price you can expect to pay for a room in the city and where you might find it. Incidentally, these booking services sometimes can get you a room in a private home for a reasonable fee. If you're toting a guidebook with room listings, check them out as soon as you get to town, starting with the ones around the railway station.* Start in the morning, if possible, or at least as early in the day as you can—better chance of getting in and more selection. The listings will also give you some idea of what you can get for the price and will indicate where the hotels are. Since they generally come in neighborhood clusters, you'll find many more in the same vicinity as the ones listed. Do ask to see the room before you decide. In the cheap hotels, you'll see some rank offerings, though they needn't deter you sheerly out of aesthetic inadequacy. I'm not a bit fussy . . . in fact, have never turned down any room if the price was sufficiently low. However, sometimes a strong resolve (and strong stomach) is needed. When looking at the room, ask if the bath is extra (also, in some places, the hot water) and feel out whether the manager might take a lower price. Off-season especially.

The average cheap room has a bed and a washbasin, usually a chest of drawers and a closet. Linen is provided (check to see if it's clean) and usually towels. But no soap. The washbasin has hot

---

*Two booklets with lists of clean and inexpensive hotels throughout Europe (but I haven't seen either): *Voyager Ltd.,* Box 24684, Los Angeles, Calif. 90024 ($1) and *Sav-On-Hotels,* from Travel Tips, Box 11061, Oakland, Calif. 94611 ($1.35).

water—let it run for a long time before you conclude it doesn't. If you're lucky, the drain will run; often they're clogged or sluggish. The toilet is down the hall somewhere and is shared. It almost never has toilet paper. Use of the communal shower or tub frequently costs extra (very little) and has to be booked at the desk so the manager can turn on the water heater. Sometimes you won't get the bath because all the hot water for the night is used up already. If it's winter, see what kind of heating the room has, and/or check the blankets. In some places I found the only way to get warm was to crawl into my sleeping bag. Sometimes the heater in the room costs extra. A final descriptive detail: if you like to read at night in your room (which I do), the available light may give you eyestrain. They use about five-watt bulbs in many places, and what you think is the night light is actually the entire illumination works. If it bugs you, buy a suitable bulb to carry with you.

In fact, however, most rooms—even the cheap ones—are reasonably pleasant. You will find that it matters more that you have a room than what kind it is. After all, you will only sleep there anyway, not take up full-time residence.

In some big cities, particularly in the railroad station again, there are various eager taxi drivers and hotel front men ready to rent a room to anyone who'll listen. The price quotes will generally be scaled too high, because they hustle conventional tourists, not just students and vagabonds. You can always do better yourself if you want to take the trouble and time to seek out hotels. In the off-season, these room hustlers can be bargained with to some extent, but it's their own kickback they're reducing, so they won't go too far.

Then there is also a breed of roomhawkers who have places for rent in their own homes or in a house they've rented for this purpose. They're on a simple money-making trip, and seek out people with back packs and other hip young travelers who won't mind taking a less than ideal room. This could mean anything from a crash pad to really elegant digs, but the price will be cheap and the experience interesting. In East European countries, people offering rooms of this kind will be ordinary citizens who need the money and whose accommodations will give you a look at typical homes and life styles.

PENSIONS AND OTHERS

Pensions are small hotels managed in a more homey way than hotels, usually by a family. Often cheaper than hotels, they are also friendlier and funkier. If you're lucky, you'll practically be one of the family, sitting around in your shorts watching the soccer matches on TV in the parlor. Breakfast is usually included; sometimes all meals may be taken there (full pension) or two meals (demi-pension). It's easy to meet the other people staying there, and thus easier to trade experiences and gather information. They're also mostly coed, so pensions are good places to meet guys and gals for whatever kind of fun you can manage. In Great Britain, the B & B or BED AND BREAKFAST signs along the roads indicate similar kinds of establishments.

Many cities have private hostels. For example, Istanbul has a place called the American Student Hostel, which is not part of IYH, but is as cheap and very much better with respect to personal privileges. Copenhagen has a private youth hostel (DIS) that is quite nice. Throughout Scandinavia there is a network of inexpensive lodgings, called KFUM, corresponding to our YMCAs. The guidebook *Let's Go* has a fairly comprehensive listing of these places for each country. Here are some other tips in specific cities:

In London there are hostels, like Holland House, where you pay a small membership fee and then get a bed for under a dollar and dinner for about fifty cents. For a list of hostels, write: Youth Hostel Association, 29 John Adam Street, London W.C. 2.

In Rome and other cities, Dutch students manage their own hostels. For a list, write: NBBS (Netherlands Office for Foreign Student Relations), Room 606, 40 East 49th Street, New York, N.Y. 10017. In Amsterdam the NBBS has all kinds of services and information at Rokin 65 and a student center at Leikeskade 105.

In Munich the students and hip people *(Gammlers)* will be in the part of town called Schwabing (hippie-ouster campaigns by the business community may change this). Some student hostels are St. Paul's Kolleg (males), Übernachtungsheim (females) and Newman Haus (both). For information on what to see and other places to stay, go to Internationales Studenten-Foyer, Adelheidstrasse 15.

In Paris: American Center, 261 Avenue Raspail.

As a step further down there are various settlement houses and religious missions, if you really feel down and out and can take it. (Generally for men only.) For example, Berlin and other large German cities have a Bahnhofsmission—a religious order operating out of the railroad station. They'll give you a clean bed in a dormitory and two very plain meals for less than a dollar a day (this in a city which otherwise has American-style prices). Copenhagen has its Kofoed Skole: fifty-cent suppers, free shaves and showers, an activity program but no sleeping facilities. There are others throughout Europe, but if you use them you'll meet the poor and needy class of Europe and may feel guilty about it if you have any money. On the other hand, you'll meet some marvelous characters. There are also free lodgings in monasteries in Greece and Italy, for example.

Staying at police stations is possible if all else fails, or they almost certainly will help you find a place if you've nowhere else. Other places to inqure for lodgings or just some floor space for your sleeping bag are at clubs and cafés—ask the bartender, the customers, any Americans you see (especially military personnel). Also, just strangers in the street—more often than not, they will do what they can to help.

The final way to save paying for a room when you're traveling is to take the night train (or bus) and sleep as you go. Most European capitals are about one night apart by train. Also, you can sometimes sleep in a moving car if you're hitching and have a long ride ahead. Sleeping in the railway station waiting rooms is okay if you have a ticket for a morning train, but they're back-busting, noisy and drafty. You may be better off in the bushes in the park across the street.

STREET PEOPLE, CRASH PADS AND COMMUNES

The rise of the counter-culture: There is a growing network of, shall we say, informal accommodations for adventurous travelers. The best guides to it are other travelers, and success in this area is strictly fortuitous: you work it out by chance encounters. Make a point of talking with other tourists who appear to be traveling on a low budget, or who look like they might know a place to crash. Find out where they've stayed and how they get by. Listen to their tips and take heed of their cautions.

Another related approach is to contact places that provide free or low-cost crash pads as a service to travelers. For example, BIT, an underground information center in the Notting Hill area of London, has a list of crash pads. Their address is given in the next chapter in the section on communes. Communes themselves sometimes welcome visitors, though more often not. One of particular interest in London is Street Aid, an informal aid and information agency. See if it's still alive. Again, BIT is the place to get information. There are similar agencies appearing all over, many only temporarily. The trick is to find out about them, which you do mostly by good luck and good listening. The underground newspapers of Europe are also sources for this kind of information, and should be read and, where possible, their offices visited or called for the most up-to-date scam.

As in America, the underground scene changes daily, often catastrophically, so you'll have to make contact with it in whatever way works for you. Don't feel badly if it doesn't work for you at all—it happens to the best of us, including me. Playing the underground game can easily turn into hipper-than-thou antics of no redeeming value. Don't worry about being hip; just be yourself and get happy with that.

For the complete story on the international underground scene, the definitive guide is a new book called *Play Power*, by Richard Neville

(Vintage, 1971: $1.95). Primarily a fascinating and droll History of Hippies, the parts that relate to the underground press (with addresses listed), the drug scene, and advice on traveling/surviving cheaply (mostly in the Near East, Far East, and North Africa) are excellent. Highly recommended. Copy the addresses you might use (newspapers and crashpads). Finally, a special service to travelers is rendered by something called the *Travelers' Directory*, discussed in Chapter 16.

SLEEPING OUT

Finally, at the lowest rung but in some ways the best, are the expedient free lodgings. There is no shortage of reasonably comfortable buildings, garages, farmhouses, toolsheds, barns and, especially, new construction. It's hard to find any village or city without several dry and accessible buildings under construction. I'm talking about sleeping out without asking anyone's permission, on the assumption that linuistic and other difficulties make it unfeasible to inquire. But if you can get permission from someone in charge of an expedient sleeping plot, so much the better—if only to spare you the anxiety of being discovered. However, underfoot vagabonds normally receive some sympathy from Europeans, so if you're found out, you may have to leave (not always), but you will not be treated like a criminal. If you're in a city and can't find anyplace else, make for the city park, historical ruins and other public grounds. If you're hitchhiking down the road when night falls, sleep in the fields under trees, or if you need more shelter due to inclement weather, scout the facilities underneath highway overpasses and bridges, tunnels and the like.

It can be difficult. Sleeping under a tractor in a German barn, a farmer came in the predawn darkness and drove it away without ever seeing me. If I hadn't awakened and groggily rolled out from under in time . . . goodbye world. Sleeping in vacant lots on fields may require clearing the turds away first. And you may be bothered by animals at night (dogs, cats, rats, mice or insects). Finding a place where you can sack out without somebody stumbling over you is often difficult, particularly in town, but seldom impossible if you keep your eyes open for the possibiities around you. Having done it a lot, I can say that casually sleeping out is perfectly feasible and, within certain limits, interesting and fun. But it is uncomfortable as a rule and it's hard to keep clean and presentable for long. The most sensible way is to do it only when you need to save some money, or when you have to because you're stranded somewhere. To do it, the essential requirement is a sleeping bag, but you should also have a ground cloth, some food and water in your pack, a flashlight and some insect repellant.

In years past, Amsterdam's central square—The Dam—has been an open-air camp for summer people passing through. The police awaken them in the morning, the square is hosed down, and then it's cool to go back. I don't know if this is still permitted. If you check with other travelers, you will probably hear of other such group sleeping arrangements here and there.

STAYING WITH FRIENDS

If you have European (or other) friends in Europe, or acquaintances or relatives, take their addresses with you and plan to look them up. Doesn't matter if you don't know them very well—just go. At worst, they'll turn you out, but it's rather unlikely. Europeans are heartwarmingly hospitable, but often have little room to spare. If you're prepared to sleep on the floor, and you should be happy to, you're all set. It goes without saying (I hope) that you don't make an asshole out of yourself by expecting to freeload and take advantage. These things can always be done with grace and good humor. Be thankful for whatever generosity you receive. More about this later, in Chapter 16.

UNMARRIEDS SLEEPING TOGETHER

A fine way to travel: young lovers enjoy the carnal and economic advantages of marriage, but without the heaviness of legality. However, what about the hotelkeepers in various countries—where do they stand? Very possibly, between you . . . bedding of unwed couples is officially against the law in most countries, and the hotelkeeper is subject to punishment for allowing it. Since it's almost universally required to show or temporarily surrender your passport when you check in, deception is difficult or impossible.

In actual fact, there's usually no difficulty. It helps to register as a married couple, letting the guy fill out the papers alone if he can. Sometimes no passports will be asked for (rare); sometimes only his. If the girl has to show and sign, she should sign both the passport name and then in parenthesis her "married" name: Jane Smith (Brown). Your explanation (offered only if asked for) is that you got married after the passports were issued. The older you are, the easier it is. Over twenty-one is much better than under, mainly to keep hotel people from getting uptight about routine police checks. Act orderly. Stay in either very good or very bad hotels—they tend to be more relaxed about the regulations.

The only place my girl and I ever had any problem was Algeria, and there it happened twice. But I found out there's no law against it (if you're over twenty-one), so you can't be refused a room because you're not married. France and Scandinavian countries offer no problem at all. West Germany is somewhat uptight about it, and Holland is reputed to be impossible (even campgrounds are checked). Luxembourg hotelkeepers are suspicious. The remaining countries are generally okay, but you may have to tell tall tales once in a while.

By the way, renting a room for yourself and then moving other people in secretly for the night is quite difficult. Front desks are usually manned all night, even in cheap hotels, and you risk some quite unpleasant scenes if discovered. If you're a group, it's better to ask for a bargain rate all together, offering to sleep some of your party on the floor.

THIS IS A BLANK PAGE.

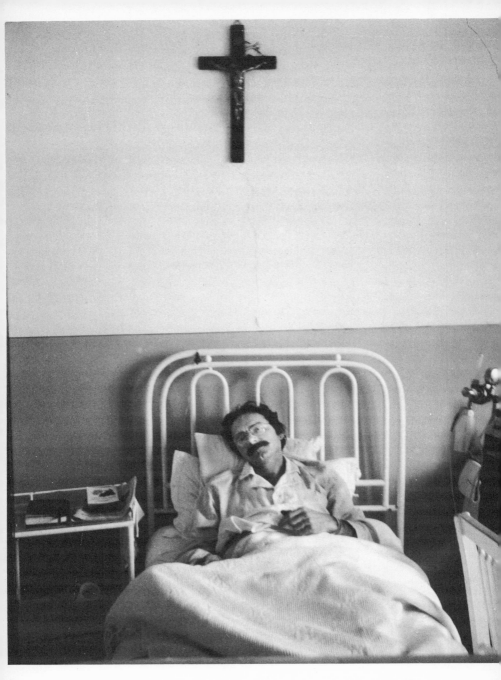

Capri, Italy: "It was on the isle of Capri that I found her" — namely the kidney stone in my gut. This picture is for real, taken while under the influence of both a pain-killing drug and the cross of God. I spent two days here in the clutches of a medical staff whose entire English vocabulary consisted of the word "pee-pee."

15 STAYING AWHILE

ADVANTAGES
ABOUT HANGING OUT
RENTING A ROOM
ARRANGED ACCOMMODATIONS
WORKING IN EUROPE
STUDYING IN EUROPE
COMMUNES IN EUROPE
TIME LIMITS

ADVANTAGES

Being a will-o'-the-wisp, floating across one border after another, haunting the capitals of Europe for a few nights at a time, is a phantasmagoric experience. What if you get tired of being a ghost and want to rattle your bones in one spot for a while? The advantages are legion. There's no better way to get to know a place than to stay there. There's no better way to meet people and find out who they really are. Certainly it's the best way to learn a foreign language, because you'll be surrounded and forced to surrender to it. Naturally you're going to save money. This always happens when you settle down in one spot. You'll be arranging for space by the month instead of by the day; you'll be preparing food at home instead of eating out; you'll have time to root out money-saving deals. Much cheaper. If you have the time, maybe you'll enroll in a school or college (git some a dat furrin larnin'). Maybe you're even going over to study in the first place. If you're short of money, what about working? Staying in one place may enable you to change the direction of cash flow from out to in. Working isn't any more fun abroad than here, but it could be a way to stay abroad when you run out of money. Or you could join the mushrooming communal movement in Europe, settling in with a group of like-minded inner travelers. Finally, staying awhile in Europe is adventurous in a different way than touring is. It's even more enriching because you get beneath the surface of things. You get involved, which is the key to living fully. Because everything is new, because every day is a learning trip, because it's exhilarating—pick a spot and find out where it's at.

ABOUT HANGING OUT

The easiest way to stay awhile somewhere, and perhaps the best way, is to simply hang out. I can't tell you how to do this because hanging out is not sufficiently defined to be able to say, "You do it this way." It's every man for himself. And just see what happens. Of course, you need someplace to stay. Generally you start off by renting a place or sharing a place, but after you've been hanging out for a while you generally move at least once, sometimes many times. After staying in a place for a time, you will hear of other places you can stay for less, or perhaps for nothing at all. You'll make friends who perhaps offer to put you up for a while, move you in with them to share expenses, or who otherwise help with lodging.

For example, I lived in Denmark for about three months during the winter. I stayed in five different places and didn't pay rent in most of them. When I did, it was only to share the rent and food costs of a group of people living together. First I stayed with friends of friends for a while. Across the street was a condemned building that some street people clandestinely occupied, and I moved in there. That was the beginning of the Sofiegarden commune, now Copenhagen's oldest. Later I boarded at low cost with a Danish family. Eventually that fell through due to domestic problems, and I moved in with some other friends. The last place I stayed was a fifth-floor walk-up without heat and without toilet, but I remember it fondly nonetheless. Yet when I first arrived in Copenhagen, I didn't know anyone at all.

Hanging out can be fun. In Copenhagen, my particular thing at the time was following the folk musicians, so I got to know most of the music clubs and the musicians that played there, and some of the crowd that frequented the clubs. It was a strange existence: quite unstructured, lonely at first, but staying there was certainly different than moving around. That winter made Copenhagen a very real place for me. I remember many silent snowfalls on late-night walks; I can still see the ice-clogged shipping channels on the waterfront; I remember living in the bustle and excitement of the sailors' district in Nyhavn . . . hanging out made it a special place in a special way. No short visit could have done that.

RENT A ROOM

Living on/off the street and hanging out is also a constant hassle, a struggle to survive. If you have a little money set aside, it's much easier on your head to simply rent some kind of steady habitation. Depending on the spot and the season, this can be extremely cheap or incredibly expensive. If you want to stay somewhere in Europe, remember it's better to stay longer and make some sacrifices, than to stay only a short time and live plush.

In Spain I saw many places I wanted to live, but I searched all over to find a cheap one so I could stay for a couple of months when I finally did settle down. In most places—even Spain, despite its budget reputation—the sky is the limit for what you may pay. Expensive rentals are always easy to find everywhere. But if you can keep looking, especially in out-of-the-way places, you can generally find something reasonable. It took weeks to find the house I rented in Spain for $22 per month, with eight rooms and situated right on a Mediterranean beach. But the rooms were like monk's cubicles—barren walls and one barred window in each room. The house was in a tiny village six miles on a dirt road from the nearest town of any size, had a bucket-type well for the water supply and a separate sea-water well for washing clothes. The garbage was thrown into the backyard, where the neighborhhod chickens and goats disposed of the organic stuff, while the wind removed or aerated the remainder. Staying in that small village for several months brought me closer to Spain and the Spaniards than anything else I could have done. I came to feel more at home there than I have in some American towns I've lived in. Someday I hope to go back there, though I've heard the road is now paved and some hotels have been built.

To find a place to rent, whether in city or country, go to a local real estate agent or rental agent as the best first step. He's likely to speak English and can either show you some places or give you the scoop on the rental situation. If you don't get any satisfaction that way, the next step in a large city is to check the newspaper ads. This is perilous if they're in a foreign language, however, and possibly no better in Great Britain either because of the classified-ad codes. In London, for example, could you translate c.h., c.h.w. and s.c.k. & b. into central heat, constant hot water and self-contained kitchen and bath? Also, visiting prospective rooms all over a strange city could turn into a bloodbath (inside your shoes). Both patience and alertness are needed if you go this route.

Where there are no newspapers, as in a village or countryside, you can go directly to the people with your quest. Find them at the greengrocer's and the café or the cantina, ask the proprietor and the patrons where you might find a room or a house to let. This works particularly well in the smaller towns, if you can summon up the nerve and the linguistic skill to approach any of the natives (who will often appear incredibly hostile and glaring until you stammer into your little number, at which point they will magically turn into some of the nicest people around). When doing this, I used to tortuously work out and practice speaking such prases as: "Is here from this village a man hiring rooms? Where is she?"

If you want to live in a big city, renting a house by yourself is out of the question unless you have more money than you should. Try to rent a room, or possibly share a house. In addition to a rental agent, go to a room-booking service and ask about monthly rentals. In particular, ask about renting a room in a private home. It's usually easier to bargain over the rate with a private party than with a hotel or pension. Another possibility in town is to offer to share the rental costs with friends who are already living there on some kind of long-term basis. If you can't find any place to stay, get the best rate you can on short-term rentals and keep looking until something turns up. Be sure to check the student bulletin boards and inquire personally of students. The longer you stay in the locale, the more likely you are to hit on something. This gets you back to hanging out again; keep your ear to the ground and follow all leads.

It's inadvisable to rent a house in advance from America, before you even start your trip. Not only will it cost more (perhaps very much more), but you haven't even seen the house, the town or the country. You may not like any of them. Advance rentals, like other advance reservations, also place restrictions on your movements. You'll be much better off doing it when you feel you're ready to do it, having the chance to evaluate the houses personally and the opportunity to shop or bargain for the best price. Despite crowded conditions, it is generally possible to find a place without advance reservations. If not in one place, then look somewhere else.

ARRANGED ACCOMMODATIONS

For a price, you can arrange to stay with a European family. I've done it informally, of course, at no cost, and it's great. But this is a matter of luck and keeping alert. By formal arrangement as a cultural sampling is something else, but may be worth investigating. One address I have: Cultural Exchange Club Ltd., 71-11 Austin Street, Forest Hills, N.Y. Write for information. Prices vary depending on the country you get fixed up in, but average about $75 per week.

If you ask, national tourist offices can tell you about similar cultural adventures that can be arranged, sometimes through their offices. A hipper way to prearrange this could be via a free ad placed in *Nomad* magazine or worked out through *Travelers' Directory*. Read about their services in the next chapter.

Since I'm addressing vagabonds in particular, I will assume you are not going to Europe primarily to work. Thus, the work I'll talk about is the kind that will help you survive after you're there, not the kind over which you'll enter into lengthy correspondence before you get to Europe. However, for those interested in formal work opportunities, I'll tell you where to go for information.

For the best information and the most addresses to contact of any readily available source I've seen on this subject, go to the library and read the chapter "Work Abroad" in *Europe This Way* by Steffensen and Handel. It gives information about work camps (in which you do anything from farming to construction to sick-room attending, about *au pair* (which means maid or governess service in a private home for room and board—a good way for girls to temporarily trade countries), plus exchange programs for trainees in specialty fields, nonprofit agencies, government employment agencies and miscellaneous other formalized work opportunities. It gives lots of addresses to contact and some good advice as well. The ubiquitous CIEE also has a job-finding service for students, aged eighteen to thirty, through their International Student Employment (ISE) service. A variety of unskilled jobs are available in stores, offices, hotels, factories and farms. Working papers are arranged. The ISE fee is $25; for prearranged jobs there is an additional $20 fee. For information and applications, write the CIEE (page 16), c/o Department ISE.

There is relatively little work in Europe for the average American—or rather, the work is there but you aren't given the chance to do it. Almost all European countries have a thing against giving work to foreigners (especially non-Europeans) as long as one native national is unemployed. Your skills and talents usually don't matter. If there is a job and you can do it, they would rather leave it open for a year or two in hopes a native will apply than give it to you. This is done not at the job level but at the governmental level, which means it is possible for you to apply for and land a job (assuming you meet the proficiency and linguistic requirements, if any) but you may not keep it long because you won't be granted your working papers by the officialdom. In Europe you need working papers in order to work, and the odds are stacked against getting them. In England, for example, the Ministry of Labor, upon learning that you have been offered a job, asks the employer to submit a statement saying that after having advertised and solicited the employment agencies for at least several months, he cannot find an Englishman to fill the job you want. Furthermore, he must state that the job is a bona fide one, meaning it hasn't been created for you. Then you submit your personal data to prove good character. Finally the government passes judgment and the answer may still be no. This is fairly typical.

Things are loosening up, however, as the labor shortage worsens. First Italians and then Spaniards were imported to German and Swiss factories to meet the demands; now Moroccans are finding work all over Europe, and they're even starting to give working papers to Americans. They're getting to the bottom of the barrel! On your part, it will take perserverance to succeed. Keep your eyes and ears open; ask continuously about places needing labor. When you hear of a place, go there and keep going there. I met an American who found work in a German factory knowing how to say only *Ich suche arbeit* (I seek work), going back every day to repeat it until he got a job . . . and eventually working papers. (He worked six months and used his earnings to go to India.) I've now heard basically the same story several times from Americans all over Europe. If you get some work of this kind, don't be surprised if it's idiot labor on a production line, at coolie wages. A friend who worked in a Danish factory told me he was expected to (and did) work harder than the other workers, for less pay, simply because he was a foreigner. This had nothing to do with his personal relations with the workers, which were quite friendly.

Other possibilities: check the classified ads in the international *Herald Tribune*. There may be jobs for English teachers and tutors, or bilingual secretaries. The best countries for job-finding are the prosperous ones, which means northern Europe.

There are ways around the work papers. Right in London, for example, are numerous agencies that provide household domestics and menials on a rental basis: cleaning, gardening, etc. It's hard work and pays a minimum wage, but they don't bother too much about work papers. Many so-called shit jobs of this type are available because nobody else will do them, and it's one way for you to get a little money ahead. In this category are also kitchen-help and chambermaid jobs at hotels and resort lodges: inquire on the premises. If there is a European you know, or one whose close friendship you've gained, he very often can find or direct you to some kind of work that will keep you going for a while on a casual, part-time or sub-rosa basis.

If you have musical talent, or just a lot of nerve, you can perform part-time or sporadically. One can live fairly well in Copenhagen, Stockholm, Brussels, London or Berlin by performing a few nights a week in a folk-music clubs that take walk-in talent. Ask students or salesmen at music stores for the whereabouts of such clubs. If you have no talent, there is always street-singing. *Let's Go II* has a nice section on this. As stated there, the street-singer is a beggar and a hustler, so the rules of street-singing have little to do with music and quite a lot to do with running. It's a hard gig because the police don't dig it, but it's still done.

Or you can be a sidewalk chalk artist adjacent to the tourist haunts. A less glamorous assignment is hawking the international *Herald Tribune,* among other publications, on the street corners of Paris and other tourist meccas. Ask a vendor how to arrange it. Panhandling is notably uncool in Europe, and will not get you much in the way of income. If you must beg to live, or feel you must, you'll do best with American tourists that you engage in conversation before you hit them up with a hard-luck tale. Work the American Express offices and the major tourist attractions.

Currently the best of all street ventures involves things you manufacture and sell yourself . . . jewelry in particular, clothing and accessories, candles, novelty items, anything at all that might sell. There are a lot of people doing this, but good quality is a requirement or you won't sell much. Use a colorful cape or other large cloth to define your business area and display your wares. Street-vendors with legitimate goods haven't been hassled too much by the police, but that varies locally and may change, also. It was once possible to street-sing with no trouble, before so many others started doing it and all were repressed. Sales locations are of vital importance. Main streets are usually taboo; too much chance of citizens' or businessmen's complaints. Side streets, public squares and parks are best . . . off the main track, but accessible to tourists. If the police tell you to move on, do so promptly and go to a completely different spot, maybe another part of town. A famous example of a place to sell is the Spanish Steps in Rome, where, however, many people have been messed with by cops. Another is Bayswater Road in London. Particularly in summertime, the street people are suspiciously watched to ensure that they won't annoy or disturb the paying customers—namely, the ordinary tourists. A street-vendor only has to sell a couple of items per day to keep going, but an average day is hard to define because you won't do it every day or in the same spot or even in the same town.

If you're in semi-permanent residence somewhere, a better way to sell all the same things is through boutiques, gift shops, head shops or other tourist service stores, either by outright sales or on a consignment basis. Approach the stores with some samples. There is a demand for low-cost handcrafted goods. Other marketplaces are the various (and famous) flea markets of Europe. The largest ones are in Paris, London and Madrid, where they occupy giant areas and draw tens of thousands of people. But almost every large city has some kind of weekly marketplace for anything at all you have for sale. Some cities have indoor arenas for this purpose, such as Vienna's Dorotheum in the St. Dorotheum Cloisters.

A final street venture is dealing dope, particularly hashish. This is a good drug to deal because you can justifiably feel morally innocent, even righteous (after all, it's only a psychedelic drug, not a killer like tobacco). It's easy to procure with a minimum investment in Africa or

141

the Near East (unlike LSD or other pills that require a factory contact). It's easy to transport (much less bulky than grass, for example). Finally, it's not difficult to sell at an excellent—more likely fantastic—profit. Alas, it's illegal, and therein lies your sole problem. My advice: nix! You risk spoiling not just your European trip but perhaps your whole scene for a couple of years. Society shows its stupidity by outlawing such drugs, its hypocrisy by choosing to enforce this particular set of prohibitions and its viciousness by the needlessly harsh sentences meted out. Don't be on the receiving end of all that shit without a good reason. If you do deal, keep it small-time to lower the risks and penalties. Keep it among friends and do it with love. Good luck.

STUDYING IN EUROPE

This prospect has limited appeal to vagabonds, but if you're already committed to the pursuit of formal education, definitely check out Europe. From what I've researched, here's a short, straight rundown on the subject: studying in Europe is cheaper than at home, median tuition is about $100 a year (but $600 in Great Britain), rooming and living costs are lower. A year's costs for everything except transatlantic transportation and diddling with expensive Schatzies should be between $2,000 and $3,000. Hangups: registration is complicated, you must know the language well and you'll probably strain your tush to keep up with their higher academic standards. Most European schools won't accept you until you're a junior (Spain is an exception). The whole thing will be cheaper and easier if you pick a smaller provincial school rather than a well-known big-city flasher. Make sure any overseas credits will be accepted by your American college, and do it in advance. Check out various junior/senior-year-abroad programs offered by American colleges. Beware, because many of these effectively segregate you from the indigenous scene and are cultural copouts. The guidebook *Europe This Way* has a good chapter called "Studying Abroad." Full of addresses to contact and advice to heed. Naturally, you should research the entire prospect and make all arrangements well in advance.

For people already there, more or less settled in a big city and not really interested in College As Seriousness, here's something: it's possible to enroll in day or night classes in miscellaneous subjects of use or interest, such as the local language. Investigating this kind of part-time program is certain to accelerate the pace of important activities like communicating with the natives, making friends, meeting sex partners and keeping in or out of trouble, whichever you prefer.

This may not be news to you, but the growth of communes in Europe· is phenomenal, especially in northern European countries, where English is most commonly spoken. Almost every kind of commune is represented: groups organized simply to share costs, totally involved extended families, work/service communes and mystic drug communes, too. Although all ages are represented, most communards are young people. However, the core members tend to be somewhat older and more settled. Although the European communal movement is part of the same phenomenon as the American one, there are differences, because the places themselves are different. Communes in Europe tend to be less romantically inspired: groups form for pragmatic reasons of lowering living costs and reducing daily alienations. They're not as interested in returning to the land or doing a teepee trip, partly because there isn't much land available in Europe. Also, far fewer communes there are drug-oriented.

The most flourishing locations are Denmark (over 200 communes), Sweden (about 100), several dozen communes each in Holland, Germany, France and England, and various communes in other countries. These figures come from my friend and neighbor Dick Fairfield, publisher of *The Modern Utopian,* who toured the European communes in late 1970. There's no possible way to know all the communes or even how many there are. They irregularly appear and disappear, change form, move, and many are strictly underground in the sense that the members don't announce their doings at all. Most of them are based on the idea of extended family rather than organized as intentional communities.

To make contact with European communes, or any given one, the best procedure is to write or visit *The Commune Movement,* c/o BIT, 141 Westbourne Park Road, London W. 11. This is the major English-speaking clearing house for all underground activities in Europe. If you're visiting, ask for Nicholas Albery or Ian King. A 48-page Directory of Communes (in Europe), including a beautiful article entitled "A Federal Society Based on the Free Commune" by Tony Kelly, is available from BIT by mail for $1. The directory includes descriptions of selected communes in England (primarily), Scotland, Ireland, Wales, Austria, Denmark, France, Germany, Holland, Italy, Switzerland and Belgium. Also, it lists available crash pads in England plus addresses of related organizations and phenomena.

A domestic source of good information is the *Alternatives Foundation,* PO Drawer A, San Francisco, Calif. 94131. This is *the* information source for American communes, but regularly attracts letters and offers from European communes as well. A $10 subscription to Alternatives includes the bimonthly magazine *The Modern Utopian* and a bimonthly newsletter that prints communications from American and European readers offering advice and seeking solutions and people. The magazine in 1972 will be publishing information, interviews and photographs gathered by Dick during his tour of European communes. Obviously this information will be of interest if you want to connect with one.

A final word: most European communes welcome American members and, in most countries, present no language barriers either. Communes in France, Spain and Italy will probably require language proficiency. English is okay for the most part in Scandinavia, Holland, Germany and Switzerland.

TIME LIMITS

In connection with staying abroad, you should know that most countries have a three-month limit on the length of time you can stay in the country with simple tourist status (some as short as one month; some as long as six months). For Scandinavia, it's a total of three months altogether in Denmark, Sweden or Norway in any combination. These time limitations are the authorities' automatic way of eliminating foreign undesirables—if they don't pick you up for anything else first. These limits won't be extended unless you can produce a bundle of cash to prove you won't be a liability to their economy. If you do have some money, or have some sent from home, you can probably get a visa extended. As soon as you get a clue that you might want to stay awhile, investigate residency requirements, etc. Numerous West European countries, however, do not stamp your passport when you enter. In these countries, of course, time limits can't be enforced with too much success. If you find a job and get papers, then of course you can stay as a worker, or you can stay if you're on a business mission or going to school. Or you can marry one of the natives (any one of them). Less drastically, you can keep moving from country to country in long-period oscillations, which is the normal procedure. If you can't work anything out and decide to stay past the limit, keep clean and carefully avoid the border and the police. When you do leave, the penalty will probably be no more severe than being refused reentry on the same passport.

A last thought about getting home if you find yourself broke and hungry and with no return ticket. Any American embassy will give you passage money home, simply to prevent you from embarrassing the U.S.A. But don't plan on it being an easy way home. If you can prove that you have no ticket, no money, no resources, no relatives or friends to borrow from, the embassy will negotiate a loan from the government to you. But you may have to wait for the money (weeks, in some cases), giving you plenty of time to starve. If you do get it, it will be a loan, not a grant, and your debt will be stamped in your passport, making it (and any future passports) invalid until you repay the money.

Berlin, Germany: There's nothing like sharing a drink together with new friends. This frivolity took place just a few yards from the Berlin wall, and is an attempt to counteract the bad vibes coming from it.

16 PEOPLE YOU MEET

THE PROBLEM
MEETING THE EUROPEANS
SEX AND ROMANCE
VISITING FRIENDS AND RELATIVES
TRAVELER'S DIRECTORY
NOMAD MAGAZINE
THE GRAPEVINE
NOT EVERYONE IS FRIENDLY
POLITICS IN EUROPE

THE PROBLEM

It seems to me that the one really big difference between what happens to a vagabond and what happens to the ordinary tourist can be summed up in a single work: people. The vagabond just naturally runs into people all the time, and they make a profound difference in the experience.

If one goes to Europe and doesn't meet any Europeans, what was all that about? Don't ask me, but I do know that a lot of tourists get no more out of traveling than the dubious social prestige of having physically occupied the premises, fleetingly. To be fair, I'm sure most Americans go to Europe with good intentions. They hope to see Europe *and* meet the Europeans. From their point of view, they're more than willing to meet the Europeans halfway—in fact, they're going all the way to meet them.

However, once arrived, their travel style simply doesn't bring them into contact with Europeans. Their preconceptions about Europe increase the difficulties, while their feelings of alienation, ignorance and frustration, which take them by surprise, make them nervous and uptight. It's hard to blame anyone because the blame lies in the kind of situation it is. Yet something needs to be done about it, and who's in the best position? The travel agents? The Europeans? Or the tourists— namely, you? Obviously no one's going to do anything if you don't. So in the end it's up to you.

Meeting people anywhere, including Europe, is a matter of mental attitude, sufficient time and physical opportunity, and vagabonding affords you all of these things. Let's look at them a little further . . .

The key thing separating people anywhere anytime is fear. Fear of harm, fear of rejection, fear of humiliation, fear of fear. So, rule number one in meeting people is to try to be less afraid of them. Remember that you will be rebuffed at times, but when it happens you simply shrug it off without going into massive melancholia. It's nothing to get shook up about. All contacts with people are based on percentages: some like you, some hate you, most are neutral. When you deal with people, certainly you know they can't all like you. So your attempt is always trying merely to raise a few more percentage points.

Wanting to travel reflects a positive attitude to begin with. You want to see, to grow in experience, and presumably to become more whole as a human being. Vagabonding takes this another step further: it promotes the chances of sustaining and strengthening this positive attitude. As a vagabond, you begin to face your fears now and then, instead of continuously sidestepping them in the name of convenience. You build an attitude that makes life more rewarding, which in turn makes it easier to keep doing it. It's called positive feedback, and it works. Vagabonding is a way of facing those fears, and beginning that feedback process.

When you go to Europe, try to give yourself the gift of time. It will keep you relaxed, keep you from foolishly rushing everywhere, keep you from spending too much money too fast and enable you to build a good head and a good attitude. In doing all this, you'll naturally meet people. To get it all together at its best, you need time to make contacts and especially to pursue them further.

Finally, you need the physical opportunity to meet people. The one sure way you'll encounter Europeans is by hitchhiking. And hitching contacts, by their nature, are direct and honest. A driver in his own car relates to you with the least pretense of all. Besides, people riding together in an automobile are expected to converse with one another—that's often why a hitchhiker gets the ride at all.

What about trains and buses? It's fairly easy to meet people using public transportation, but the passengers are not expected to entertain each other as part of the price of the ticket. Even when they do converse, certain pretenses are played out because they are not in a private place. Nevertheless, you should view your train and bus rides as opportunities to meet the natives, and not just as a way to get from Hodmezovasarhely to Mynydd Eppynt. In a second-class train compartment especially, the entire compartment may get involved in some kind of mutual exchange. Lots of soldiers ride the trains, and you'll find them very easy talk to, perhaps becuase they're usually young. Workers and farmers and their families are also companionable, more so than the businessmen and professional types (who you'll see less frequently in second class). Impromptu compartment parties sometimes develop when the passengers (or maybe you) pull out a bottle of wine, a sack of food and/or a willingness to talk and laugh. Offering cigarettes around or matches for lights are some ways to break the ice. In the corridors, listen for sounds of singing or instruments coming from a compartment of happy young people; maybe you can join in.

For those traveling by car, encountering people in a meaningful way may be difficult. That's why I earlier gave the advice about picking up hitchhikers and suggested that car-campers circulate around the campgounds once in a while. In any case, the motorist in Europe should remind himself to get out of his car and leave it behind as often as he can reasonably manage to do so.

Whatever your travel means, you should make some attempts to go out of your way to encourage encounters and make the most of them. You must understand that the reluctance you'll feel, the embarrassment over your ignorance, perhaps even a helplessness you'll feel—these are all quite natural and normal. Don't worry about them. At least, don't let them deter you from being open to experience. Relax! You're supposed to be having a good time. When you're in a public place and under the amused gaze of the Europeans, remember that being a tourist is okay . . . it's not a crime against society. You're as much a human being as anyone else there, so don't get to feeling paranoiac—it either constricts you into stomach cramps or goads you into eventually obnoxious overreaction. You can't successfully meet people if you're soured by suspicion or hostility. Let part of you worry about making your schedules, solving your problems and keeping up appearances in restaurants, pubs, railroad stations and the like. Hold back another part of you that can transcend your tourist crisis of the moment and savor the whole experience—keep a sense of balance and a sense of humor about it all. ("Well, here I am—little Ted Jones from Des Moines—actually visiting Venice, Italy . . . imagine that! Venice, where I've fallen into the canal and am going down for the last time . . . Far out!")

The place you stay is another good bet for meeting people. Youth hostels are deliberately set up for encounter, but pensions and hotels are not bad either. Wherever people spend time together is fine. There are no tricks in it at all. If you want to meet people and can get into the right head about it (not be afraid), you will do it as naturally as breathing. The American Express offices around Europe and money-changing lines in banks are special cases of where to meet other Americans in a hurry, and that's fine too. You can trade trip experiences, get some good leads on things to do, agree to go off and have a drink together, maybe even join up with some other people for an afternoon or a year. Just don't make the people in the American Express line your only contacts.

A last thought about people-places, and that's the ferries, particularly long-distance ferries—all-day or overnight ones, are great, not just for meeting people, but for relaxing, for pleasure. The boat's throb gradually quiets the travel-jangled nerves, the marine vistas are tangy previews of Heaven, and the passengers get to feeling all together after awhile—in good spirits and open to approach. There's something about sea air that breaks down people's reserve.

You don't have to make all the efforts. Europeans frequently tangle with tourists quite voluntarily, offering help, friendliness or just idle chitchat. Most often it's help—the sorry plights to which tourists are naturally prone call forth European good samaritans in droves. Simply looking lost or stranded will sometimes be enough for someone to volunteer help, often in halting English. I've been given directions, shown to buses, walked long distances by people going out of their way, had phone calls placed, received assistance in buying tickets, been offered food-drink-tobacco-money, had bags carried, photos taken of me with my camera, been given my daily bread and had my trespasses forgiven. Amen.

During a long wait trying to hitch a ride across the Algerian-Tunisian border, Stephanie and I were approached by a young man who had been watching us for a while. He tried to tell us something, but we couldn't comprehend. He persisted, in mime and speech, until we understood there would be scant traffic across the border, that there was a train station in town and finally that we should go there now because the train was waiting. It would leave in twenty minutes, and he offered to take us to it. After brief consultation, we agreed he was right. Rather than get stuck, we'd take the train to the first town on the other side of the border.

He led us through town to the depot, where a mob scene awaited. A hundred or more Arabs were milling about a customs office, clearing the border formalities. We had no idea of what was required or where to go, and very little time in which to do it. Panic. The same young man began to ask questions in Arabic, posted another boy to watch our packs, then literally pulled and tugged us from one desk to another, pushing people aside so we could fill out forms, process our passports and get our bags examined. It was total confusion, and we just managed to get on board as the train pulled out, amidst people wailing and stampeding after it. Our last view was of the young man waving goodbye to us as we chugged away.

There's more. We didn't have any tickets. When the conductor came, we didn't have any Algerian money because we hadn't got to a money changer yet, and we didn't have any Tunisian money left because I'd purposely spent it all before we came to that last Tunisian town. The conductor refused to take any other currency, and looked exasperated. (I could see us getting put off the train with no money in a roadless stretch of mountains in Algeria.) When the conductor left us at last, though, he assured us everything would be taken care of (?) Or I think that's what he said—there was no way to tell. Much later we crossed the border and came to the first Algerian town. Whew.

The customs-clearance precedure took three hours, while the train stood in the station. Questions and papers. More confusion. Were we going to be allowed in? What about the train fare? Many dark suspicious glances in our direction. Finally the station agent asked us to come with him. The train pulled out. The next thing we knew, the agent was checking us into a cheap hotel. He ordered the hotelkeeper to advance us some Algerian money, and directed us to a place to eat. In the morning, he met us at the hotel, walked us to a bank, where we changed dollars to dinars and repaid him the loan. The train fare was never mentioned. He wished us goodbye and good luck. We shouldered our packs, hiked through that far-out town of Souk-Aras and hitched a ride into the mountains on a gravel truck. And so our adventure continued, but it took a bunch of good samaritans to get us over that one short stretch of it. It will happen to you a lot.

SEX AND ROMANCE

Speaking of making friends . . . .

Part I: Sex, or How to Get Laid. This is for men. Getting laid in Europe by a genuine European lass is not going to be easy, especially if you think of it in terms of just "getting laid." The situation is basically the same as in the States, except worsened by language and cultural differences. Also, American men don't rate too well—as a stereotype—with European women. They tend to think of the American male as someone who is coarse, neurotic, materialistic and superficial. How do you like them apples? However, that's just a generality; there are frequent exceptions.

As in any sexual conquest, mutual attraction and opportunity are the key factors. The real problem for travelers is lack of opportunity, mostly stemming from lack of time. Given enough time, you learn where to meet European women and, in time, pursue a relationship beyond mere acquaintance. The best places are wherever

151

you can comfortably encounter women and be with them long enough to break the ice. Aboard trains, for example, or boats and ferries. In music clubs and discotheques. At the homes of friends and relatives. In youth hostels and pensions.

If you do meet a European woman and she likes you, it may be surprisingly easy to arrange a liaison. She's more likely to be sexually liberated than her American counterpart, and will go to bed sooner and enjoy it more. European women are beautiful in a way seldom seen in America. They are confident of their femininity and sexuality, sophisticated and sensitive. Maybe you'll be lucky. Women in Scandinavia and Northern Europe afford your best chances. Then East Europe, where women are very curious about Americans. Southern Europe and North Africa range from difficult to impossible, primarily due to religious and cultural factors.

But don't despair. There is another outlet: sexual success is much likelier if you stick to the American girls traveling in Europe. Like you, they are eager to spice their European adventure with the salt of sex, and the resultant action is *heavy*. No language problems, either. In fact, all Americans traveling in Europe find themselves falling in with other Americans automatically and easily. All the usual barriers between strangers at home simply don't exist. Most important, this instant friendliness solves the problem of meeting girls because you can literally meet them anywhere at all, anytime you recognize them to be Americans . . . in the street, at a restaurant, in a museum, etc. And American girls in Europe don't play second fiddle—they are fresh and exciting, too.

Part II: Romance, or How to Find Love. This is for women. Finding love in Europe, offered by a genuine European gentleman, is going to be easy if that's what you want. Surprised? It's true, but there is a small price. European lovers are traditionally impoverished, and need their meals and expenses paid to keep up their strength. There is a large informal army of gigolos stationed throughout Europe, looking for American women to service, usually in hopes of making a little spare change as well. This prospect need not be as repelling as it sounds. These European men are often genuinely charming, handsome and exotic. They speak a passable English and are fun to be with, for they exude life and vitality. They can be marvelous guides to a city or country, showing you an insider's Europe. And they're reputed to be good lovers. The point is that suave and romantic European men are readily available, but the sincerity of their affection is to be doubted.

American women traveling in Europe have the reputation of being easy lays and of having money. What could be more enticing? So, if you are an American woman, especially young and pretty, you will be appreciatively noticed by many dark-eyed Lotharios. It's a turn-on experience, swelling out your own natural beauty. Be open to possibilities and see what happens. Part of the excitement of travel and vagabonding is unquestionably a sexual excitement, so don't try to repress it out of existence. As a free person in Europe, you will know the heady sensation of being stared at, appreciated, desired. Dig it.

European men are enormously varied, but generally tend to be more gentlemanly, more self-centered, more confident than American men. Unfortunately, they do think of women primarily as sex objects, but are so gracious that it's not readily apparent. In the south of Europe, especially Italy, stares and whistles from the men may be followed by a pinch or goose to the ass, or perhaps even a patting of your left breast. This will often by done by a man showing off for his male friends nearby, who will be hooting and laughing. This can be tough to take, especially when they're not the least bit subtle. If it happens, try to ignore it and pass on. If it continues, don't be afraid to make a scene by cussing him out or even slugging him with your fist or purse. This never happens if you're with a male escort.

Then there are the American tourists, whom I spoke of just before. These are the cream of our society, so don't short-change our own out of mere cultural prejudice. Love an American; they're clean.

Please liberate yourself from the possibility of pregnancy. Bring whatever you need to enjoy sex without fear. See "Medical Advice" in Chapter 17.

VISITING FRIENDS AND RELATIVES

Certainly this is the easiest, perhaps the most rewarding, way possible to get to know some Europeans. It doesn't matter how slightly you know them, even to not knowing them at all. It doesn't even matter if you don't have any.

On my first trip to Europe, I knew no one there. Not one soul. But I did a clever thing, and so should you. I canvassed my friends for addresses of their friends and relatives in Europe. Came up with a list of perfect strangers all over the continent. After I got over there, finding their houses was one thing. However, finding the courage to knock on their doors—sometimes knowing they spoke no English—was frankly terrifying. But I steeled myself, gulped and began rapping. As for the results . . .

In Wales we were warmly greeted and put up for several days, given solicitous tours of everything to see in Cardiff, taken out to dinner, and spent each evening talking until the small hours. These marvelous hosts were the parents of a secretary I knew slightly in the office where I worked.

I mentioned before that the car-camper I took to Europe on my first trip was a used car. The story in full is that I bought it from an English couple living in California, who gave us the addresses of both their sets of parents in England. Well, we sought them out too, and it was the same good scene: we played cricket on a lawn in the Midlands, were even shown the birthplace of George Washington's mother (!). The other parents, in London, first baby-sat my daughter while we went out on the town, then gave us their flat for a few days. All this because we bought their children's car? Not really, but it allowed us to knock on their door. After that it was up to us, and up to them. What you will repeatedly discover is that Europeans are willing to be friendly if you take the first step to show your own friendly intentions.

In Switzerland we couldn't exchange a single word at first with the parents of another office friend. A linguistic panic stuck everybody about equally. But by day's end we'd been taken on a personal tour (including the biggest waterfall on the Rhine river and the town castle), generously fed and offered a place to stay. Four hours passed, with everyone jabbering and miming, before any of us thought to ask each other's first names!

In Germany our addresses were on vacation, but their neighbors took us in for an afternoon, hunted up some other nearby relatives instead and directed us to them after making phone calls. There we stayed the night . . . and I still get Christmas cards from those people.

On another trip, in Sweden, the family of another secretary friend simply took me into the family for a week. I stayed in several houses during that time (belonging to the parents and grown sons). It was a small town, and I got to know the life style a bit. I went to the movies, to the beer halls, played chess, talked with Swedes a lot, went on walks through the snow. The family treated me like an old friend. Then I hitchhiked out of town the same way I'd come in . . .

But wait! These were only the relatives of friends. When I finally got around to my own relatives, anything I can say is inadequate. I simply couldn't believe how much attention and love were lavished on me by total strangers speaking this weird foreign language. This was in Poland, of which my entire previous knowledge was gained from Polish jokes. I'd never known that any of my relatives even existed, except in a very vague sort of way. My parents never told me anything, and I never asked. Until this time. I wrote my parents for some Polish addresses and set out from Copenhagen with another American I met there.

Thus began a series of what were for me among the most moving experiences of my life. We had one wild time after another, skylarking our way across Europe into the land of my forebears. Everywhere we appeared on a relative's doorstep, we were received with at first incredulous questions and then fantastic, tumultous welcomes. There were family reunions and feasts, incredible meetings with incredible people, and all the fuses in my defense system against people were sizzled out of existence by massive overloads of hot human emotion. We were poked and patted and kissed and fed and bedded. We stayed in log cabins, we caught rides on horse drawn sleighs, we were kept roaring drunk on vodka. Return of the Prodigal. Heavy.

Poland is a harsh place. The winters on these northern plains blow cold and white; the towns are shabby and the countryside bleak; suspicious strangers brusquely fend each other away. But this same chilling environment invests friendships and family life with a special warmth. The sense of human closeness is greatly heightened as if to compensate for the starkness and hostility surrounding the circle of family and friends. I'd never experienced such intensity before; it left me stunned and touched. Later I made a return trip, and it happened all over again. I decided I can't go often, simply because I can't handle it.

I don't know if you'll have a similar experience with your relatives in Europe, but more than likely they'll be delighted to see you. The sense of family is strong in the "old country," and your visit will be an occasion of the heart. Actually looking up those people who've stared at you out of photographs, discovering their personalities and seeing them function in their own environment, can be a mind-blowing experience.

So do it. Get all the addresses you can before you go. Relatives, friends, relatives of friends, relatives of relatives, friends of relatives, friends of friends. Collect all of them, even if the connection seems remote and the chance of visiting is slight. Your contacts in Europe can easily make a merely good trip into a memorable life experience. The more Europeans you meet and get to know, the better your trip becomes. If possible, have whoever gave the address write to say you may be visiting. Otherwise, you do the writing if you can, but wait to know for certain that you are, in fact, going to visit. Go unannounced if there's no other way. Don't be shy. Europeans are curious about Americans and will want to see you. The chances are they'll be warm hosts even if the common acquaintance is only the friend of a friend of your Aunt Tillie's gardener, and you've never even met him.

TRAVELERS' DIRECTORY

Here's a special way to meet people. Quoting from information provided: *"Travelers' Directory* is the international registry of hip travelers who enjoy meeting others everywhere, whether around the corner or around the world. The book lists their names, addresses, telephones, ages, interests, and offers of hospitality to other travelers passing through.

"Published annually since 1960, *Travelers' Directory* is now being published every six months to keep pace with its rapid growth. (The number of listings has more than doubled over the last two editions.) New listings for the forthcoming edition are now being accepted. As always, copies of the new edition will be sent only to those travelers listed in that edition, so only listees will know who else is listed. No extra copies are ever printed. Each copy of *Travelers' Directory* is numbered, bears the listee's 'underground passport' to identify him to all the others in the book.

"Listees also receive a year's subscription to the Directory's own magazine, *Trips,* an entertaining publication written by and for the listees themselves. It features photo-stories about Directory Listees, articles about their travel experiences, invitations to all listees for free weekend Directory parties in different cities, details of the Directory's charter flights and conventions around the globe, plus competitions, humor, even gossip.

"Such bonuses, however, are incidental to the primary purpose of *Travelers' Directory*. The main reason people decide to be listed is that they enjoy meeting others with similar interests wherever they travel. They know they have friends to welcome them to any city in the world where there are Directory listees, and that seems to be just about everywhere: London, Paris, Rome, Stockholm, Bombay, Tokyo, Sydney, you name it. Listees live in almost every major country on every continent, as well as in such out-of-the-way places as the Canary Islands, the Panama Canal Zone, Hong Kong, even Antarctica. Although listees collectively speak dozens of languages, every one speaks English, the international language used throughout the Directory.

"Since a listee must submit his listing himself every time he wants it published in the next edition, all addresses and offers are current, and couldn't possibly be more than six months old."

It costs just $3.00 to join up and be listed. For your application form, write: *Travelers' Directory,* c/o Peter Kacalanos, 5102 39th Avenue, Woodside, N.Y. 11377. Tell Peter I sent you.

NOMAD MAGAZINE

Here's another related travelers' aid. John Wilcock, the founder of *Travelers' Directory* (above), author of numerous travelers' guidebooks, editor of numerous underground magazines, is starting a new magazine called *Nomad.* Herewith a description from information supplied:

"*Nomad* is a magazine for the modern wayfarer. *Nomad* is the essential magazine for international hitchhikers, people making their way across country and around the world, whether on foot, by bicycle, boat, bus, train, or horseback. *Nomad* makes the world smaller and everybody in it brothers and sisters. Want to share a ride across the country? Want to swap your pad in Chicago for one in Tangiers? Want to drive a car to Mexico or take a bus from London to India? Do you want to go by jeep across the Negev Desert and down into Africa? *Nomad* is the magazine that will help you do all these things and find people to do them with. Every international wanderer is a potential *Nomad* reporter. One day it will be understood that if you're short of bread on you way from Nepal down to Madras, a written report fired off to *Nomad* will bring you a small check at your next American Express pick-up. There will be a free classified covering all services in which money is not involved: swapping apartments, driving cars from one point to another—all these things are free to advertisers. Send us your free classified ads (keep them short); send us reports about your travels or your commune; send us 'survival-type' articles of use to anybody. Anything used will be paid for. *Nomad* press cards are free for the asking."

Need anything more be said? To find out about subscribing, to get press cards, to place ads, to submit material: John Wilcock, NOMAD, c/o Other Scenes, Box 8 Village PO, New York, N.Y. 10014.

THE GRAPEVINE

Whenever you encounter another traveler, in whatever circumstances, tune in your psychic antenna. There is a travelers' grapevine/news service that abounds with information on every conceivable aspect of traveling: cheap places to stay, unusual things to see, personal contacts to make, underground news and rumors, black-market conditions, ways to save and/or make money, and so forth. It is particularly easy to get assessments of other countries, cities, hostels, sights on your own intinerary or around which to plan a new itinerary. All this is worth tapping from any source, and youth hostelers are among the good sources. However, all Americans and other travelers overseas are easy to approach and speak to.

If you're hitchhiking, other hitchhikers can give you direct information about things closest to your own scene, so make it a point to talk to them now and then, even though you are basically rivals if you encounter them on the road. Hitchers do like to share their experiences, so approach them and gas awhile. Trading news and telling tales is one of the pleasures of the road—dig it. If you have a car, pick up the hitchers. You're doing yourself a favor, too.

Meeting people who live the tales is of course another great part of the trip. They are mostly people like yourself . . . other hitchhikers and vagabonds . . . and many of them are glorious characters, So why not you? It's common knowledge that you'll be traveling as part of an unusual and rewarding company. Most vagabonds are middle-class idlers, such as students from every country there is (and some there aren't), teachers on sabbaticals, researchers on grants and undercover agents on duty. Naturally, there will be droves of hippies, that international troupe of contemporary gypsies who strain the boundaries of the unbelievable. There will be street people, drop-outs from every scene and place, including a special military contingent of deserters and draft dodgers. There are gadabout groupies following itinerant folk singers, nomadic truth seekers accompanying roving mystics, budding talents in all the arts tracking down the aesthetic treasures of Europe and maturing their own creativity. And the drug dealers and drug users, and smugglers and agents, the American expatriates and foreign expatriates, and bums and drifters and hustlers . . . You name it! That's our gang!

NOT EVERYONE IS FRIENDLY

There are some less-than wonderful people you'll meet, too. To start with, you may encounter some anti-American sentiment in the form of someone who shouts "Yankee go home" at you, or throws you a finger or just clobbers you or your car with a rock. There aren't many of these around, but they do exist. What you do about it is up to you, I guess, but don't let it fluster you too much—and don't take it as a sign of the majority opinion. America is unquestionably fucked up and seemingly intent on destroying the world, but individual Americans aren't blamed for it.

If, perchance, someone does start coming on abusively or unpleasantly, take the better part of valor and quietly split. Fighting for your country's honor is not required, and probably unjustified anyway.

158

The same thing is true of a purely personal altercation—for example, with drunks on the street or in a bar. Flash them the peace symbol instead of the finger, shrug your shoulders and leave.

Perhaps the most unfriendly people will be those paid to act that way—namely, the police, border officials and other government representatives. As a general rule, the most human, humane and sensible rule is to treat them as human beings, which will predispose them to return the favor. Hopefully. More about this in the next chapter.

POLITICS IN EUROPE

More than in America, politics is traditionally a matter of everyday concern and controversy. If you meet any Europeans at all (or exiled Americans), you will talk politics, probably sooner than later, perhaps immediately. It helps to know something about European politics, especially the national politics of whichever country you're in. You can't possibly make points faster than by showing that you're conversant with topical issues and personalities, and in this case—and in this case only—you're entitled to express your opinions.

In any case, remember that such discussions are primarily a social pastime and will not noticeably change the course of history. Accordingly, if you disagree with or detest someone else's views, it's not necessary to express that feeling if it means getting people uptight or punching someone in the nose.

However, you will be asked about Vietnam and the Indochinese War, racial oppression, Black Panthers and American violence, such as the Kennedy murders. These are common questions put to Americans. I've talked about these issues with Russians in Warsaw, Congolese in Budapest, Cameroon students in Berlin and European nationals everwhere. Vietnam is the paramount issue, and has been for years, everywhere in Europe. Opinion is divided, or was, at least—the war is not universally deplored. Many Europeans, especially Germans (who feel protected by American troops) and Spanish (who are fanatically anti-Communist), still support the official American position. In traveling through Arabic North Africa, it's probably uncool to delve too deeply into the Israeli matter. Of the Arabs I met who did talk about it, all of them deplored the Arab-Israeli conflict. However, I never brought it up myself.

All Europeans are curious about America itself, but especially in the Communist or Socialist countries. (As long ago as 1965, a Polish child about ten years old asked me, "Why is President Johnson making death in Vietnam," just after he asked me, "Do you really have color television in America?")

They want to know about job opportunities, living conditions, civil rights, politics and hippies. Some will tell you of their dissatisfaction with socialism, of poor conditions and of lack of freedom. I met numerous people hoping to be able to leave for the West someday and one person actively plotting to escape. But others speak of the achievements of their governments, the glorious future of socialism and the decadence of capitalism. It is all most instructive, and I urge you to participate.

Poland: Truly a visit to the old country. This looks just like the old photo albums except for the tall guy in stripes. These are my uncles and aunts, who live in log cabins with dirt floors, and are some of the best and most incredible people I know. The language barrier was virtually impassable, but non-verbal communication via the heart was fluent.

17 EVERYTHING ELSE

This is the catch-all chapter, for those things that don't fit anywhere else.

LANGUAGE PROBLEMS

These will be made easier if you don't get uptight about them. People can communicate without a language in common, but this requires patience, poise and imagination. Or maybe just enthusiasm. Any other language you know, or bits thereof, will pay off. It really is worth reviewing that high school or college German, French, Spanish. Use it whenever you can. Most Europeans are pleased when you attempt their language, however much you botch it at first. If you plan to be around for some time (even as little as a month), you should make an attempt to learn a language. You'll progress quickly by being on the spot and you'll gain respect from the natives. Carry those little phrase books to start you out. The ones put out by Dover are good, and the Instant Language series even better. However, don't be surprised at how many Europeans speak a passable English, particularly in northern Europe. It's becoming harder and harder to find places where no one

163

speaks your glorious tongue—thanks to tourists, soldiers and business-men. However, rest assured that you will find some. When you do, relax, revert to your best grunt and sign language and keep on truckin'. Think how funny you must look . . . learn how it feels to be a dumb foreigner.

Specific tips: English is universal in Scandinavia, very common in Germany, Holland and Switzerland. In the British Isles, English is the native language too, but this may be small comfort when you find yourself missing most of what the natives are saying. It's not altogether different; just a matter of retraining your hearing. Places where natives rarely speak English include Spain, France, Greece and the East European countries. English is rare in North Africa too, where most people speak both French and Arabic. Wherever you may be, the people most likely to speak some English are the teen-agers and young adults and, naturally, people in the business of dealing with tourists: at hotels, shops and agencies.

Try to avoid letting a language problem deter you from doing anything you'd normally do. Non-verbal communication can be most eloquent. The most important element in any positive communication is mutual respect—the rest is a matter of academics. It's so easy in Europe and Africa to be afraid to do something because you're disturbed by not knowing the language or the customs. You've got to fight this attitude by following through on your initial impulses; by disregarding the problems and doing what interests you, going where you like and engaging whomever you're interested in. So long as you respect the situation and the people involved. If you don't attempt to grapple with this problem, you're going to miss a lot of the fun of your trip. Being afraid and shy all the time gets you awfully bored.

The best language to know in Europe (after English) is German. If you've ever studied any, review it, for you can use it throughout Europe and be understood. This is partly the result of the German occupation in World War II, but also due to the mass distribution of German tourists and businessmen. And your German needn't be very fluent—a viscous sort of pidginDeutsch will suffice because that's exactly the kind most non-Germans speak. A word on France: the French like the French language to the exclusion of all others. They often won't understand or will pretend not to understand anything other than fluent French. This includes imperfect French, too. But even the French—despite contrary rumors—are human, and will respond if you're not put off by some of their initial coolness and insolence. No matter where you are, a willingness to communicate, a respect for your listener and a sense of humor will speak for you when your tongue cannot. Remember this and practice it.

RACIAL DISCRIMINATION?

Are black people and other non-whites hassled in Europe? Not that I've seen or heard. I've spoken with black and oriental travelers in Europe—all report no especial discrimination. Although some racial scenes have occurred in England, incidents of racial prejudice are apparently far fewer than in America. Some black travel agents have said their clients, to the contrary, receive preferential treatment in many places. My observation is that the relative rarity of non-whites makes them objects of curiosity, which ranges from mild to intense. It also gives them a visibility that makes it easy for them to meet people and to keep their trip at a high energy level.

A particular inducement to black tourists in Europe is the chance of meeting black Africans there, mostly students. This seldom happens at home because Africans prefer to take their higher education in Europe, particularly East Europe. These students usually speak English (or if not, then French) and are easy to approach and rap with. Without exception, every black African I've met there is no ordinary dude.

Numerous agencies specialize in black travel, and you can probably find one in any American city with a large Negro population. But between you and me, cool that agency scene and don't get booked into some black package or first-class shuffle just to prove a point. Europe is wide open, so do it whatever way you feel like.

BORDER CASH NEEDS

All countries expect you to bring money, but some may require you to exhibit it before you can cross the border. (No vagrants need apply, right?) Whether you will be asked how much money you have, whether you will then be asked to actually show it and, finally, how much money you need in this case—all depend on the place, the time and particularly your appearance. It's easy to travel without a lot of money, but if you actually look like you're traveling without a lot of money, then you'd better have a lot of money, or you won't get into some places. Countries that require visas normally require currency declarations, so you must state on paper the amount of money you're bringing into these countries. Sometimes you must also account for your money exchanges while there. In all such places, the amount depends on how much time you say you're going to spend in that country. Assuming that you have a ticket out of the country or back home from Europe, you can safely multiply $5 per day by the number of days you say you'll be in that country, and that will satisfy the border officials if they ask. If you don't have that much, tell them you'll be there for fewer days, or that you're just passing through. Or lie about it, because being asked about your money does not necessarily mean you will have to show it. In fact, if necessary, it is possible to lie you way through most borders. However, you can do this only if you appear relatively straight and prosperous. Have a story handy in case they do ask to see your money and you can't produce it.

The same thing applies to your round-trip ticket, only more so. You must have one with you, or be able to show enough money to buy one. Your ticket home will probably be looked at more than your cash, especially if you look "undesirable." If, from your other world, you happen to own something like an American Express or Diner's Club credit card, this can obviously be a most useful tool for traveling with relatively little money. Having the card shows you are a person of substance, with the obvious capacity to buy tickets, eat lots, rent rooms and generally be the all-American tourist. But you don't actually have to use it for anything, so it needn't cost you any money. In fact, a good credit card can be thought of as a vagabond's insurance policy. No matter how bad things get, you know you can always get a room, a meal, a train ticket or whatever you need to solve an ultimate travel problem.

If you can possibly bring extra cash, do it. More young people get refused entry or deported for lack of money than anything else. A few hundred dollars in travelers' checks that you don't intend to spend, only exhibit, may save you much trouble. You can live from day to day as cheaply with it as without it, yet be able at any time to pass a solvency test if demanded to do so by border officials or police.

ON BEING SEARCHED

I've been searched at only three borders: East Germany, Greece and Spain. Regarding the first-mentioned search, you can expect a hard time from some of the East European border people. Depending on what the political climate is at the time, you may be warmly greeted or coldly messed with. Going to Berlin, the East Germans stopped the car in which I was hitchhiking and completely searched it from bumper to bumper, including putting rods down the gas tank. I showed everything in my bag and on my person, down to the last loose button, and they even looked at what I had written in my journal even though they couldn't read it. They almost didn't pass me because they didn't think I sufficiently resembled my passport photo. (Which reminds me that this can be a problem in other places too. If you are long-haired or bearded and your passport picture is short-haired or smooth, the border people could insist that you rectify the discrepancy with a pair of scissors before they'll let you in. For this reason, it's a good idea to get your passport picture made when you have reasonably long hair or a start on the beard.)

166

The search at the Greek border was almost certainly a punishment because I was coming from Turkey. Those two neighbors don't like each other much. I have heard numerous stories about searches entering Turkey, mainly to catch dope and contraband smugglers.

Searching people entering Spain from Morocco via the Tangier ferry is nowadays mandatory if they look anything like hippies or weirdoes. Actually, the authorities are looking for dope. Plain-talking, cigar-smoking, gross-looking Americans with paunches, sport shirts and ugly wives with teased hair seldom have to open their bags. Stephanie and I had to completely unpack our packs and unroll our sleeping bags. Then, after repacking, we were frisked before we could leave (she was taken aside to a little room for frisking by a policewoman). The latest word is that if you have a Moroccan or Turkish stamp in your passport, you will be searched at other borders too.

Any country can search your stuff, so watch out. Looking straight will help, of course, as will having an automobile, but there are no guarantees. In fact, however, most border officials will not go out of their way to trouble you, especially if you're not out to trouble them. Be cooperative, be dignified (don't fart), and they'll let you in.

SMUGGLING AND BLACK MARKETS

It's a fact that the East European and various non-industrial countries have scarcities of quality-manufactured products and luxury items. Also, countries with weak currencies have markets for relatively stable monies, such as American dollars, and also for contraband gold. The almost universal laws prohibiting psychedelic drugs automatically place these at a premium (and narcotic drugs too, of course). As a traveler, you may have the opportunity to turn a profit by buying goods, money or dope at par where you are and then transporting these across borders to finally resell above par. However, smuggling is definitely a hassle on your head and mainly the province of dedicated operators (of whom there are very many—smuggling is a large and traditional business in Europe). You're unlikely to become a smuggler (aside from dope, which is a special category) unless asked by someone else—a stranger or possibly a driver who picks you up—to carry something over a border for him. Unless you get really turned on to the idea for some reason, I'd advise not doing it. Since you're ignorant of the chances involved, it could be a real sucker's setup. Successful smuggling involves knowing everything: the risk, the land, the language, the customs, the commodities and particularly bribery.

Dope is something else. A lot of ordinary heads cross borders with a little stash for personal use. So far it's been easy to do this at most borders, particularly once you're away from the supply areas in the south and east of Europe. Watch out around Turkey, Greece, Spain, Morocco. Whether you're attempting to smuggle a little or a lot, the big hurdle is the border. Put on your best clothes and prepare your toilette. It's common knowledge that most smugglers tip off border agents by their own overt or covert nervousness, so keep cool and don't crap in your pants, sweat profusely, jiggle your elbows or drool a lot.

A word of warning: Canadians and Americans come under the most suspicion because they're the biggest users and dealers and they've got the money to do the business.

One of the most heavy borders will be the American one, upon returning from Europe. If you are planning to smuggle some hashish or whatever into the States when you come home, lots of luck, but remember these guys and their trained dogs are itching to get their hands (paws) on you. Professionals smuggle enough through to make the risk worthwhile in the first place (supposedly), but also know how to keep the risks at a minimum (supposedly). Amateurs don't (supposedly). In any case, I know a number of amateurs who either carried or mailed some dope home and who are now in jail or on probation. Actually, the odds are in your favor, but a sure penalty in any case is a great deal of head-messing and stomach-churning. If you want some stuff just for your own use, it's not worth it.

If you mail dope to yourself, or hide it in the vehicle you're having shipped from Europe, receiving it at the other end does not necessarily mean you're home free. Once discovered, a lot of contraband dope is repackaged or put back where it was, and allowed to pass on by ... with a string of feds just out of sight to nab you red-handed so they'll be sure of conviction.

However, black-market selling on a small scale is mostly legal or quasi-legal, and you might consider it. All countries allow you to bring in personal goods and money in reasonable amounts. If you want to sell these, it's usually okay (or at least nothing they can prevent). For example, if you happen to bring in some new nylon shirts to a place where they don't have anything like that, you can sell them at a big profit and it's cool. Of course, you'll get paid in the local currency, which is likely to be worthless anywhere else. In lots of countries, there is no end of marketable items of this kind, from *Playboy* magazines to chewing gum, but you need explicit knowledge of what is selling at the moment (needs change) and who to sell it to. For example, I met a guy on the train to Poland who was bringing in two cartons of small plastic tubes. I asked what for. It turned out they could be used to make ball-point pens (then a rarity in Poland), and he was planning to live six months on the profits. On the other hand, scarce items make great gifts for people you'll meet. In addition, maybe you should bring a few small made-only-in-America gifts: coins (Kennedy half-dollars), political buttons, novelties.

Black-market money-dealing is a better proposition, and it's reasonable to stretch your cash in this way if you can. Most countries that require you to declare your currency and account for your spending have a black market, so carry undeclared dollars. However, don't carry them in your wallet because a spot check by authorities would reveal a discrepancy between what you declared and what you actually have. Rates vary, so do some haggling until you learn what the realistic rate is. Be suspicious of moneychangers—some are agents. For that reason, the safest moneychangers are expatriate friends, foreign relatives, people you know at least slightly, and children.

AVAILABILITY OF DOPE

Meaning psychedelic, not narcotic, drugs. The situation in Europe, like America, is constantly in flux. Nevertheless, some things can be said about it that won't change too much or too fast. For a starter, there sure is a lot of it. Hashish is far more common than in America and much cheaper, simply because the sources of supply are much closer—North Africa and the Near East. Marijuana is less common, although in North Africa you can smoke kef instead. This is something like grass, but stronger.

Buying cannabis products anywhere is not too hard with a contact or two, or even off the street. Selling it is the same. But buying or selling, be wary of potential narcos or informers. For large-scale buyers or sellers, this is crucial because it's where most dealers make their big mistake.

European authorities are increasingly cracking down on drug traffic and use, and the end is hardly in sight. In general, people caught using or holding it will be expelled from the country; sellers and smugglers will face jail terms. But not always. Simple possession means three years in Turkey and six years in Spain, and they are actually locking them up in droves. In mid-1970 there were 250 young Americans in European jails for dope violations. Besides Spain and Turkey, France and Greece have tough laws.

Acid is readily available too, but less than in the past. Certain places become acid-head centers, but this changes from year to year. Acid is more available in the north, where the chemistry sets are located. I haven't heard anything about mescaline or mushroom trips in Europe.

The flourishing drug scene in most of Europe is sharply contrasted by East Europe, where it is virtually nonexistent. Young people there not only don't use drugs, but frequently haven't even heard of them. If they have, they tend to put them down as capitalist decadence.

In Poland I met a soldier and his girl in a bar one night and got to talking (in rudimentary words and sign language) about grass, which they'd never heard of before. He said he'd like to try it sometime. By an odd coincidence, about then I happened to find a few joints in my stash. So we retired to his girl's house, whose father (an army sergeant) was already asleep. To make a long story short, she wouldn't try it, but he and I got ripped. Soon he got sick from too much vodka beforehand and started to moan. His girl immediately freaked out and woke her father, who drowsily listened to her tattling about how I'd messed her cat with my "funny cigarettes." I could only speak a few words of the language to try to quiet her down, keep the sergeant from calling the cops and reassure the soldier he was not going crazy—all while I was totally stoned. The sergeant finally concluded we were all pie-eyed drunk (he had never heard of grass either), shrugged his daughter off and went back to bed. Be careful who you stone!

For more information about this whole topic, refer to *Play Power* (page 129).

GETTING MAIL

American Express offices are the standard places to receive mail when abroad, and for that reason are usually overcrowded, often with long waits and rotten service. So don't use them exclusively. Cook's offices have the same facilities, with more offices and better services. American embassies also have mail services, but are not as numerous or convenient. Finally, you can pick up mail at any post office c/o Poste Restante, which is like General Delivery. However, think some second thoughts about this. Unless your business agent back in the States has to keep in touch with you, or unless it's really important for you to be sustained by epistles of love from home, I'd advise not planning to get too much mail. It's great for your ego, but mail stops are troublesome and just another restriction on your freedom.

MEDICAL ADVICE

Take along a small medical kit containing things like:

Aspirin	Suntan Cream
Band-Aids	Diarrhea Potion
Thermometer	Insect Repellant
Burn Ointment	Antihistamine

Aspirin and *Band-Aids* are self-explanatory. In addition, you may want *compresses* and a *disinfectant*. A *thermometer* is no necessity, but useful because sometimes you may feel sick or feverish but not be able to prove it in order to take any particular action. *Burn ointment* is good to have, though its most frequent use will be for sunburn. Try to prevent this with a *sunburn preventive*—a must if you're hitching because of all that standing in the sun. When you get the runs, and you're likely to, that bottle of no-shit will come in handy. I've always used *Donegal*, a no-prescription remedy in an unbreakable bottle; it seems to plug things up pretty well. (You buy it here. In Europe, buy *Entero-Vioform*.) So-called tourist stomach is not from bad food but from change of diet, together with the tension, excitement and fatigue that always accompany travel. It really isn't necessary to avoid drinking the water anywhere, but maybe you'll feel better in some of the grubbier places by imbibing only bottled water, beer and wine. The *insect repellant* will help if you're sleeping out, not just from mosquitoes, but ticks, chiggers and crawly things. *Off* is good; *Cutter's* is better. *Antihistamine* or general cold-relief tablets are worth carrying: stuff like *Coricidin* or even *Contac* (if you're an organically oriented person, heavy doses of vitamins C and B will stifle a cold). For upset stomach if you're prone, an *antacid* may ease a bad time.

For girls only: take a sufficient supply of *birth control pills* to last the trip, or a *diaphragm*. Otherwise, keep your legs or your fingers crossed. If you're absolutely certain you'll remain chaste no matter what happens, then you're too uptight. Life is strange . . . anything can happen, even the best of things. Be tolerant enough to allow them to happen. *Tampax* (or Kotex—whatever suits your style) . . . just a starterpack in your purse for convenience. You can buy more anywhere.

If you do get sick or injured, get help the same way you would at home. Ask help from bystanders, the police, etc. Find a doctor. Most American embassies and tourist information offices have lists of English-speaking doctors if you want one of those. Stephanie had to go to a French doctor once in Morocco and I had to go to an Italian hospital for a couple of days in Capri. No one understood what we were saying either time, but we received the right treatment anyway (I think). However, if your problem isn't obvious, you may need an interpreter. For more or less self-curing illnesses, like colds, flu, diarrhea, you need a place to rest up and wait it out. At times like this, you'll appreciate having somewhere to go and/or someone to take care of you.

Other things to do: get your shots. Smallpox shot is required, and at least tetanus shot is recommended, especially for travelers who may be sleeping out and roughing it more than the average junketter. Tetanus germs, by the way, are present in the earth wherever animals have been. Travelers with chronic ailments should bring a medical report from their doctor detailing the condition and its treatment, *and* it should be translated into the appropriate languages or it may not do any good if you need it. Any necessary medications for these ailments should naturally be brought in sufficient quantity. Have your teeth checked beforehand and get the work done here. Being abroad with a toothache is a bummer, with a dentist perhaps hard to find or an appointment difficult to arrange. Eyeglass wearers should bring an extra pair or write down their prescription somewhere just in case. There's a place for this on your shot card.

LEGAL ADVICE AND COPS

Contending with European police is, on the whole, more pleasant than here at home. First of all, they're less inclined to kill or maim you with no provocation (they're often even unarmed), probably because they haven't been raised on the doctrine that violence is venerable. Furthermore, your status as a visitor will rate you preferential treatment, compared to their own. Tourists are forgiven all kinds of little faults and transgressions—especially if you are cooperative and apologetic, rather than pissing them off with some kind of tough-guy crap. You may get off with just a warning, where a local would get thrown in jail. If you're caught at something unforgivably illegal, you may still get off with mere deportation or an escort to the border.

Remember that your tourist shield of immunity is easily perforated or shredded if you are in fact guilty of some horrible crime or look like you're guilty, or if they think you are guilty. So it isn't much after all, except that they are invariably polite, even when arresting you. Bear in mind that all policemen are different, not only individually but as a result of national characteristics. I have little experience in these matters, since I am quiet and law-abiding by nature, but herewith a few observations:

English: polite and efficient, but with a hard streak underneath that can't be trifled with. Unimpressed by paperwork and explanations.

German: brusque and efficient, but cautious not to overdo it or appear too Gestapo-like. Impressed by paperwork and rational explanations.

French (Les Flics): tough and cynical, but with a human streak. Dislike to bother with trivial matters.

Italian: quick to be exasperated, but more tolerant and human than most.

Scandinavian: quite neutral; as eager to do you in as help you out—depends on the circumstances.

Spanish (Guardia Civil): mostly simple peasant types who can be influenced or persuaded if you deal with them at their own level, but quite harsh or inflexible if you don't.

North African: relatively simple types again, but proud. Open to rule-bending if you can get them to like you.

East European: frustrated and angry people as a rule; will go out of their way to trouble you as an entertainment. Careful. The political police are more suave, however.

The first time I was picked up by the secret police in Poland is a case in point. They snatched me off a railway platform with my "spy" camera in hand, and were rather pleased about it. As the grilling proceeded in a back room, a uniformed commandant paced the floor, impatiently screaming for my head. It looked bad, and I figured it was all over for me. But I kept cool, pleaded my innocence and hummed the CIA fight song. Later I was dramatically transferred to the provincial jail, sitting between two plain-clothes agents in the rear of a black sedan, which sped through the streets scattering pedestrians. There I was interrogated all over in English by a well-dressed gent who kept chain-smoking Russian cigarettes that wouldn't stay lit. A photo expert was brought in to develop the film from my camera. While waiting to see the results, we sat around genially rapping about life and times in America and Poland. I asked, "Why aren't there any signs prohibiting photography on the railroad platform?" "Aha, clever . . . if we had signs prohibiting photography, they would reveal the presence of secret objects worth photographing." So I said, "But that's crazy, comrade . . . what secrets could there be? There's nothing but trains and passengers." "Aha, clever Yankee . . . you want to trick me into revealing the secrets." And so it went. But friendly. The film returned badly developed but not incriminating. Free at last. They returned my possessions and even gave me a replacement roll of film, which I thought was quite fair of them. And I got the hell out of there. It was a month and several countries later before I discovered just *how* fair they had been. When I loaded up the roll of film they gave me, I discovered it contained exactly four exposures of film on the entire roll—precisely the same number that had been unused on the roll they developed that day.

If the police really come down on you with incarceration and all that, you have the right to communicate with an American government official to arrange legal assistance. Anytime you need a lawyer, by the way, American embassies have a list of English-speaking ones in the area. If you lose your passport, report it to the police and/or nearest embassy as soon as possible . . . your trip is all over for a while. For this reason, always take your passport with you everywhere, even to the john. Many travelers carry them in special neck pieces or belts, which is a good idea.

173

In most of Europe, especially the north, prices are all fixed. But in the south and in Africa, and to some extent everywhere, you can haggle successfully over some prices to save money, especially during off-season or whenever business is slow. The ability to bargain skillfully has its rewards: you'll gain respect from sellers, feel less like a tourist, enjoy the spectacle and save money. Some people are born to it; others abhor it; most people are somewhere in between. In any case, you'll improve your skill by practicing it, and you should attempt to haggle when you can. Here are some tips.

First of all, how does one know when to bargain? Common sense is the best guide, along with an exploratory inquiry if you have some lingering doubt. A rule of thumb: wherever the owner is present, bargaining is possible to some extent, whether the shop is an elegant showroom or an Arab tent. Another indicator is whenever there is a glut of whatever is for sale—for example, empty hotel rooms during the off-season. To proceed intelligently, you need to know the real value of the item you covet, whether it's merchandise, a room or a service. Try to discover the value beforehand from the fixed-price stores, from tourist literature, or by making inquiries.

Next, browse casually until you see what you want or need. Communicate your serious intention by holding the item in your hands and/or start asking basic questions about it. When the price is revealed, be surprised at how costly that little mother is. Make a counter-offer if you choose to, but for less than you expect to pay, knowing the dealer will in turn be shocked or amused. It's part of the game. If he's at all interested in selling to you, though, he'll quote a new price sometime before you leave the premises. If he does, try again. Examine the goodie, try it on or whatever, make counter offers. Give reasons why his last price is too high: you can't afford it (you're only a vacationing sharecropper); there's something wrong with it (smells funny, too greasy, excessively hot), etc. Finally, return the object to indicate that you're losing interest. The shopkeeper may now come through with his final price, a realistic one. If you agree, there's your bargain. If not, the final ploy is a last-ditch offer made as you leave.

Bargaining can get involved, so be sure you want something enough to work for it. But be friendly throughout and keep it light-hearted. Best bargaining times are early in the morning (the day's first customer is considered lucky and the hotels are emptier) or late in the day (when the shopkeeper wants to close his dealing day on the upbeat). If you're naturally shy or temporarily subdued by the foreign environment, bargaining can be a most difficult undertaking. (It always is for me.) Nevertheless, try it once or twice to loosen yourself up.

As for things to bargain over, you will see in Europe and North Africa the finest and loveliest wares in the world, many of them being things you didn't know existed before. You will want to bring some things back with you, so plan on budgeting something extra for this purpose. Every country has its specialty goods that are either among the best of their kind or the lowest priced of their kind, or both. The nicest things after you come home are the things you can't buy here, for they become both remembrances of the trip and beautiful rarities as well. Bear in mind that you will have to pay duty on these things when you return home. You're allowed $100 in value without payment of any tax, but above that you must pay a duty, of which the amount depends on the kinds of things you bought and their value—typically about 25% of the "fair retail value." Full details are given in the booklet "Customs Hints for Returning U.S. Residents," available from a passport office or customs office (or Bureau of Customs, Washington, D.C. 20226).

Save receipts to prove what you paid. Many merchants will write you phoney receipts, but these won't fool a good customs man, particularly if the stated value is way below the actual value. If you bring in dutiable items, ask the customs man which ones to declare in order to get the best break on the cost of duty. Believe it or not, they will help you save money if they can. Remember that you can mail gifts under $10 in value from Europe without paying any duty at all.

Another category of goods are the things available at home, but at much greater cost. A free port is one of the best places for such purchases, particularly for items like expensive cameras and lenses, where the savings may be considerable. You'll have to pay duty on these things but you'll still save plenty. Make these purchases at the start of the trip if you like, say at Kennedy International Airport in New York before you catch your plane to Europe, or on board ship in the duty-free shop.

In dealing with Europeans, how far can you trust them? That's certainly an all-American question. On the average, I'd say they're more honest than you are. Of course, you should use your own judgment, but don't be more suspicious simply because you're dealing with "foreigners." Trusting Europeans comes naturally, I think, although I've met some tourist types who constantly guard everything, add the bill multiple times and count their change until it's smooth. I was swindled out of some money in Italy by a guy who knew he was taking almost all (of the little) I had. This was the only time I lost anything substantial by trusting everyone—but of course he wasn't Italian, this guy. He was American.

Another ugly American was a hitchhiker on a bus in Turkey. We had to change buses at some wild-looking place, with no one speaking any more English than "Hi, Joe." After some milling around, we found the bus and had to unexpectedly pay a bit more. The hitcher paid with a paper note and waited for change. He didn't get it immediately, and he began to yell about his change, swearing at the "crooked" Turks, threatening sundry mayhem. The bus was full, the people around kept gesturing that everything was okay, but he kept it up. Of course, his change was brought—the driver simply had moved the bus to somewhere he could change the bill. It was a minor incident, but embarrassing. Naturally, it developed that the American was loaded with dough and was being tight on principle. The people who wouldn't miss losing a little money are usually the most asinine about it. Of course there are crooks and cheats, and you will get nicked now and then. The basic attitude to have is—so what? It will happen less in Europe than here, especially if you keep away from the tourist checkpoints and stay close to the ordinary citizens.

DOCUMENT YOUR TRIP

Cameras and film mean extra weight and inconvenience, but they're worth bringing along. Mere possession of a camera sharpens your awareness of your surroundings. In the process of "looking" for pictures, you "see" everything better. It's a travel intensifier. I think it's better to shoot black-and-white film than color. It's cheaper to buy and process (or you can develop and print it yourself later), and you're more likely to get better pictures (since color requires better lighting and more critical exposure). Don't photograph places and views available on postcards and commercial slides. They're cheaper and probably better than you could take, anyway. Photograph what is meaningful to you: people you meet, traveling companions, street scenes, out-of-the-way locales. If you don't bring film from America, don't worry: European film is excellent and usually costs less than Kodak. Watch for photo restrictions. In most museums photography is prohibited or regulated (the Louvre in Paris is a notable exception). Don't photograph military installations. In East Europe airports, train depots and factories are also on the forbidden list, and they do enforce this. As mentioned before, on both my trips to Poland I was picked up by the police for suspected photo violations. Also, I know of some American students held five days and then deported for photo violations.

If you are taking your own camera abroad and it's a good one, don't forget to register it with U.S. Customs before you leave. Otherwise, they may think you bought it overseas and force you to pay duty on it when you return. This applies to any quality product made in Europe that you take there with you; either register it first or bring the U.S. sales receipts. For serious photography enthusiasts, I've found the best lightweight rig to have is a 35-mm range-finder camera with two interchangeable lenses: a wide-angle and a short telephoto. The normal 50-mm lens will be extra baggage if you have the other two, and I suggest the range-finder type over a single-lens reflex because it will be smaller, lighter and quieter. There are restrictions on the amount of film you can bring into and take out of various countries, including the U.S.A., but I've never been bothered about this at any border. By the way, it's not a good idea to mail your film home because the U.S. Customs may ruin it by x-raying. Likewise, on airlines looking for hijackers with x-rays. Carry your film with you, and tell somebody about it at the boarding gate.

Bring some sort of hardbound journal or diary in which to record your thoughts and impressions. Use your postcards to illustrate the journal, and make sketches, too. You may not be this way again, so these things will be valuable after you get back home. Along with this, you might want to save various maps, tourist folders, museum guides, reproductions, tickets and other memory-laden paperwork.

WHAT NOW?

The end of the book is at hand, which raises an important question: What now? How do you make the transition from whatever you're doing now to this vibrant experience of vagabonding, live, out in the world? Guidebooks are attempts to bridge the gap between different places in space or different states of being. However, people often want their guidebook to *be* the experience. They read about something and then feel no desire to experience it themselves. Their "guide" does it for them.

I believe that a guidebook fails if it "does it for you." That's why this book is primarily an exposition of options, suggestions, possibilities ... I've told you a lot, but not what to see, where to go, how to do it, etc. That's all for you to choose yourself and to experience yourself. I've merely tried to help you make intelligent choices, and especially to kindle your enthusiasm for doing it. Now my job is about done, and you'll be on your own. Of course, that's right where you should be. Once you're on your way, on your own trip, this guidebook doesn't apply any more. Go live your own.

As for me, I felt qualified to write this book because I'm *not* a syndicated travel hotshot, just an ordinary maverick nobody. Facing something new and adventurous, I get both bright eyes and butterflies, both feverish in the head and weak in the knees. Overcoming doubts, I do what I sense is right for me, and sometimes even what I want to do.

177

It works, so have a go at it yourself. The road is calling.

Let me hear about your own experiences, or comments and suggestions for this book, or whatever. Write to: Ed Buryn, P.O. Box 31123, San Francisco, Calif. 94131.

HAPPY VAGABONDING!

"Halleluja, I'm a bum, hallelujah, bum again."—anonymous song

THE TERRITORY

THE TERRITORY

APPENDIX 1

COUNTRY BY COUNTRY LISTINGS

This final section alphabetically runs down the list of European and North African (and a few other) countries, with something specific to say about each. There's no rigid consistency, but I try to cover hitchhiking conditions, something about car-camping and usually some impressions and observations. Look it over. Some of it will be useful and interesting, some not.

AFGHANISTAN

See "Near East."

ALGERIA

See "North Africa" for a general rundown on things Arabic, then read this. Algeria is the most European of the North African countries, a heritage from French colonialism. Prices are higher here than in Tunisia or Morocco, and there may be some harassment at the border for hippies and long-hairs. Be aware that Algeria is not a tourist country at this time—the Algerian revolution happened just a few years ago, remember. You need a visa to get in, tourist offices are scarce, money is hard to change (only certain banks do it), there are no American Express offices, no American embassy, etc. There is some official hostility to Americans, but none whatever on the part of the people. A lot of well-known Americans are moving here!

The visa is easy to get in the United States by mail. Send your passport plus $3.50 and self-addressed envelope to the address on page 20. Overseas, go to an Algerian Embassy or get it at the border, but the latter may cause some delay. If you're a long-hair, you may have to get a haircut at the border. In mid-1970 long hair is okay coming into Algeria from Tunisia, but not from Morocco. They're working the hair clippers even on the trains, so be advised. (Long hair in Europe or Africa is seldom objected to inside the country, only at the borders.)

181

On the whole, Algeria is more modern, more European, than its neighbors. Notwithstanding the revolution, the French influence lingers strongly, especially in big cities like Algiers and Oran. Sectors of Algiers are like imitations of Paris, with elegant boulevards, smart shops and French restaurants. Yet there are amazing contrasts. The medina of Algiers is the most medieval in all North Africa—a fantastic jumble of alleys over a large area that rises steeply uphill behind the new town. Some parts are explosions of life activity conducted at panic pace; other parts are silent, shadowy byways, where your footsteps echo and you keep looking over your shoulder. And very few tourists here, so you feel too visible for comfort. The vibes in this medina are not too good, but the young kids will be anxious to show you around, especially to all the locations where *The Battle of Algiers* was filmed. In this way you can also get out onto some rooftops for an unforgettable panorama over the medina rooftops down to the sea and the port.

In Algiers a good location is the Square Port Said, near everything and with a good selection of hotels and restaurants nearby. The main entrance to the medina, near which are also some far-out-looking Arab hotels, is adjacent to the main square—Place des Martyrs.

In one of the many milk bars around town, be sure to try a chantilly of some kind—a whipped cream specialty that is much thicker and heavier than ordinary whipped cream, and the like of which I couldn't find anywhere again, even in Paris. Algeria, at least along its north coast, varies greatly in its scenery but is predominantly hilly and mountainous. This makes for gorgeous scenery, but it also means cold and snow if you're traveling through in winter or spring. North Africa in general stays cold until April, so don't be surprised if the hot desert sands you went south to find in January are somewhere beneath the snowpack. Roads are excellent and empty; miles and miles between towns. Easy to camp out anywhere.

Hitchhiking in Algeria is excellent. The rides tend to be long, more often with Europeans (French background) than Arabs and, as everywhere else in North Africa, there's little traffic. You'll see hitchhiking Arabs with some frequency, but you'll seldom be picked up with them. The Algerians you will meet run the gamut from lean Arab farmers in pickups to paunchy French executives in big Citroen sedans. You should have a lot of people-adventures. One of ours was this: a trio of mad Arabs snatched us off the road and held us virtually captive for a half-day because they liked us so much. They drove suicidally at 85 miles an hour over hilly, curving roads, taking turns doing animal imitations while knee-slapping and belly-laughing, telling jokes and swearing at other drivers. Just having a ball. Somehow getting to town in one piece, they wouldn't let us go till they bought us a beer. As a pre-luncheon snack it was delicious, but led to another and then a third. We insisted on going and staggered out to the car. Naturally we wound up at another bar for more beers (no food). Sometime later everyone agreed we couldn't hold much more and offered to help us get started. They drove us well out of town to a treeless stretch of highway, and after loud farts and fond alcoholic goodbyes, sped away again. In a few minutes a heavy rain began falling, with no shelter in sight. So, already sopping drunk, we also got soaking wet . . . a liquid hitchhiking tale.

AUSTRIA

Hitchhiking here is just middling. Some rides will come from the natives, but a lot will come from Germans passing through. (This is a personal observation for all of Europe: wherever you are, you can expect to get rides from Germans. *Achtung* and bless 'em.) I only hitched north-south over the Brenner Pass and not to Vienna, which would have given more information, but I got the feeling that the Austrians would get you there sooner or later.

The scenery and the towns are picture-postcardy, like Switzerland. In fact, Austria and Switzerland are somewhat alike in being conservative, quaint and alpine. Austria is more rococo and ornate, however . . . especially Vienna. This is an imperial city of palaces and castles, formal parks and imposing buildings. Statues sprout from the ground as readily as trees. Good town to walk in—do the Opera Ring around the town center, than go into the Centrum. And it's a music town, of course. Dig the Vienna Philharmonic.

Innsbruck, deep in the valley of the Inn river, has a fantastic setting. The old town (Altstadt)—the several streets that are the remnant of it—is great to stroll around in and let your imagination go back some centuries. It's near the river too—a glacier-fed torrent backdropped by an alpine escarpment so sheer it looks unreal. The Altstadt has cheap hotels and restaurants. By the way, Austria is noticeably cheaper than the other countries of Western Europe. Particularly outside Vienna.

Roads are good but mountainous, of course. Casual and commercial campsites are numerous. Roads are constantly patrolled to assist motorists in trouble.

BELGIUM

This is Europe's most densely populated country, and space is scarce everywhere. Remembering the many shoulderless roads, there might be a problem finding good places for hitchers to stand. But it's a small place and won't be much trouble to traverse.

The countryside is flat, green and lush. The towns are bustling and somewhat chaotic as a result. Big emphasis on commerce of all kinds. Ostend on the coast is a step back to a Victorian world of riding pedal carts down the tiled seaside esplanade beside the wooden cabanas. Brugge is a delightful Flemish town of canals, spacious squares and step-tiered roofs. In summertime the streets are decked out in huge flags and standards depicting regal crests and medieval scenes. Brussels sprawls for miles, has huge open traffic circles and squares, and it's every man for himself in the traffic snarls. Many tree-lined streets, unexpected avenues leading off others, distant views of spires and large buildings in all directions.

Off the main motorways, the roads are pretty bad. But interesting—cobblestoned, uneven and dippy. Campsites are relatively easy to find. Had one memorable camp in a tiny farm run by a family that sold us eggs in the morning. While fingering the eggs and unable to understand the language, still was able to learn that the proprietor was an ex-truckdriver who worked all over Europe for twelve years, preferred Scandinavia for the culture and Spain for the weather, had owned the campground for a year, moved his parents in, and the eggs cost 36 cents. Not bad for a lot of arm-waving, grunting and wild guessing.

Belgium is great for bicyclists: the country is flat, distances short, lots to see. The roads have special lanes for bicycle traffic. Scooters and bikes are easy to rent.

BULGARIA

Hitchhiking from Yugoslavia, I got a ride straight through to Istanbul that took me through Bulgaria from border to border in the dead of night. I can report that the road (a main highway) was winding, cobbled and in poor condition. And dark. I remember going through Sofia at two A.M.: empty drab streets draped in Communist flags, all signs in Russian, and one memorable sight—on a sidewalk a young man was beating up a kneeling teen-age girl as a passer-by ignored it all. Presumably this was a rare occurrence, but made a vivid impression on me.

The reports on Bulgaria say it has cheap living costs, especially food and transportation. Beautiful scenery, colorful people and virtually no tourist facilities ... meaning you can expect hassles, confusion, frustration. Not always fun, but it will be adventurous and unforgettable. Once there, Balkan tourist agency offices can find you housing. Trains are reported to be extremely crowded—buy your tickets days in advance and board the train an hour or two in advance.

For motorists, the Green Card insurance is not valid, but cheap insurance can be arranged at the border. For information about tourism

184

and travel arrangements, write the address on page 20. See the heading "East Europe" for more information.

CZECHOSLOVAKIA

I've only been to Prague, which I thought to be one of the two or three loveliest cities in Europe. On the train into Prague I met an architecture student who loved his city, knew it intimately and insisted on spending several days showing it to me. Too much to tell and more than I can remember, except that it is a classic European capital with Gothic, Renaissance and Baroque influences, better preserved and less westernized than any other major European city.

The people are noticeably difference from other East Europeans; in particular, there is an ambience of vitality and openness that is distinctly Czech. They are less suspicious, more outspoken and spirited. Testifying to this is a great number of clubs, coffeehouses, theaters and other creative and social arenas in which to meet the Czechs. I was there before the 1968 occupation, however, so don't really know how things have changed. For tourist information, write the address on page 20. For visas, contact the Czechoslovakian Embassy, 2349 Massachusetts Avenue N.W., Washington, D.C.

DENMARK

Impressions of Copenhagen in wintertime: cold long walks . . . canals lined with ancient multi-storied European houses, state buildings turreted, domed and shingled with green copper roofs. Bicycle traffic everywhere, red-coated mailmen, fascinating shops (the Stroget walking street is one of the great world streets). Raadhuspladsen (town hall square) at night in the snow with neon-lit crowds, the gaudy KAR cafeterias, the Russian hats worn by the men, the marvelous-looking women and hot-dog (polser) carts in the main streets with nose-burning Danish mustard. Ah, such a good place. A hive of activity; endless things to see and do.

Lodgings are hard to find, even for Danes. Check around the main station; get a room through the station's room-finding service. To get information about hanging out, go down to the Christianshavn area where lower-class types and hippies live, near the Kofoed Skole (cheap meals). Explore the country by train (25% discount on round-trip tickets), by bike or scooter (rentable, and the countryside is flat and pretty), or by car. There are many official campgrounds in the fields, forests and beaches of this tidy and friendly country. Casual campsites are hard to find, and the Danes will frown on the activity. Danes are fun-loving people, but they are rather controlled and conservative too ... something like the Germans, but with milder temperaments. They tend to admire Americans, just as Germans do.

Hitchhiking is accepted but slow in the countryside, where you will play the waiting game. I've made it up and down the Copenhagen-German highways numerous times without special difficulty, except at the ferries. These can be tough going either way. The problem is like that at borders: there is no traffic except that going on or off the ferry, which is definitely limited. (On my last trip, in winter, there were three cars on the boat, which is a large ocean-going thing that can hold an entire traffic jam.) If you don't get a ride in the ferry crowd, there'll be no more traffic at all until the next ferry (an hour or more later). The best technique is to solicit the drivers on the auto deck as they're getting ready to disembark. If this doesn't work and you don't want to wait, try taking the train far enough inland to start encountering the normal interior traffic patterns.

EAST GERMANY

Definitely not a tourist mecca, but there is plenty to see if you can take the uptightness of the country. Suspicious and hard-nosed people at the bureaucratic and official levels, and somewhat freaked-out at the citizenry level (through friendly if you can allay the initial suspicions and fears). Walking around East Berlin (1966) was heavy. Grim and forbidding, as they say. Lots of staring burghers, blocks full of bombed-out buildings, the whole city generally shabby, but also unique and fascinating. Architecturally speaking, East Berlin is more interesting than West Berlin. The west side of the Wall is the usual glass-and-chrome skyscraper scene, whereas the east side is classic old-German and much quieter, ghostly and touching. Visiting is not difficult—you can go across from West Berlin by foot or subway via Checkpoint Charlie on Friedrichstrasse.

Police and officials apparently love to hassle everybody; many openly anti-American signs and such; much paranoia. Interesting! Freaky! Hitching to Berlin from the west, then taking the train out toward the east were approximately equivalent experiences for me. Lots of frowning officials searched everything in sight, issued orders and generally kept things on the nervous side.

I hear that things are better now, but don't know for sure. *Let's Go II* (1968) reports that tourists are welcome, prices are cheap, campsites are available and hitchhiking is good. It's probably all true. There certainly is a lot to see in places like Leipzig and Dresden, as well as Berlin, and the countryside must be something else. Sounds like a worthwhile adventure, all the more so because not many tourists are doing it. For tourist information, write the address on page 20, or go to a travel agency either here or in Europe. You'll need to buy a visa and vouchers. For more about this, see "East Europe" also.

EAST EUROPE

(Bulgaria, Czechoslovakia, East Germany, Hungary, Poland and Rumania) Far out. Behind that verbal barrier called the Iron Curtain lies a whole different world that the vagabond should gravitate to as surely as the soul seeks adventure and the pocketbook seeks a bargain. For most tourists, East Europe is still terra incognita, and therefore you can get your traveling pure and unpolluted by the previous hordes. And Western Europe has no corner on the sights and culture of the continent: East Europe is a treasure house of beauty and humanity, enhanced by being undiscovered.

All these countries require visas, the purchase of travel vouchers and currency declarations. However, they're easy to visit because all (except holdout Albania) want to cash in on that tourist dollar. What it means for you is an adventurer's paradise: low costs, spectacular countries, few tourists. Many people are afraid to travel in East Europe through ignorance of conditions there; some even morally unwilling to—because East Europeans are "Commies." In fact, there is no danger, though there usually is a distinct lack of normal tourist facilities. This is good, as I see it. Regarding the flag-wavers and Red-hunters, all I can say is that there are millions of wonderful people who live in those countries. They live under a somewhat different system, but that has little to do with their human qualities. I've found East Europeans to be less sophisticated than West Europeans, and hence more earthy, more honest and different. Because they're more isolated from the West, they're interested in tourists in a way not found elsewhere.

Travel arrangements can be made by any travel agent (for an additional fee of around $20) or directly through the addresses given in this section—see the headings for specific countries. Generally you will have a buy a visa issued for a certain number of days, and then you must buy that many days worth of travel vouchers at a daily rate that depends on the quality of accommodations you will use—first-, second- or third-class hotels, hostels, camping or private homes. If you are visiting friends or relatives, you can use the last-listed class; otherwise, request the hosteling or camping rate. Costs for the vouchers vary, of course, but should be around $3 to $6 per day. When you get there, you exchange the vouchers for that amount of local currency. The vouchers are their way of guaranteeing that you will spend a certain minimum amount during your visit, and at the official exchange rate. It's possible to extend your dollars once there by trading them on the black market, but quite often you'll have trouble spending what you get from your travel vouchers anyway. Black-market dealing is good for buying local wares at an effective discount, but you run some risks. See Chapter 17.

Low-cost rooms are generally available without reservations. They are many hostels and student quarters as well. Also, keep your eye peeled for room-hawkers around the tourist and transportation offices. Their services are forbidden but common, and are generally a good value for the money, especially with a little bargaining or if there is nothing else available. Ample organized campgrounds are provided for tourists, but casual camping is discouraged or prohibited. Hitchhiking is possible, reportedly even good, but there are problems. Since auto-stopping will require an unknown amount of time to cover a given distance, it makes visa and voucher planning somewhat difficult. Furthermore, the roads are poor and auto traffic is slight. East European trains and buses are among the cheapest on the continent, comfortable for the most part (except unbelievably crowded some-times) and fascinating travel experiences. *Let's Go II* includes excellent listings on East Europe, and this is your best source of budget addresses.

Refer to the individual-country headings for further descriptions of each (Bulgaria, Czechoslovakia, East Germany, Hungary, Poland and Rumania).

ENGLAND

See "Great Britain."

FINLAND

Like Bulgaria, this is well off the tourist routes. Even I didn't get there. Apparently it's a camper's paradise in summer. Organized campgrounds are plentiful, with unlimited casual camping. Although not too developed in tourist facilities, there are complete services for finding rooms, providing tourist information, even a program to meet English-speaking Finns. The land of the sauna bath and the northern Lapp country, Finland, I would guess, is offbeat but not primitive, quiet but different. Hitchhiking is a question mark; depends on how conservative Finns are.

This is a small world unto itself, because it is Europe's largest country (bigger than Texas) and essentially a land of contrasting regions. Paris holds it all together, but there is also the Riviera, Brittany, Normandy, the Basque region, the Auvergne (central) region, Alsace-Lorraine and the Savoy Alps. Each has its own hallmarks, moods, people and climates.

Paris is noble and grandiose, with a sense of infinite possibility. Anything that can happen has been happening here for a long long time. Like other things French, it is many things, many cities in one, and the possibility of choosing among them at will is one of the secrets of its fascination. And it pulses with life. The swift but serene surge of the Seine contrasts with the unimaginable traffic and populace jamming the streets and thronging the sidewalks. I came prepared to dislike Paris as a big tourist shuck, and left loving it. One of the great cities.

Parisians and Frenchmen generally are something else. They are a quick people, egotistic and insolent by nature, but also amusing in that they overplay their roles so. On the whole, they are formidable—strong characters, dramatic, colorful. One time hitching through France, having just left Spain, Paul and I tried (with occasional success) to pass ourselves off as Spaniards. We spoke pidgin-Spanish to uncomprehending Frenchmen, and they dug us. We were the kookiest Spaniards they'd seen, and thought we were great. Maybe you make it with them by being even more nutty than they are. Reputedly the French are anti-American, but they don't really single out Americans alone. They're equally unimpressed with everyone until they know them individually. Their seeming unfriendliness is just impersonality. The French are a bit fed up with tourists . . . all tourists, and even hitchhikers, are just more tourists to the French. They like themselves best of all, which only proves they have funny tastes.

Hitchhiking in France is disappointingly bad. Rides are few, although the traffic is heavy, and the few rides are short. Officially, you need a police permit to hitchhike, but don't bother about it unless you have to because of police confrontations. As to why the hitching is bad, I think that urban Frenchmen tend to regard hitchhiking as being insufficiently stylish, not grand enough to engage their sympathies. And most rural Frenchmen are actually rather conservative types—picayune and suspicious—and will pass you by unless you look neat and super-straight. Put on your best duds for hitching.

P-R-O-V-O-Y-A is a number you dial in Paris if you want a ride out of town bound for anywhere in Europe. This is an organization that arranges rides for hitchers for a $2 registration fee. Get details from: Provoya, 16 rue de Provence, Paris 9e. I've heard of this several times but haven't used it and don't know anyone else who has. Anybody?

For motorists, France is one of the world's roadiest countries. Almost nowhere you can't go. Excellent roads, even the secondary and offbeat ones. Organized campgrounds are frequent, and casual camping is not difficult, except in the industrialized north. By private auto is probably the best way to see France. But their public transportation, especially the train, is fast, frequent and efficient. There's so much to discover in France, most of it unknown to Americans, that a good sightseeing guidebook is essential. Get one or more of the Michelin Green guides—there are sixteen of them covering the various regions of France (of which nine are available in English).

GERMANY

See "East Germany" or "West Germany."

GREAT BRITAIN

(England, Scotland, Wales). My first impressions of England: 1) weather—can't escape it: cold, windy, rainy, uncomfortable. Dress to keep warm and dry, any season. 2) friendliness—everywhere, without exception. People eager to give directions, to explain, to help. 3) the sights—storybook villages, charm and architectural beauty, kempt and cultivated lands, countrysides often a lush quilt stitched together with trees and hedgerows. (The industrial towns of the Midlands are, of course, not like this. Liverpool, for example, is buried in soot and has a raw, mean quality that stands in contrast to the charm of southern England. The Liverpool tunnel, which submarines beneath the Mersey River, is Hades-like.) English villages all have individual character, as, in fact, do the individuals. The toughness and pride of Englishmen as a breed can be seen to originate in these surroundings. Everywhere stand artifacts and symbols that daily remind an Englishman that he has a heritage, a tradition, a background—and whatever else he may or may not be, he is, by God, an Englishman . . . in short, he is somebody!

I preferred Wales to England for a special reason. Not that Wales is more beautiful or that its towns are more charming, for the opposite is true on the average. However, England seems too cultivated, too controlled, too charming. Wales is still rough around the edges, and craggy. Here lies its greater appeal—it's more real, somehow. Along with the harsh and spacious countryside, the spare-looking stone towns, is also an underlying sense of poignance. It invests the land and its people with a mysterious sadness and apartness.

Scotland is different yet. Far less populated, more austere, with distinctive hills and terrain. Edinburgh is a likeable small capital: a city

190

of tall black spires, turrets and chimneys. It's gay and active, with greenery and statues and the throngs on Prince Street all surmounted by historic Edinburgh Castle. London impressed me as the most civilized city I've ever seen. Throbbing with life and vitality, charged with excitement, it is convincingly cosmopolitan. The street faces include Indians, Africans, continentals and Americans—a world cross-roads. Commerce and traffic are the dominant mode—sights, sounds and sensations testify to a lack-nothing cosmopolis. It has what must be the best civic transportation network ever developed—subways, buses, taxis, urban railroads—but, alas, everything closes up at midnight, including the transportation scheme. Incredible number of things to see. Grab your detailed guidebooks.

Great Britain is one of the best of all European countries for ease of hitchhiking. Remember that traffic drives on the left, so you hitch left-handed too. Have a good map when you're in England—some parts are a macadamized maze, and you'll have to keep your bearings and your wits about you, along with a stiff upper lip, of course. Some of the English gas-station maps, (which are not free), are incredibly detailed . . . excellent. Most English roads have no shoulders, so finding a suitable place to stand, park or camp may be a problem. Heavy traffic is the rule everywhere, and the country roads are frequently narrow, winding and hilly—all this together with left-hand driving makes for tortuous but interesting motoring.

For complete road and sightseeing information, visit the offices of the AA (Automobile Association). Any fair-sized town will have one. If you belong to AAA at home, you rate honorary membership privileges in the AA in Britain. There is also the RAC (Royal Automobile Club). Both the AA and RAC independently maintain networks of roadside motorist service huts. These are manned, and stand ready to help with anything you need. These clubs also provide leaflet-type short-form city maps that are extremely useful.

GREECE

Originally the place where it all came from, Greece has since become the place to get away from it all. Greece is a backwater Mediterranean society resting on a substratum of glorious antiquity. Gorgeous and peaceful in the country, bustling in the cities, its ruins testify to a distant, wild greatness that lingers bittersweetly into the present. Highlights for me: the island of Crete, overnight by boat from Pireaus/Athens (deck class is only a few bucks). Fantastic, mythic island—very wild in spots, and hitchable, too. Rent a motorcycle in Iraklion and go into the mountains to see the Minoan ruins (Phaestos especially) and drink in the magnificent panoramas. Delphi: a spectacular mountainside site reminiscent with its walls and pines of a Sierra canyon, but littered with marble fragments and temple columns. Fun to watch the guided-tour groups trying to look intelligent. And the remains of ancient Athens are worth the whole trip: the Parthenon an interplay of gale winds, weathered grandeur and small human forms gliding surrealistically about.

Hitching is not too good. Tourists are your best bet. Many roads, except the main north-south to Athens, are poor and not much trafficked. You may get stuck awhile in spots. Bail out on a bus, if necessary. They are many and cheap. Try catching some of the coastal or island boats; crusing the Aegean or Ionian seas is heady stuff. Bring your own food if you travel deck class. Camping out is easy anywhere in the country.

Be advised that, as of 1970, the famous hippie settlement at Matala on Crete has been shut down by the police. The problem again (and again and again) is too many people in one place. I was at Matala in 1966, when there were about a dozen adventurers there living for free in the caves and leading idyllic lives at this isolated, classically beautiful site. *Life* magazine did a story on it in 1968, and in early 1970 there were 500 hippies crashing there. Moral: if you find a spot you like, don't expect it to stay that way.

The takeover of the Greek government by the military has apparently produced a petite fascist society with the usual contemporary characteristics: long hair is forbidden, as is rock-and-roll music; there are curfews and many other presumptuous restrictions on both residents and tourists. Free-living vagabonds will probably find the "new" Greece to be intolerable; straight touristic types probably won't be able to notice any changes at all. Same old scene.

HOLLAND

See "Netherlands."

HUNGARY

For me, the 48 hours spent here on a transit visa were hectic and full. Not much time, but I used every bit of it. As so often happens, I met some people who took over my visit and gave me a whirlwind sightseeing and cultural experience. This time it was a black African student who showed Julian and me around during the daytime, while a Hungarian railroad worker fed and housed us during the nights. It was a memorable visit, but my overall impression of Budapest was negative— gray town, gray people (however, this was 1966—very long ago). But we ate lunch at the Lenin University cafeteria, and the girls there are knockouts. For our last supper we went to an elegant restaurant, showed our waiter all the Hungarian money we had left and asked him to bring us something to eat in exchange. The resultant spread was simple but ample, and it was marvelous fun listening to a really awful dinner band massacre authentic Hungarian rhapsodies and threnodies.

Your visit to Hungary requires the purchase of vouchers at the rate of either $6.50 per day for an ordinary visa or $4.50 per day (7-day minimum) for a camping visa, plus the cost of the visa (around $5). You can get it at their official tourist agency (Ibusz) in Vienna, or, in America, write the Hungarian Consulate, 2437 West 15th Street, N.W. Washington, D.C. Or you can get a transit visa, which eliminated the necessity for vouchers.

I don't know much about the countryside outside Budapest, but I'm sure car-camping is the best way. For all assistance, accommodations, etc., while you're there, you'd best get next to the Ibusz people—the Hungarian language is like nothing you've heard before, and you won't pick it up in a week or so.

INDIA

See "Near East."

IRAN

See "Near East."

IRELAND

Another place I haven't seen and don't feel like making guesses about. But I saw an article about hitching in Ireland. The writer (Bill Grout) says it's his favorite country: the natives are delightfully loquacious, the landscape is unspoiled by freeways and traffic jams, sleeping costs at youth hostels/breakfast houses/farmhouses is around $2.50 and the only problem is rain (lots of it). Another thing: Ireland is the only place I know offhand where you can go caravanning—and well you might ask what that is. Well, for about $100 a week in Ireland you can rent a horse-drawn gypsy-type wagon equipped for camping. Then, off you trundle/clank into the Irish mist, on a variety of routes in the southwest of the island (around Tralee and Dingle Bay). Don't worry about getting lost; the horses know all the routes, and the neighbors there know all about you, so it sounds good for a relaxed, offbeat adventure. If you split the cost amongst three or four people, it's fairly cheap, too. For information, write the Irish Tourist Board (page 21).

My own admittedly inadequate adventures in Ireland consist of landing at Shannon Airport twice for an hour. Each time I bought bargain-priced goods at the excellent free port there. That's all I know about Ireland at this time. Stay tuned for future adventures.

ISRAEL

Various sources agree this is the best hitchhiking country of all. Apparently even girls can hitchhike alone with no qualms whatever. (If the Israeli girls are all as tough as the hitchhiking sabra in *Portnoy's Complaint*, I can understand why.)

Small but immensely important, idealistic but bone-tough, here's a country where people need and help each other. It's also a young people's country—modern and swinging. Disadvantages: tourists occasionally get murdered (along with the natives—no discrimination here)but until and if there's a full-scale war wiping both sides out, I think it would be a neat place to go. An Israeli stamp in your passport will prevent you from being admitted to Egypt and other gung-ho Arab allies. Ask the Israeli border people not to stamp your passport, and you can then visit Beirut, et al., via neutral Cyprus. Within Israel, bus, car or thumb are the ways to travel. Youth hostels are the places to stay. Individual is the way to be. Working on a kibbutz is easy to arrange, whether or not you're Jewish; there's even a hippie kibbutz now—a collective farm for American drop-outs 24 miles south of Tel Aviv.

ITALY

Immensely varied scenery, climate, culture, people. Although there is a certain Italian quality, count on every place being different. For example, Venice and Naples are nearly opposites—the first being calm, cool, elegant, no cars; whereas Naples is chaotic, hot, earthy, with a carnage of auto horns and exhaust fumes. Yet Naples also has Capri nearby, which compares with Venice for beauty and charm. Rome is a great place to visit for a while to take in the vast amount of sights, but is otherwise an uncomfortable, noisy, exhaust-filled, even ugly city. Florence is a special place, probably representing the best combination of Italian qualities (art, history, beauty, vitality) with less evidence of the worst (overcrowding, pollution, low living standards, political unrest). Verona in the north is worth a visit—few tourists, friendly, many interesting things to see. Sicily is still like Italy used to be before

194

it was overrun with cars: just beautiful. Palermo is Italy's most attractive large city; Siracusa is fascinating for its extensive ruins and port atmosphere. But hurry—even in Sicily they're building the freeways and introducing the ugliness of Progress.

Hitching in Italy is okay, but depends on who you are to a large extent. If a girl alone, the drivers will fight each other to pick you up. And feel you up in the car. Two girls will find it easy, and have each other for protection. Italian males tend to lose their minds when they spot any hitchhiking female, even with a guy. In the latter case, they've no intention of giving you two a ride, but will honk to get the girl's attention, then appraise her charms and leer. A guy alone will find fair-to-good hitching all over. A couple will encounter poor-to-good, averaging fair, hitching. The wolves won't pick up a couple, so the possibilities are leaner.

Like other countries with freeways, the Italian autostrades are both good and bad: nice for fast travel, but difficult to get to. Hitching right on them (as opposed to at an entrance) is illegal, and the police will order you off if they catch you. However, unlike some other countries, the Italians aren't hard-nosed about it, and will be polite with you if you are with them. Always try to walk or take city buses as close to the freeway entrance as you can. Almost no traffic is going where you are if you're merely somewhere en route to the freeway. In the interests of efficiency, raise the odds by choosing your hitching point carefully.

LUXEMBOURG

No one is likely to go here except the Icelandic Airlines travelers, who wax in numbers. Luxembourg—city and country—is one of the offbeat places of Europe. It reminds me of Hobbitown because it's small, uptight, and has the feeling of Dark Riders about. Spend a day there and walk around—the city topography is complicated, and there's a trace of supernatural eeriness lingering in the canyons and the cliffs of the old fortress. A tour of the latter, with its casemates (fortified caves), is highly recommended.

The people hereabouts eye you with distrust, and the atmosphere is provincial. Some of the hotels may turn you away if you look weird, and I've heard the hitchhiking is poor. Take the Icelandic buses to Germany or France to get your trip started; it's probably a mistake to try to hitch directly out of (or into) Luxembourg. In fact, there isn't much traffic through here—if you look at a road map you'll see that although Luxembourg is right in the heart of Europe, the roads through it are not really on the way to anywhere else at all.

See "North Africa" for a general rundown on things Arabic, then read this. Newly discovered by hippies, travel agents, filmmakers and other exponents of Progress, Morocco is changing rapidly behind the pressure of heavy people and money influx. (Flux you, too!) It's the in-place, the target for all kinds of tourists, ranging from Hilton Hotel hoppers to dream-dealing druggies. Indeed, Morocco has something for everybody, and is a kind of paradise. History, culture, climate, scenery, inexpensiveness, plus something indefinable (maybe dope) make it the best visit of all. Entry into this neat place may be difficult for you, however, if you are male and possess long hair like a female (on your head, that is). Ah so. Almost everyone so arrayed will be messed with, and how long is long in this case is arbitrarily up to the border bosses. At this time long-hairs can enter only under exceptional circumstances. I met one Canadian who lied his way in as a cowboy movie actor, but he backed up his fib with $1,000 he was "planning to spend in Morocco." A French couple with lengthy locks made it after hours of pleading, during which they made the symbolic gesture of discarding their back packs and buying suitcases instead (more respectable). Most long-hairs simply get turned back, even in private cars, and this is true of all entry points, whether from Algeria or from Spain via Tangier, Ceuta or Melilla. There's almost no way left, except possibly via the Canaries. The international long-hairs at the quay coffeehouses in Algeciras, Spain (the main jump-off point for Morocco), rap for hours about how to beat the border.

It's a fun game, but I advise cutting your hair. It's no big thing, unless you feel your identity depends on your hair style or brand of hair spray. Anyway, once inside, you can grow it back. More than that, as a long-hair you put yourself in a certain bag that may isolate you in the long run. So many same-looking "hip" people are "making the scene" these days, it's almost time to start issuing horoscopes to tell the players apart. Often the purpose of wearing hippie uniforms is to be recognized by others in the clan so everybody can sit around at a sidewalk cafe, look far-out and act stupid. Man, this is what the straight people have been doing for decades in their own costumes.

Train service is good in Morocco but connects only the main towns. Buses do the rest, and can be wild. Roads are quite good generally, but fade away rapidly around the Atlas Mountains. Nevertheless, by car is the best way to explore the incredible back country, with its isolated villages and undisturbed scenes from another way of life. Camping out anywhere is easily accomplished—just pull over and stop the car . . . open space is the rule.

Hitchhiking in Morocco is generally excellent, except on the routes into Tangier. These get the most traffic but yield the least rides, with more hitchhikers trying than anywhere else, too (which could be why it's bad). The interior route from Fez to Marrakech, along the Atlas Mountains, is hard to hitch and sometimes closed by snow well into spring; it's actually much faster to hitch via Casablanca and the coast instead (the way the train goes). Rides in Morocco should be among the most interesting you'll get anywhere because of the cosmopolitanism of Morocco: rich and poor, native and tourist, straight and hippie. Morocco has a bad reputation for solo hitchhikettes, but I met several girls who hitchhiked alone with no trouble.

Of the main cities, Fez, Marrakech and Rabat are the most interesting. Tangier is flooded with tourists and hustlers, and Casablanca is modern, crowded and dull. The coast towns of Agadir and Essouira are very big on the hippie circuit and are probably worth going to (hippies do have excellent taste in selecting places to hang out).

Marrakech is the big one, and the place to stay is in one of the numerous fleabag hotels in the alleys behind the CTM (bus station) at the Place Djemaa-el-Fna, the happening place in town. The rooms are around $1 a day or less, you share one toilet in the building and there is no bath at all. But there's usually a roof for sunning while stoned, and the public bathhouse is nearby, up the same alley. Dope is illegal in Morocco, but in Marrakech it's cheap, available and common—hash, kef, and hash cookies. The government of Morocco has officially declared war on drugs in a well-publicized campaign (they wouldn't want to lose their American air bases, would they?). We'll see how it goes, but watch out for double-dealers. The old Arabs smoking in the alleys will probably be unmolested, but you better be cool.

New topic: in the new town, about the prettiest in Morocco, on the Avenue Mohammed V is a shop called Photo-Bertrand. Here at reasonable prices you can buy outstanding photographic prints of authentic Moroccan scenes—fine souvenirs.

Fez has a bigger and much less touristed medina than Marrakech, with far fewer hustlers and much better vibes overall. It's a beautiful city nestled in hills, and has the most authentic feel of any big town in Morocco. There are cheap hotels in the new town, which has an active street life . . . crowds and sidewalk cafes. The main attraction, though, is the medina (actually two different medinas in one) and is the best preserved in all Morocco.

Rabat is notable for its history as a pirate capital for hundreds of years and for its beautiful setting: a white city built on hills and cliffs above a coastal inlet. The battlements are silent now, but you can feel the ages blowing in the wind. There are some stunning tourist sites—the Kasbah, the Museum of Muslim Art with its adjacent garden and Moorish cafe, the Hassan Tower and Mosque, the Chella Necropolis . . . all knockout places.

NEAR EAST AND BEYOND

Just a few general pieces of news put together from hearsay: Iran, Afghanistan, Pakistan and India are hitchable, but not easy. No traffic, primitive conditions, omnipresent weirdnesses make it unreliable, uncomfortable and adventurous. Moreover, bus fares are dirt cheap. General comments: visas are needed for all these countries; get them in the neighboring country. You need passport pictures and usually a couple of days' wait. Shots may be required if there's an epidemic around, which there may be.

Cost of living extremely low—cheap food and accommodations. Living conditions, life styles, cultural things will all be new to you. Exotic people, strange adventures, weird sights abound. Also dirt, dysentery, lice and poverty . . . all of which you may get.

Dope is everywhere: hash, gunja, opium. Smoked openly on the streets by some natives, but not by you. Watch out for dealers—they might either burn you or turn you in. Safest place to buy is from foreign residents you know or meet. Some hostility to Americans, growing hostility to hippies. Some evictions of young foreigners (those without money) have been going on, especially in Katmandu (Nepal). Smuggling and black-market dealing . . . lots. Anything you don't declare or have written into your passport can be sold. Otherwise, you've got to have it when you leave the country. The market varies but everything from tape recorders, cameras, watches, to gold, guns and gunja (extra-potent Indian marijuana) is dealt. Lots of people go to jail for these games, but lots don't. In India and Pakistan: English commonly spoken; it's the official administrative language. Trains cheap: buy third-class tickets, then ride in a higher-class car—the conductor will permit it. People friendly, apparently a lot of hospitality at all levels. Cars drive on the left, one evidence of much remaining English white supremacy. Another: everyone drinks milk tea, like the British. For more info, read *Play Power* (page 129).

NETHERLANDS

(Holland). Hitchhiking is slow, but not a problem. You'll get lots of short rides from locals going to the next town. Try hitching north from Amsterdam over the hook of Holland for a look at some of the most placid pastoral expanses of Europe. Holland also is not nearly so uptight with young people and long-hairs as some places, such as Spain, Italy and Morocco. In fact, here's a quote from the chief of police of Amsterdam: "For us, each foreigner is the same. Large hats and long hair do not play a role. We only mind about the law."

Casual car-camping is more difficult than usual here, but

organized campgrounds are of good quality, generally. All roads are excellent. The bicycle paths and flat terrain make this ideal cycle touring country. But the electric trains are fast, frequent and not exorbitant in price.

Amsterdam is an unusual (somehow) town. Buildings lean at all angles, canals and boats are everywhere. Has a pleasantly provincial atmosphere (though upraised with the likes of Rembrandt), and is happily scaled for human beings—easy to walk or bike all over. Be certain to check with the tourist office for all manner of friendly information and help. Amsterdam is where Anne Frank lived; the house is open—see it.

NORTH AFRICA

By this I mean Algeria, Tunisia and Morocco. On my last trip I went especially to learn about these places—for me, long gone in mystery and mystique. I'd heard various conflicting tales, but the net effect was a kind of scarey ignorance. Now, after doing it, I'm pleased to tell you that the experiencing there is the best. I repeatedly felt that for this time, at least, I had stumbled onto some kind of adventurer's cloud nine. Here is a huge land of surpassing beauty, disarming friendliness, low prices, delightful climate, exciting, exotic, and with marvelous hitchhiking, too. Come see for yourself.

Hitchhiking is paradoxical in these countries. The major highways are mostly peaceful, tree-lined lanes with no traffic whatever. You don't see many cars in an hour . . . yet you're almost sure to get a ride from one of them. After a place like France, for example, where literally thousands of little iron boxes sputter by before one stops for you, it blows your mind to be where the average is about one out of four. Do hitch the trucks, wagons and everything else that moves, except buses and burros. You'll often get rides in trucks, unlike Europe. Also, hitch even cars loaded down with passengers and luggage . . . it's amazing, but sometimes fully loaded cars will stop anyway and the driver will rearrange his entire load to make room for you.

However, you should plan to know or learn some French along this route. Or Arabic, if you think you can handle that (!). It would be a shame (mostly for you) to miss out on communicating with the people you meet. They are friendly to a fault, often being unwilling to let go of you. Most of your rides will come from the Arabic rather than the European segment, and the Arabs are a trip. They are soul people who practice brotherhood every day rather than just bullshit about it on Sundays.

Stephanie and I got left in a Moroccan town called Kenitra, on the way to Tangier. It's a bad place because an American air base squats on the outskirts and the town has really been fucked over by this influence—as so often is the case. Anyway, we waited all day for a ride (our longest wait in North Africa) while many Arab hitchhikers were picked up all around us. Finally, in late afternoon, a small car with three Arabs stopped and squeezed us in. We were a bit freaked at the start by various happenings we didn't understand—by an early brusqueness on the driver's part, by one of the Arabs who had a gun and by a French dialect we couldn't follow too well. More time was killed because our driver ran errands all over town, leaving us waiting (and confused) with the engine running. Out on the highway, he stopped several more times—at a little village, at a canning factory, at a truck stop. Besides that, his car barely ran (he always left the engine running because the batteries were dead). Our progress was slow, it was getting late, and we were in a hurry (always a mistake).

Gradually the car emptied, conversation waxed and our driver warmed to us. He apologized for not being able to take us all the way (because his car had no headlights), but he promised to help us. When we came to his town—the end of the ride for us—he told us he had a friend we'd like to visit. In rotten French I replied, "Thanks, but it's very late—how about taking us to the highway instead?" This while pointing at the setting sun, trying to get across the idea that we had to split down the pike before dark and had no time for visiting. Ignoring this, he drove off the highway into the back streets of this new nowhere town. His friend turned out to be a well-to-do octogenarian in a long robe and red fez, who fondled a two-year-old daughter (!) and strained his orange-blossom tea through a wide white mustache. Then lots of awkward small talk, dragging.

Antsy to get out, I pointedly suggested we leave. "Monsieur, it's getting dark and we'll be stranded . . . let's split." This was ignored; we had another cup of tea, and more talking with long pauses. Ultimately, we left. Nearly dark. Only after some boys pushed the car to start us off did our driver tell us what was happening. "I took you there," he said, "because had the old gentleman liked you, arrangements would be made for someone to drive you further. But he didn't offer it. You see, you must relax and take the time to be friendly . . . that is how it is done here."

So we blew that one, but still had to get to the highway. Our man now drove us to it, but then, damnit, he still wouldn't let us out. Instead, he drove slowly out of town, repeatedly checking his rearview mirror. After awhile a car overtook us, and as it passed, he energetically waved it down. The other driver halted and our man (now in Arabic) went into a rap with the occupants, pointing at us. And talked them into giving us a lengthy ride.

The beautiful part is this driver's commitment to get us a ride one way or the other, and his means of doing it. His various attempts were based on soul and on the precept of people reacting to other people's needs. It was a learning experience about the Arabic temperament.

These hitching comments don't apply, by the way, to girls traveling alone. Travel with a guy, or you probably won't dig the Arab soul too much, mainly because you'll be too hassled to be aware of it. Truth is, the Arabic men, like the southern European men, think of women primarily as sex objects, and will brutalize your humanity more than you care for. Girls do hitchhike alone in North Africa (and Italy, Spain, Greece and Turkey) but I don't recommend it for the average American girl—you're going to be messed with sooner or later.

All large cities in North Africa are, in fact, two entirely different but adjacent cities: the medina and the *ville nouvelle* (new town). The new town is the modern European sector, usually French in character, with tree-lined boulevards, shops and hotels. Clean, expensive and uninteresting. The highways always go through this part of town, so you'll see it as you hitch in or out. (Or drive in, or arrive by train.)

Once you arrive, leave this sector and head for the medina, which is the original Arabic town, often completely behind ancient stone walls. Here is where you find the cheap hotels and restaurants, the tourist sights—like the kasbah, or fortress, the mosques (barred to non-Muslims), the souks, or covered streets, where anything can be bought at prices settled by bargaining—and all the enchantment and ugliness that characterize Arabic Africa. Every medina is different but fascinating. They are mazes of winding streets and alleys that teem with people and animals, with noise and smell, with exotic and amazing sights at every step. They are heavy places to experience because everything is strange and sometimes scarey: people constantly staring; merchants, beggars and kids hustling you; freaky things all around; easy to get lost . . .

Well, the trip here is to learn to dig the medinas—to put aside your fears and prejudices and just do it. Follow some of those side alleys around the corner, go into some of those dark shop entrances. Despite what you think, they're not dangerous places. The best way to see a large medina is with a guide, and I don't mean one of those straight cats with an official badge, being dogged by a laughable mob of sport-shirted, camera-toting tourists. Every medina has an informal guide corps consisting of kids from about six to sixteen. The best ones are about ten years old because they know everything and are less likely to shuck you than the older ones.

When you arrive in the medina, select one of the kids and turn yourself over to him. If you've made a good choice, you've got it made from them on. Your guide will get you into a cheap hotel, show you the native restaurants, take you to the tourist sights, score you some hash, bring you to the shops and bargain with the shopkeepers for you, carry your pack and, in general, treat you like gold. Which of course you are: take whatever story they tell you with a grain of salt; they're in it for the money, and many, if not most, get kickbacks from whereever they take you. But don't discount their friendliness, which is genuine. And some may work very hard to show you around. Pay them something for their services, but not too much—less than they ask for, if they do ask. In big tourist towns, like Marrakech and Tangier, they're overpaid a lot, so it's a good idea to find out ahead of time that they're not going to take you to the cleaners. Unless they really do a lot for you, the tip you give will be some fraction of a dollar, not some multiple of it.

About bargaining: don't get up tight. It's supposed to be fun for everybody. The final prices are generally about half the starting prices, but sometimes you may have to haggle for an hour. It's great sport if you have time and really want the item in question.

NORWAY

Dead-of-winter impressions: snowbound Oslo is out of an old Sonja Heine movie—an odd haze hangs over the white crispened streets, the sun sets dramatically into misty red clouds, future Olympic champions frolic and play with skis/sleds/ice skates, men tied onto the steep roofs shovel snow into the streets. Thick icy rime plates the sidewalks like verglas (an old woman of about seventy did an incredible heels-over-head flip at a bus stop for me), the cold freezes my mustache into steel wool and the snow is asshole-deep wherever it hasn't been cleared.

So winter is probably not the best time to visit. Many roads are closed, even the main one from Oslo to Bergen (though trains run all winter). I've been told that summer hitchhiking, especially in the northern regions, is very good. I was able to get some rides in winter, but it was simply too cold to stand around for very long. However you do it, you should try to get into the interior mountain region (gentle barren slopes) and to the fjords (wow). For the former, any travel means is good, but for the fjords, take one of the boat rides.

Oslo is a small-time capital—rather straight-laced—but is a first-rate art center: Munch Museum impressed me as much as any other in Europe; likewise the Vigeland sculptures in Frogner Park. There's also a national gallery, a folk museum and three ship museums.

PAKISTAN

See "Near East."

Also see "East Europe." A hard place, where I've been on two different trips and got picked up by the police both times (story told elsewhere). Land of strangeness, or how to return to the Dark Ages in one easy step (actually to the 1930's, because Poland today strongly resembles America back during the Depression). Warm gushing humanity versus cold bureaucratic government. Poles are a paradox— intellectual tradition and peasant heritage; tragic history and fierce heroic pride. Rampant black market (around 100 zlotys per dollar instead of the official 24), shortages and endless lines, rotten service everywhere, gray vibes—yet the people as individuals are strong, humorous and unforgettable. (One big downtown Warsaw restaurant routinely admitted it had run out of food the day before; was offering just rolls and coffee. Upon reordering rolls, I was told they'd run out of those too. Did I want more coffee? But I had a good time talking with the waitress, whose relatives lived in Detroit.)

Warsaw: 80% rebuilt and machine-gun scars in the remaining 20%; people friendly to and enormously curious about Americans; women among the most beautiful in Europe. Kraków: old-world and Gothic. Zakopane and Krynica in the mountains to the south offer winter sports, and the Baltic Sea in the north affords summer bathing and beachcombing. Oświecim (Auschwitz in German), with its World War II extermination camps, is achingly unforgettable. Ironically, everything about this major international tourist attraction is modern and glittering—exactly the opposite from the rest of Poland. The Polish language is incomprehensible (in common with other East European languages), but you'll meet English-speakers here and there who'll be eager to practice with you. German is understood fairly widely, and some French. But prepare for a linguistic scramble.

Visas ($4) can be obtained from the Consulate General of Poland, 1525 N. Astor Street, Chicago, Ill. 60610. The per diem (voucher) rate of about $3.50 per day will serve for tourists who camp, stay in tourist or youth hostels or stay with relatives. For tourist information, write to the address on page 21.

Trains and buses go everywhere and are cheap, exciting and crowded. Poles are easy to meet here, but communicating with them will be a problem. A phrase book will help. Roads aren't too good, but serviceable. Campgrounds are available, and casual camping is okay and easily found. Hitchhiking is reportedly good (for Poles, anyway).

PORTUGAL

I haven't been there. Reportedly the costs are low, the camping is

203

excellent (some campgrounds are government-operated and luxurious), the people are conservative and uptight and the landscape is beautiful— also, great beaches.

RUMANIA

See also "East Europe." Another blank for me. Reportedly the easiest of the East European countries to visit. The language is more comprehensible than most, the tourist facilities better developed and the people easily approached. However, money is on everyone's mind: anything you want can be bought and anything you have can be sold. One columnist (Leonard Wolf) says he was "treated to the most heartwarming hospitality mingled with the most naked avarice."

Visas and tourist information can be obtained from Carpati, the official tourist bureau: see page 21 for the address.

SCOTLAND

See "Great Britain."

SPAIN

A warmly hospitable country but, alack, it's about as bad as France for autostoppers. Here, however, the causes are different. Private vehicles in Spain are still less numerous than other countries (except in Barcelona and Madrid, where the congestion is awesome). Most intercity traffic consists of trucks, official cars and tourists. Only the last-mentioned is normally a good possibility for autostoppers. The shortage of distance cars means anyone going a long way usually has a load of friends and relatives—empty cars are infrequent. Part of the problem in Spain is that the vast majority of autos are Seat brand, which is a Spanish-built Fiat—tiny. Two hitchers with packs are a full load. Finally, the average Spaniard with sufficient means to own a car tends to be more cautious and conservative than the *campesino*, who shares what little he has. Precarious as the Spanish middle class has been, one can't blame him, but the result for you, the hitcher, is fewer rides.

Don't be discouraged. You can always rescue yourself on a bus, which is cheap. Do experience Spain, because its dramatic landscapes and vivid people will etch themselves indelibly into your trip memories. Spain was a high point for me, even though I was at times discouraged by lack of rides. By the way, you shouldn't be wearing a beard in Spain if you want rides from the natives. I stood, bearded, in one spot for three days in southern Spain. My ride came only after I had the brush removed. Spaniards don't wear any facial hair, and it freaks them to see it. (Any bearded or mustachioed natives you see will be gypsies.) Last time over I met a Spanish hitchhiker who told me the trick to getting rides in Spain. You must be well-dressed according to European standards: suit, tie, short hair, tidy suitcase. He said the same applied to France. He'd made it in five days from Madrid to Paris, which is good on that route. If you're not well-dressed, this stretch could presumably take forever; for some hitchers, it probably has.

Spain is notable for the immense number of commercial campgrounds it possesses, especially those in the luxury category. The landscape is dotted with motorists' Disneylands . . . but casual camping is generally not difficult and is particularly pleasant on the beaches. Remember that the shiny-hatted Guardia Civil will come prowling around, though. Spanish buses are modern and efficient; the trains tend to be dilapidated and dreary. For motorists, the main roads are good. The back roads range from good to impassable. Exploring the side roads into or through the mountains of Spain is a highly recommended pastime. Doing this will also give you a welcome respite from the rampant commercialism and the runaway destruction of the Spanish way of life by the developers and real-estate interests in the touted tourist areas.

SWEDEN

Some hitchers say this is a tough country for them. I've always had exceptional luck, with frequent rides with lovely people. Most Swedes you'll encounter speak English, too. You'll find this is Europe's most prosperous country, and for this and other reasons, much like your own U.S.A. They've even switched over to driving on the right side of the road. The Swedes are not cold-hearted personalities, as some claim, but they are more independent and self-contained than most people. As a result, they don't particularly *need* you, which you may or not interpret as coldness.

Sweden is an expensive country, so it's a good one to cut costs in by hitching, camping, sleeping out and grocery-store shopping. Get away to the north country to escape the tourists and find a land of Arctic prairies and northern lights. Or take the Gota canal by boat through the lake district.

TUNISIA

See also "North Africa." In some ways, the best in North Africa, although for me not as beautiful or exotic as Algeria or Morocco. However, it is less frequented by tourists and is friendly and funky. Tunis was the first place we landed in Africa (via the boat from Sicily—$14—a good way to come in) and soon dispelled any concerns felt about Africa. The natives are not restless; they are downright friendly and eager to help out. (Our first night in town, a clerk called every hotel for us until he found us a suitable—i.e., cheap—room.) Prices of everything are much lower than in Europe, hotel rooms are clean, food is delicious. The national dish is couscous, a spiced meat-and-vegetable mix served on a heap of steamed semolina. You'll also find it in Algeria, Morocco and Paris, but the best I had anywhere was in Tunisia for about 30 cents. Yogurt is big here, and delicious, though unflavored (mix it with raw table sugar for sweetness).

For things to do, there are great beaches with clear turquoise waters, and the whole country is a vast archaeological treasure house. Visit the Bardo Museum in Tunis, with collections housed in unending gigantic rooms, to bend your mind.

Hitchhiking is exhilarating in Tunisia because it's easy and it's fun. The countryside is lush and gently rolling, the climate warm. You stand (more likely, sit) by a road without a car in sight in either direction, and no hint of any on the way, either. Maybe an occasional bus or truck chugs by, lots of foot-traffic-cum-livestock looks you over if you're near a town, and probably a congregation of children hovers nearby. Occasionally an adult chases them off, but they keep watching from a distance—to them you're a good BET (Being, Extra-Terrestrial). In one town we had a crowd of about thirty kids gathered in a quarter-hour before our ride came along.

Most rides in Tunisia will be short unless you get lucky with a cross-country tourist, but the rides come almost as frequently as the cars.

TURKEY

Wild and stunning land. Similar to North Africa in its combinations of wealth and poverty, of the modern and the primitive, and especially the jarring force of a basically different culture.

Istanbul is where East meets West, and the encounter serves to catalyze a human ferment that is frightening at first, and at all times fascinating. Built on hills that face the narrow straits of the Bosporus, the city is dramatic, exotic, unique. Narrow streets and narrower alleys are solidly packed with autos and pedestrians vying for momentary

206

supremacy. Smart shops stand next to ramshackle peddler's huts, while people pass by in every manner of dress, from tuxedos to rags, from women in veils to porters bent double under gigantic loads on their backs. Auto traffic is simply unlike anywhere else—pedestrians literally risk their lives attempting to thread the juggernaut vehicular flow, most of which consists of older-model American cars (!).

Then there are the sights—the famous, fabulous mosques, the covered bazaar (like the African souks, but more extensive, and where bargaining is definitely in order), the Byzantine splendor of Topkapi Palace, and the museums, squares and parks.

The food is another trip. Turkish food is a special category unto itself—things like a long bread loaf filled with cottage cheese and a fried egg on top, or a bowl of bread soaked in yogurt and sugar, topped with parsley. Plus famous shishkebab, saslik and pilav. The people are gentle and friendly—easy to engage in "conversation," ready to assist if they can. Watching some kids play soccer in a schoolyard, Julian and I were invited to play. We were hesitant at first, but they urged us on. So into the fray we jumped, ultimately scored three exciting goals, with a crowd of spectators cheering the "American" side—so loudly, in fact, that a school official broke up the game because classes were being disturbed by the uproar.

Prices for rooms and food are extremely low if you seek out the native places rather than the tourist places that cater to the European population of the city. It's walker's town . . . so absorbing that you can cover miles without realizing it. Take the ferry across the straits and explore Asia . . . it's good for some picnicking in the countryside.

You can hitch in Turkey, but the bus is spectacularly cheap. Edirne (on the west border) to Istanbul is about $1 for 230 kilometers. Other destinations are comparable in price. Best hitching route into Istanbul by far is down the main highway from Belgrade, Yugoslavia. This road funnels virtually all traffic from Europe going to the Middle East (you can get a transit card through Bulgaria at the border). Go this way if you're planning to go on beyond Teheran or other interesting points. Or come up from Athens—lots of tourists on this road.

Important: the hippie scene in recent years has become a real burden. Drug busts (three years, minimum) are common . . . fuzz and informers are everywhere.

U.S.S.R.

I didn't go. When I was close and wanted to, I couldn't afford the vouchers. If you stay in hotels, the Soviet Union will be expensive (minimum of about $10 per day). But if you have a car or can get a ride in one, camping visas are cheaper. However, like all visitors, you will have to file (3 months in advance, from the U.S.A.) an itinerary of campgrounds with dates, and spaces will be reserved. There is no such thing as traveling without a schedule or without preconfirmed reservations. Hitching is forbidden and the rule is enforced. Russians are reportedly easy to meet and talk to, as long as you don't talk politics. However, Russians must camp apart from foreigners. Campers wanting to save money should bring their own canned fruits and vegetables. Also, spare parts, tire pump, toilet paper and patience.

WALES

See "Great Britain."

WEST GERMANY

Excellent hitchhiking. Not only has a large, prosperous auto-owning middle class, heavy traffic and a friendly people sympathetic to the *Weg-Wanderer*, but a super system of autobahns (freeways) for fast motation. Autobahns are the fastest way to go, but you have to know some things, like: hitching on an autobahn itself is illegal, and you can catch a fine on the spot for doing it. Police cars are always crusing the autobahns, so watch out. Station yourself at an entrance—exit *(Einfahrt-Ausfahrt)* instead, but watch out for the cops here too. In 1968, hitchhiking near an entrance to an autobahn was also made illegal. So far enforcement of that is rare. They claim hitchers cause traffic congestion, but another reason is a gradually intensifying crackdown on hippie types. This repression, by the way, is not just a Germanic phenomenon, but a world-wide one. (Have you visited the U.S.A. lately?) So get downwind of the entrance and display a sign to give the motorists a clue that you want to make the freeway too.

Picking an entrance with enough traffic is crucial. At some mid-autobahn interchanges or under poor conditions (bad weather or no-action entrance) you may have to get on the autobahn itself, next to the mainstream of traffic. It's risky—the question is, what comes first: your ride, the police or someone who'll run you over? If the police do nab you, your best bet is to plead ignorance of the charge and of the German language too. This puts the burden of communication on them, which is a difficulty that may incline them to let you off more easily. You'll find the German police to be businesslike and impersonal, but nothing to fear if you don't give them a hard time.

Hitching in Germany with its autobahns is reminiscent of hitching in the U.S.A. with its freeways. One big difference is that you'll get that

208

ride faster in Germany. Sometimes the superhighways complicate things for the hitcher, and you'll yearn for the simpler routes, where you can stand on the shoulder.

For Berlin travelers: you can hitch all the way, even through the East German corridor. But any ride you get has to take you the whole way (about 200 kilometers), and the driver has to go through extra red tape on your account. You'll have to get a transit visa at the border (fill out papers and pay a couple of dollars). Ask the friendly border guards on the West German side (that's our side) to solicit rides for you if you've gotten just that far and need one.

I personally like Germans a lot and, as the saying goes, some of my best friends are Germans. As a matter of fact, the hospitality shown me personally by Germans probably exceeds that of any other country I've visited. Yet Germans certainly have their bad sides. When they're gross, no one can be more so. The German methodicalness in everything does make them lack an élan, a creative vitality. Everything is well ordered and under control. For a more interesting side of Germany, leave the modern cities and go into the countryside to the old towns, to the forests and hills, to the idyllic Rhine and Moselle river valleys. Commercial campgrounds are numerous, but casual camping is easy.

YUGOSLAVIA

I've had good luck hitchhiking here, but you need luck because this can be high adventure indeed. Yugoslavia is Europe's most primitive country (though not its poorest) and you'll see sights out of a century ago if you get away from the two main north—south highways (the coastal route and the Belgrade—Sofia route). But be careful about winter and spring traveling—Yugoslavia is just about all mountains. And spectacular ones. Many roads are closed by snow, or little frequented if they're passable, so you can get stranded but good in bitter weather that you may not soon forget. Be warned that some of the main highways shown in pretty colors on the maps are actually dirt roads in bad condition. Also, in winter there's little traffic along the coast, and all the ferries to Italy (from Zadar, Kotor, Dubrovnik) are not running, further reducing traffic.

APPENDIX 2

REFERENCE BOOKS AND MAGAZINES

INDEX

212